Auditory Interfaces

Auditory Interfaces explores how human-computer interactions can be significantly enhanced through the improved use of the audio channel.

Providing historical, theoretical, and practical perspectives, the book begins with an introductory overview before presenting cutting-edge research with chapters on embodied music recognition, nonspeech audio, and user interfaces.

This book will be of interest to advanced students, researchers, and professionals working in a range of fields, from audio sound systems to human-computer interaction and computer science.

Stefania Serafin is Professor in Sonic Interaction Design at Aalborg University in Copenhagen.

Bill Buxton is a partner researcher at Microsoft Research and Adjunct Professor of Computer Science at the University of Toronto.

Bill Gaver is Professor of Design and a co-director of the Interaction Research Studio at Goldsmiths, University of London.

Sara Bly is an independent consultant focused on user practice, particularly in designing technologies to support collaboration

Auditory Interfaces

Stefania Serafin, Bill Buxton,
Bill Gaver and Sara Bly

Routledge
Taylor & Francis Group

LONDON AND NEW YORK

Cover image: Stefania Serafin

First published 2023
by Routledge
4 Park Square, Milton Park, Abingdon, Oxon OX14 4RN

and by Routledge
605 Third Avenue, New York, NY 10158

Routledge is an imprint of the Taylor & Francis Group, an informa business

British Library Cataloguing-in-Publication Data
A catalogue record for this book is available from the British Library

Library of Congress Cataloging-in-Publication Data
A catalog record for this book has been requested

ISBN: 978-1-032-19646-6 (hbk)
ISBN: 978-1-032-19645-9 (pbk)
ISBN: 978-1-003-26020-2 (ebk)

DOI: 10.4324/9781003260202

Typeset in Goudy
by Apex CoVantage, LLC

Access the Support Material: www.routledge.com/978-1-032-19645-9

Contents

Figures

Tables

Preface

0.1 Introduction

This book is directed at designers and researchers in the field of human-computer interaction (HCI). It is devoted to the thesis that HCIs can be significantly enhanced through the improved use of the audio channel. Our focus is narrow and deals specifically with one aspect of sound: the use of nonspeech audio to communicate information.

There are significant potential benefits to be reaped by developing our capabilities in the use of sound. Examples of where sound is already used extensively are process control, flight management systems, and user interfaces for the visually impaired – for example, to facilitate navigation. Even the sounds of the disk drive and printer on personal computers convey information that provides useful feedback as to the state of the system.

The objective of the book is to collect and stimulate research in the field and provide the historical, theoretical, and practical background that will enable participants to "tool up" to undertake such work. The book assumes an intermediate level of understanding of user interface design and computer programming. However, no special background in psychoacoustics, audio, or music is assumed.

0.2 Overview

The book begins with an introductory overview, including a few representative case studies. This is followed in Chapter 2 by some necessary theoretical background on psychoacoustics and musical perception. The intent here is not to deliver a course on psychology; rather, it is to distill key issues from the literature and to discuss their theoretical and practical ramifications as applied to the use of nonspeech audio at the interface. Recent research topics, such as embodied music cognition, are introduced.

Chapters 3 to 6 discuss particular classes of use of nonspeech audio. Chapter 3 deals with the use of audio as applied to data analysis. The approach is comparable to the use of graphics in scientific visualization. The motivation is to utilize additional sensory modalities – in this case, audio – to permit the user to apply a wider set of skills and resources to understanding complex phenomena. This is accomplished by mapping some or all attributes of the data to parameters of the sounds that are used to "display" them. Central to the success of the approach is the selection of sounds, the mapping of the parameters, and the human perceptual system. These issues are discussed using a number of relevant case studies from the literature.

Chapter 4 deals with embedding nonspeech audio directly into the user interface. Here, the focus is on expanding the vocabulary of user interfaces from windows, icons, and mice to include sound. This could be characterized as a move from graphical user interfaces (GUIs) to perceptual user interfaces (PUIs). A number of case studies are discussed. Some, not surprisingly, deal with developing user interfaces for the visually disabled. Part of the emphasis is on showing how such work is equally applicable to the so-called able-bodied user.

A major bias in the book, and in our approach to user interfaces in general, is the notion that the way to address the complex functionality of systems is to base their operation on existing everyday skills. With respect to audio, we have all developed an extensive set of skills that help us navigate through complex spaces and heighten our awareness of our environment. This we have accomplished through a lifetime of living in the everyday world. In the next section of the book, we develop this thesis in the context of a discussion of the theory of everyday listening.

Chapter 5 builds upon the theory of everyday listening. The examples presented illustrate the use of natural sounds and their power when applied to complex applications. The theories of everyday listening are applied in Chapter 6 to the design of auditory icons, such as everyday sounds designed to convey information about events.

Chapter 7 introduces sonic interaction design, an emerging discipline at the intersection of sound and music computing and interaction design. Chapter 8 discusses multimodal interactions and the power of sound to affect and be affected by other modalities. Sonic feedback is beneficial when it is important to focus on time, given the higher temporal resolution of the auditory system versus, for example, the visual or haptic channel. On the other hand, when providing information regarding spatial position and distance of objects, other kinds of feedback, such as visual feedback, might be more beneficial. Chapter 9 examines sound for spatial interfaces that are becoming relevant, especially with the commercialization of hardware technologies for virtual and augmented reality applications.

One of the problems in dealing with nonspeech audio is that the practical part of audio has not generally played a large part in our background. Consequently, Chapter 10 is a type of road map to help the neophyte navigate through the complexities of putting these ideas into practice.

Chapter 11 summarizes what we have discussed and speculates about the future.

The book has two main purposes: to advocate the use of nonspeech audio and to bring attendees up to speed so that they are equipped to begin to pursue work in the field. This final synthesis section, then, is intended to isolate gaps in our knowledge and to identify "good" problems and areas of activity that will help advance the state of the art.

The book was started by Bill Buxton, Sara Bly, and Bill Gaver in the early 1990s and completed in 2020 by Stefania Serafin. The book, therefore, reflects the early research on auditory interfaces together with recent developments in the field.

0.3   The authors

Stefania Serafin is currently Professor in Sonic Interaction Design at Aalborg University in Copenhagen, where she leads the Multisensory Experience Laboratory and is responsible for the Sound and Music Computing Master education.

Bill Buxton has been an active HCI and UX researcher/practitioner for over 45 years. This includes work in computer music and digital audio. He is a partner researcher at Microsoft Research and Adjunct Professor in Computer Science at the University of Toronto.

Bill Gaver received his PhD in everyday listening and auditory icons from UCSD and is currently Professor of Design and a co-director of the Interaction Research Studio at Goldsmiths, University of London. He has published and lectured on the use of auditory icons and is the developer of Apple Computer's SonicFinder for the Macintosh.

Sara Bly was a research scientist at Lawrence Livermore Laboratory and Xerox PARC. She did research on the use of audio and video media in supporting collaborative design. In her PhD thesis, she did some pioneering work in the use of audio to present statistical data. She continued this work in collaboration with Buxton and Gaver.

Acknowledgements

Social media sometimes can turn out to be useful. It happened when BIll Buxton wrote a twit looking for a researcher to complete the Auditory Interfaces book he starter with Bill and Sara in the 80s. Stefania took the challenge and the result is this book.

We would like to thank Lasse Sørensen and Francesco Ganis for providing the images and sound examples for the book.

We would also like to thank our families, friends and colleagues who make our life cheerful and meaningful.

1 Nonspeech audio

An introduction

1.1 Introduction

This book is devoted to the thesis that human-computer interaction, or human-computer interface (HCI), can be significantly enhanced through the improved use of the audio channel. Our focus is narrow and deals specifically with one especially neglected aspect of sound: the use of nonspeech audio to communicate information from the computer to the user.

Unless we are hearing-impaired, nonspeech audio plays a significant role in helping us function in the everyday world. We use nonspeech audio cues in crossing streets, answering phones, diagnosing problems with our cars, and whistling for cabs. By virtue of such usage, we have built up a valuable set of everyday skills. Our thesis is that these skills have real potential as an aid in helping improve the quality of human interaction with complex systems. To date, however, these skills have not been utilized to their full potential, and this rich mode of interaction has had little impact on how we interact with computers. Based on our own experience and pioneering studies by others, as well as the latest research on auditory displays, we feel that this should and can be changed. Helping to bring this about is our motivation in writing this book. Video games illustrate the potential of nonspeech audio to effectively communicate useful messages. In games that use sound effectively, informal observations show that an expert player's score is lower with the audio turned off than it is when the audio is turned on. This is a clear indication that the audio conveys strategically critical information and is more than a nonessential frill. As it is in play, so can it be at work. There are significant potential benefits to be reaped by developing our capabilities in the use of sound. Examples of where sound is already used extensively are process control, flight management systems, and user interfaces for the visually impaired. Even the sound of key clicks, disk drives, and printers on personal computers convey useful feedback about the system's state.

There is established literature on what the human factors community calls auditory displays (Deatherage 1972; Kantowitz and Sorkin 1983; Hermann 2008; Kramer et al. 2010). The increasing interest in auditory display, sonification, and auditory interfaces led to the founding of the International

DOI: 10.4324/9781003260202-1

Community on Auditory Display (ICAD) in 1992 (Walker and Lane 1994), which runs a yearly conference on these topics. The close link between HCI and ICAD is evident in the flow-on of the three waves of research paradigms in HCI: auditory displays are classified as first-wave human factors, work on earcons (Blattner et al. 1989) is framed in terms of second-wave cognitive science HCI (Duarte and Baranauskas 2016), and the sonic studies of Gaver (Gaver 1986) anticipated the third-wave phenomenological paradigm that considers sound in computation as a dimension of everyday life, with aesthetic, emotional, and cultural connotations (Jeon et al. 2019). The proliferation of technology into new domains required a recognition that technology and the interaction with that technology are embedded in more than physical (first wave) and cognitive (second wave) constraints. Rather, technology and people's interaction with that technology must be considered embodied. In this perspective, embodiment has come to be a term of reference that is used to collect together the range of considerations that characterize third-wave HCI.

Nowadays, different communities examine the role of sound in HCI. From the previously mentioned ICAD focused on auditory display, to the Digital Audio Effects Community (DAFX) (www.dafx.org) examining sound from a more engineering and signal processing perspective, to the Sound and Music Computing Community (SMC) (www.smcnetwork.org), a research field that studies the whole sound and music communication chain from a multidisciplinary point of view and traditionally has a more European connotation. By combining scientific, technological, and artistic methodologies, it aims at understanding, modeling, and generating sound and music through computational approaches to the New Interfaces for Musical Expression (NIME) community, which started in 2001 as a workshop on the Human Factors in Computing Systems (CHI) conference, and has now established itself as one of the main venues for studying new ways to interact with sound and music. This book builds upon this work, examining the range of applications where nonspeech audio is used and will be used in emerging interfaces.

As the size of screens of many multimedia devices is rapidly shrinking and the use of such devices is becoming extensive and powerful, we turn to auditory displays to offload the visual sense and use sound to interact with devices. We have traditionally not only relied on the visual display but also on haptic feedback. Typing, for example, is an experience that includes haptic and auditory feedback (clicking sounds of a keyboard). As keyboards are being replaced by touch-screen alternatives, we are losing the haptic interaction and feedback we used to get from physical keyboards. This can lead to more misspellings or slower writing. However, the lack of haptic feedback can be compensated for by auditory feedback to help with the user-machine interaction, which can improve the experience of interacting with the device. Auditory displays can therefore become an alternative to visual displays when it comes to interacting with a mobile device, as some of the examples in this book will show.

Unlike visual stimuli, sound does not need to be paid attention to or be in the field of view to be perceived. Even when we are in a state of sleep, we are subconsciously processing sounds, and when these are loud or important enough, we awake from our sleep. For these reasons, audio has been the principal choice for alarms, notifications, and alerts, especially in situations in which an operator moves to different locations and can miss information provided on the visual display.

1.2   What about noise?

Let us address a question that inevitably comes up. It usually goes something like "I work in a crowded office, and the last thing I need is more noise to distract me" or "When I'm thinking, what I really want is absolute silence."

Let us assume that we could create a perfectly silent workplace. An anecdote by that 20th-century master of sound (and silence), composer John Cage, describes what that would be like. He recounted that after sitting quietly in an anechoic chamber for about half an hour, he was struck by the fact that he heard two sounds: a high sustained sound and a low pulsating one. On asking about them after the fact, he was told that one was his nervous system and the other was his circulatory system.

This anecdote serves to illustrate that there is no such thing as silence. In performing our day-to-day tasks, we are surrounded by sounds. Some help us; others impede us. The former are information; the latter are noise. However, despite their potential effect on our performance, we exercise little influence over the ambient sounds of our working, playing, and living environments.

An underlying thesis of the work presented in this tutorial is that we can benefit by exercising greater control over the sounds around us. Namely, by effective design, we can reduce the noise component and increase the information-providing potential of sound. Our ambition is to promote the acquisition of an understanding that will support the design of audio cues that will improve human performance in computer-mediated tasks: "designer sound" for computer systems.

1.3   Figure and ground in audio

Audio brings some important and interesting properties to the repertoire of the user interface designer. One of the more interesting is the ability of most users to monitor a number of nonspeech audio signals simultaneously while performing a motor/visual task.

This can be seen in driving a car. Consider that driving a car at 80 m.p.h. on a motorway is a critical task in which error could result in death. Nevertheless, one can perform the task with the radio on while holding a conversation with the passenger. Despite concentrating on the conversation, one can still monitor what is on the radio and, if of sufficient interest, interrupt the conversation to point out a favorite melody. While all of this is going on, one could well be passing another car and, in the process, changing gears. A clicking sound confirms that the turn signal is working, and if the car has a manual transmission, audio cues (rather than the tachometer) will most likely determine when to shift. And throughout all of this, one is immediately aware if the engine starts to produce some strange noise or if an ambulance siren is audible.

In contrast with the driving example, the use of audio with the computer is very much impoverished. Our belief, however, is that this need not be so. Although the example's task space is full of sound, most of it is functional and, therefore, not noise. It helped the driver and passenger achieve their agendas and performance potentials. What the research we discuss in this tutorial is aimed at is the use of sound in computing to achieve the same thing.

1.4   Sound and the visually impaired

Visually oriented interfaces obviously prevent independent living for the blind. Already, back in 1987, some universities in the United States required all first-year students to purchase a Macintosh computer. Bowe (2000) pointed out that this is tantamount to saying, "No blind people need apply." Recently, more attention has been placed on the use of sound to aid visually impaired or partially visually impaired individuals. As an example, Bruce Walker and colleagues at Georgia Tech have been working for several years on developing audio-based technology to help visually impaired people perform several tasks such as navigation (Wilson et al. 2007) and, more recently, for mixed-reality applications (May et al. 2020). The applicability of this work extends beyond the visually impaired. There is a case to be made that if we saw the real world in the same restricted way we see our computer displays, we would probably not be able to be certified for a driver's license. As our displays become more visually intensive, the visual channel becomes increasingly overloaded, and we are impaired in our ability to assimilate information through the eyes. In such instances, the same audio cues that help the totally blind user can be applied to help the normally sighted.

Table 1.1 A brief taxonomy of auditory display techniques and where they are described in the book

Name	Brief explanation	Chapter
Sonification	Sound is used to convey information.	Chapter 3
Earcons	Musical sounds are used at the interface.	Chapter 4
Auditory icons	Everyday sounds are used at the interface.	Chapter 6
Sonic interaction design	Sound is used in an interactive context.	Chapter 7
Multimodal interfaces	More than one sensory modality is involved.	Chapter 8
Spatial auditory displays	Sound is conveyed in a 3D space.	Chapter 9

Mobile phones, portable music players, and kitchen appliances incorporate sufficient technology to produce pleasant, functional, and informative sounds, but the designs of their interfaces are often limited to simple alarms or speech. We argue that the field of auditory display design could benefit greatly from an efficient means to capture and transfer design knowledge for designers to build on their expertise in the field and apply it in different contexts.

1.5 Auditory display techniques

This book focuses on different auditory display techniques. Table 1.1 presents the techniques, a definition, and a reference to the chapter where they are introduced. It goes without saying that these terms overlap. For example, sonification can be achieved using either auditory icons (or earcons) or spatial auditory displays. Notice that this book focuses on nonspeech sound-based techniques. Therefore, spearcons (speech-based earcons) that use temporally compressed speech to represent objects, items, or processes with sound (Walker et al. 2006) will not be considered.

From a taxonomical perspective, one could say that sonic interaction design is to sound and music computing and that auditory display as interaction design is to HCI.

1.6 Some examples

In the last decades, several researchers from a variety of disciplines have begun using nonspeech sounds as part of their user interfaces. This exploratory work divides along many dimensions: scientific data analysis and environmental cues, musical and everyday (or natural) sounds, enhancements to visual displays, and replacements of visual displays, as well as sound for immersive environments and new interfaces for musical expression.

In such applications, existing work has appeared in two modes: sounds as dimensions for multimodal data presentation and sounds to provide feedback and other information to support interaction. Early examples of the former are works by Bly (1982), Mezrich et al. (1984), and Lunney and Morrison (1981). In these examples, data variables were mapped into sounds, and the resulting musical notes were then played to the user for analysis. Early examples of the other trend, using audio to support interaction, are Gaver's SonicFinder for the Macintosh (Gaver 1989a) and Edwards' text editor for the visually impaired (Edwards 1989). Both use sounds as cues to events in their computing environments, although in very different ways; however, in each, actions such as selecting files, locating windows, or searching for text strings are accompanied by sounds that provide feedback to the user. These and other examples will be discussed in more detail in later chapters.

These kinds of sounds can be categorized as musical sounds, sounds created by specifying pitch, loudness, duration, and waveshape, or everyday sounds, sounds perceived in terms of events in the natural environment, such as a door slamming or people applauding. Thus, musical sounds focus on the properties of the sound itself, while everyday sounds focus on the source of the sound. In early examples by two of the authors of this book, Bly et al. (1985) mapped their information into properties of musical sounds, while Gaver (1986) used familiar everyday sounds. The topics of musical sounds and everyday sounds will be discussed in depth in the following chapters. For all of the authors, issues revolve around the perception of sounds, the information the various sounds convey, and what information is best presented in the different sounds.

Much work is oriented toward reducing the visual workload by providing additional or redundant information in sound. Some researchers have worked to extract the necessary information from visual displays and encode it into sounds so that visually impaired users can use computers effectively. Other examples do not necessarily attempt to replace the visual display but rather augment it. A few results suggest that some information may be more readily accessible to all users when presented in sound than when presented visually.

Most of the work thus far has concentrated on the use and effectiveness of sounds in relation to visual displays. However, Gaver, Blattner, and others address the issue of what sounds to use. They devote much of their work to considering the capabilities of sounds, both in the perception of the sounds and the kinds of information their sounds might encode.

1.7   Sound in collaborative work

Another area where sound has particular relevance is in computer-supported collaborative work (CSCW). Of particular relevance are situations where people in remote locations are collaborating synchronously on some computer-mediated activity. Here, the problems of HCI are compounded since participants have to maintain an awareness of their collaborators' activities. This is in addition to the regular overhead of monitoring and directing their own. Since one can only visually attend to one thing at a time, this especially taxes the visual system – even more so when all participants do not see the same thing on their screen.

Pioneering work with the ARKola system (Gaver et al. 1991) has demonstrated how nonspeech audio can be used to create what might be called a shared acoustic ecology for the participants in the shared activity and thereby enhanced the sense of telepresence, or shared space.

More recently, new collaborative interfaces for musical expression, such as the Reactable, have demonstrated how designers need to carefully control both the sounds and the way we interact with them (Kaltenbrunner et al. 2006).

The nonspeech audio in this approach functions as an awareness server by allowing each user to hear what others are doing in the background while concentrating on their own activities in the foreground. As the state of the art advances, we will be able to hear what is happening, where it is happening, and who caused it – all using the audio channel and existing skills that we have acquired from a lifetime of living in the everyday world.

1.8   Function and signal type

Functionally, nonspeech audio messages can be thought of as providing one of three general types of information: alarms and warnings, status and monitoring indicators, and encoded messages. Typically, different types of audio cues are used for each.

1.8.1   *Alarms and warning systems*

These are signals that take priority over other information. Their purpose is to interrupt any ongoing task and alert the user to something that requires immediate attention. They normally only sound in an "exception" condition. They are usually loud, easily identifiable sounds with sharp transients. In the car driving example, this is illustrated by the ambulance siren. Doll et al. (1986) provided an interesting discussion of the contrast between principles of ergonomics and practice in the use of auditory signals in modern fighter aircraft. Status and monitoring messages provide information about some ongoing tasks. The nature of such cues very much depends on the type of task being monitored.

The key click produced when typing on a conventional keyboard is one example of how audio cues can provide status feedback for short discrete tasks. In typing, the sound cue only indicates whether the key has been pressed or not. However, Monk (1986) showed that one can go beyond this. In an experimental situation, he showed how mode errors could be reduced by a third by having the pitch of the sound associated with each keystroke depend on which of two modes the system was in. Likewise, Roe et al. (1984) showed that audio feedback provided a powerful cue, complementing tactile and kinesthetic feedback in operating a membrane switch.

For ongoing continuous tasks, sounds providing status information are usually sustained tones or repeating patterns that are audible for the duration of the process that they are monitoring. In such cases, unlike alarms, these messages are designed to fade rapidly into the background of the operator's consciousness so that attention can be directed to some other foreground task. They are designed to come back into the foreground only when there is a significant change in the process being monitored. The design of this type of message exploits the fact that the human perceptual system does not remain conscious of steady-state sounds. In contrast, it is very sensitive to change. Hence, if a steady-state sound representing an ongoing background task stops, then that transition will bring the fact of a change in state to the user's attention. The sound of a washing machine turning off is one such example. In the driving example, any change in the normal background sound of the car motor is another.

Humans are capable of monitoring more than one such signal in the background, provided that the sounds are appropriately differentiated. As with alarms, however, if more than one simultaneously requires attention, then it is likely that the user will become confused and performance will be affected. An actual case in which this was evident was the Three Mile Island power plant crisis. In this case, the operator had 60 different auditory warning systems to contend with (Sanders 1987, p. 155). This example illustrates that although we can recognize and simultaneously monitor a number of different audio cues, we can normally only respond to one or two at a time.

Encoded messages are used to present numerical (or quantitative) data, such as statistical information, in patterns of sound. The complex and varying sounds used in this type of application contrast with the one or two penetrating sounds used with alarms or with the steady-state tones or patterns used in status monitoring.

The design of this class of messages often exploits our capabilities of pattern matching and recognition. In some cases, such messages are much like musical melodies. The usage has a lot in common with Wagner's use of leitmotif, Prokofiev's use of motives to represent the characters in *Peter and the Wolf*, and the sounds in the video game Pac-Man.

1.9   Audio cues and learning

Just as we do not know the meaning of the themes in Prokofiev's *Peter and the Wolf* without being told, we are not born knowing the meaning of a foghorn, fire alarm, or police siren. They must be learned. Furthermore, the quality of their design with respect to human perceptual and cognitive capabilities affects how easy or hard this learning process will be. If audio cues are to be used in interactive systems, then the quality of their design is important. As graphic design is to effective icons (American Institute of Graphic Arts 1982), so acoustic design is to effective auditory signs or earcons. If audio cues are to be employed, they must be clear and easily differentiated. To be effective, they require careful design and testing.

In his work, Gaver makes the point that we can accelerate the learning process by using everyday sounds in the interface (Gaver 1989a, 1986). As pointed out by Blattner et al. (1989), this use of everyday sounds is analogous to the use of representative (as opposed to abstract) graphic icons.

Gaver's work is directed at exploiting our skills built up over a lifetime of everyday listening. His intention is to design user interfaces that use the same skills employed in everyday tasks, such as crossing the street. An example of such a skill would be our built-up association of reverberation with empty space: all other things being equal, the more reverberant a room, the more space.

Gaver proposes that such cues be used to convey information about a computer's status, and because the cue is based on existing everyday skills, they will be quick to learn and not easily forgotten. A way of using our sense of reverberation, for example, would be to have a reverberant "clunk" every time that we save a file and have the amount of reverberation indicate how much free space is left on the disk. Similarly, on the Apple Macintosh, placing a file into Trash could be accompanied by an appropriate "crash." These are concepts that Gaver developed in his article, which describes the rationale behind the prototype SonicFinder for the Apple Macintosh.

Much of the work in nonspeech audio interfaces has been based on mapping attributes of data onto the parameters of sound. These techniques depend on using the listener's knowledge of this mapping as the basis for communication. Doing so has its benefits and builds upon our skills acquired in listening to music, for example. It is important to note, however, that Gaver's approach is quite different. His use of sound is based on a theory of sources. That is, what is important is what you think made the sound rather than the psychophysical properties of the sound itself. This is a distinction that is developed in Chapters 5 and 6.

1.10   Perception and psychoacoustics

In the preceding sections, we discussed the importance of design in the use of acoustic stimuli to communicate information. One of the main resources to be aware of in pursuing such design is the available literature on psychoacoustics and the psychology of music.

Psychoacoustics can be defined as the branch of psychology concerned with the perception of sound and its physiological effects. A widely used reference in acoustics and psychoacoustics is the book by Zwicker and Fastl (2013). Psychoacoustics tells us a great deal about the relationship between perception and the physical properties of acoustic signals. Music and the psychology of music tell us a lot about the human ability to compose and understand higher-level sonic structures. In particular, the literature is quite extensive in addressing issues, such as the perception of pitch, duration, and loudness. It is also fairly good at providing an understanding of masking, the phenomenon of one sound (e.g., noise) obscuring another (e.g., an alarm or a voice). These and other topics are covered in Chapter 2.

Under a different name, acoustic design has had a thriving life as music. Although music perception is not a part of mainstream human factors, it does have something to contribute. In particular, classic psychoacoustics has dealt primarily with simple stimuli. Music, on the other hand, is concerned with larger structures. Hence, melodic recognition and the perception and understanding of simultaneously sounding auditory streams (as in counterpoint) is of great relevance to audio's use in HCI. As a reference to this aspect of auditory perception, see Bregman (1994), Deutsch (2013), and Roederer (2012).

1.11   The logistics of sound

In the past, one of the biggest problems in exploring the use of audio signals was a logistical one. For example, Bly had to build special hardware and a custom computer interface in order to undertake her work (Bly 1982).

Some important past developments have changed this situation dramatically. One significant change was due to the adoption of guidelines by the music industry for a common protocol for interfacing electronic sound synthesis and processing equipment to computers. One of these standards is known as MIDI, the Musical Instrument Digital Interface. An excellent general introduction to MIDI can be found in the work of Loy (1985). Recently, the availability of low-cost hardware and software technology has made it possible for any designer to create sounds and complex interactive sonic environments to be used with different computer interfaces and environments. Frauenberger et al. (2007) investigated which guidelines and principles are used in the design of auditory icons and which guidance is needed to improve the quality of auditory design. Their ultimate goal was to develop a methodological framework to make the design knowledge needed to build efficient auditory interfaces available and accessible in the form of design patterns. In an online survey to which 86 participants responded, they questioned the role of audio in HCI; the context of use is seen as a key property to inform the design and must play a prominent role in a holistic methodological framework.

The completeness of the auditory design space also appears to be an issue. As perceived by many HCI designers, this space consists almost exclusively of speech, not considering nonspeech sounds as powerful means to convey information. It is therefore important for a framework to make explicit the range of possibilities that the auditory interaction channel has to offer. Designers are also users, and many of them have had disappointing experiences with audio in the user interface. This resulted in prejudices and disbelief in what audio can do for their designs. It seems to be a common pattern that audio is directly associated with annoyance and is not considered a serious alternative to the visual channel.

Sound can also provoke strong emotional responses, which is both a strength and a weakness of the mode. Guidance for designing sound for user interfaces has to incorporate a way of conveying good practice regarding aesthetics. An appropriate form of communicating such subtle values in designs is difficult to shape and will inevitably be a source of debate. A last important point of discussion is that the majority of design tasks in HCI are nowadays supported by design tools at various levels. As paper and pen already constitute powerful tools for designing graphical user interfaces. In the past, the lack or inaccessibility of tools in the auditory domain hindered the creation of prototypes or auditory sketches. A design framework must link its methods to powerful tools that allow the creation of external representations of ideas and concepts.

Nowadays, the programmable audio hardware that is installed on all personal computers, together with the availability of several software tools, allows all designers to easily sketch and sculpt sound objects. This book provides guidelines on how these sounds can be designed. Several tools for sound design will be discussed in Chapter 10.

1.12   Summary

We believe that the audio channel deserves more attention. This is shown in the papers cited in this introduction and in later chapters. This research is a beginning, and it is clear that there is still a long way to go before the channel is used to its full potential. Nonetheless, it demonstrates the potential of the approach and whets the appetite for more.

2 Acoustics and psychoacoustics

2.1 Introduction

The raw material that we are working with is sound. Our purpose is to develop effective ways to use sound to convey useful information. It is the relationships that we can construct using sound that enable its articulation. The design space, therefore, is largely constrained by the type and richness of the sonic relationships employed.

The objective of this chapter, therefore, is to investigate the properties of sound that afford the construction of such relationships. The working assumption is that the better we understand such properties, the more effectively we can use sound. It is sometimes said that design is choice. If that is so, then the quality of design is affected by the richness of the alternatives that one has to choose from and the criteria used in selection. Here we hope to provide the acoustic and perceptual foundation to support both. There are three classes of relationships that can be used to encode meaning into sound:

- Intrasound relationships: These are relationships established among the parameters of individual sounds themselves. For example, a message or datum may be encoded by establishing a particular relationship between the pitch, timbre, and duration of a sound.
- Intersound relationships: These are relationships that are established between or among sounds. It is through the pattern of sounds that meaning is conveyed. A simple example would be assigning a specific meaning to a particular motif.
- Extrasound relationships: These are relationships that are established between sound and entities that exist outside the domain of sound. For example, the sound of knocking on a door tells us about someone wanting to enter rather than something about sound.

While these classes are not mutually exclusive and can be used in combination, they provide a useful vocabulary for our study. First, they help us categorize the work of others for comparative purposes. Second, they help us in the process and rationalization of design. Third, they help guide our study

DOI: 10.4324/9781003260202-2

of raw materials. They help us know what to look for and recognize properties of sound that can be exploited (or avoided).

Utterances in the vocabulary of nonspeech audio take the form of one or more audio events. Our working model is that of each event constituting an instantiation of a sonic object. One can best think of an object as having some more or less invariant parameters that identify it as emanating from a particular source and one or more other run-times or instantiation variables – that is, parameters that may change on or during each instantiation.

The notion of the source of a sonic object is important. It is closely related to timbre. Timbre is the parameter of the object that causes us to associate the sound as coming from a trumpet or flute, a closing door, or breaking glass. As a matter of fact, the Acoustical Society of America (ASA) Acoustical Terminology definition 12.09 of timbre describes it as that attribute of auditory sensation that enables a listener to judge that two nonidentical sounds, similarly presented and having the same loudness and pitch, are dissimilar.

Within the design space of nonspeech audio, one can choose from among the repertoire of object classes (i.e., sources or timbres) and then set the parameters that control their instantiations, such as pitch, duration, and loudness. Just as we have classes of sonic relationships, so do we distinguish between two classes of applying parameters to the instantiation variables:

- Fully formed objects: These are sonic objects whose instantiation variables are fully specified when the sound is initiated. For example, if we want to create an audio display of an existing 3D data set, we might use one dimension to determine the object used and the other two to determine the pitch and duration. When the object is invoked, all parameters are fully specified.
- Evolutionary objects: These are sonic objects in which one or more instantiation variables are updated (continuously or discretely) during the lifespan of the object. For example, we may want to monitor a sensor by mapping its temperature to the pitch of a sustained sound object. In this case, for example, as the temperature goes up, so does the pitch.

Like the categorizations discussed previously, these distinctions don't specify what mappings to use. That is a much larger topic. Our purpose in this chapter is to lay out some of the options that exist to be used in such mappings. We now proceed to look at the properties of sound and our perceptual system.

Hopefully, the previous discussion will change what follows from a basic course in (psycho)acoustics to a hunt for properties and opportunities that can be exploited in later designs.

Our discussion has to do with applied acoustics and psychoacoustics. Thus, although we cover a wide range of topics, this discussion is not comprehensive in either depth or breadth. For more information on acoustics, see, for example, Kinsler et al. (1999), Rossing (2007), Truax (2001), and Zwicker and Fastl (2013). For more information on psychoacoustics, see Boff and Lincoln (1988),

Zwicker and Fastl (2013), Cook (1999), Scharf and Buus (1986), and Benade (1990). For more information on music acoustics, perception and cognition, see Rossing (2007), Deutsch (2013), Pierce (1992), Rossing and Fletcher (1991), and Rossing (2007).

2.2 Acoustics

Sounds are pressure variations that propagate in an elastic medium (for our purposes, the air). Our ears are essentially very sensitive barometers that perceive these pressure variations and transform them into a form that can be accommodated by the brain. There are a number of useful ways to analyze these pressure variations. One is to represent them as waveforms, which are a time versus amplitude representation.

2.2.1 Waveforms

Figure 2.1 shows the waveform of a sine wave, with the amplitude of pressure variation on the abscissa and time on the ordinate.

This kind of graph shows sound in the time domain. This is a periodic wave – that is, it repeats itself. The time it takes to complete a full cycle is called the period of the wave and is equal to 1/frequency, where the frequency is the number of cycles per second. The actual wavelength of the signal is the distance that sound can travel in the interval of one period. This can be expressed as

$$\lambda = cp \tag{2.1}$$

or

$$\lambda = c\,/\,f \tag{2.2}$$

where λ is the wavelength, c is the speed of sound, p is the period of the wave, and f is the frequency of the vibration. The sine wave shown in Figure 2.1 can be considered the simplest kind of waveform (for purposes which we will soon discover).

A SINE WAVE

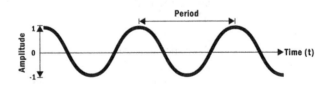

Figure 2.1 A sine wave visualized in the time domain. The horizontal axis denotes time while the vertical axis amplitude.

Sound Example 2.1: *A sine wave: A sine wave is presented at three different frequencies: 100 Hz, 1,000 Hz, and 10,000 Hz. The sequence is presented twice.*

2.2.2 Fourier analysis and spectral plots

Sine waves are never the result of natural events. In fact, there are no mechanical devices that create perfect sine waves. Even the sound produced by a tuning fork is complex, particularly at the attack. However, because of their mathematical properties, they are extremely useful for acoustic theory. In particular, Fourier analysis allows the expression of any (well, almost any) complex wave as the sum of a number of sine waves of different frequencies, amplitudes, and phases (see Figure 2.2). The instantaneous phase represents an angular shift between two sine waves and is measured in radians (or degrees). As an example, a sine wave and a cosine wave are 90° out of phase with each other. Figure 2.3 shows

COMPLEX WAVES

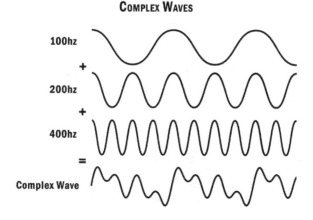

Figure 2.2 Three sine waves of different frequencies may be added to create a complex wave. Conversely, complex waves may be analyzed into their components via Fourier analysis.

PHASE

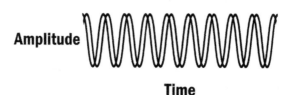

Figure 2.3 A sine and a cosine wave at frequency 440 Hz. The only difference between the two signals is the phase.

FREQUENCY VERSUS TIME DOMAIN - SIMPLE

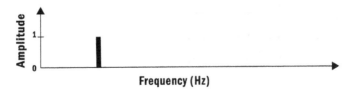

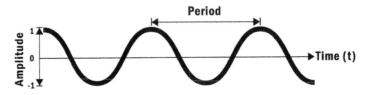

Figure 2.4 A sine wave shown in the frequency domain (as a spectral plot) and the time domain (as a waveform).

FREQUENCY VERSUS TIME DOMAIN - COMPLEX WAVE (HARMONIC)

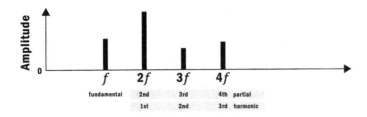

Figure 2.5 A complex wave that is harmonic.

an example of two waveforms that have the same frequency and amplitude but different phases.

When a wave is analyzed using the Fourier transform, the result may be shown in a spectral plot (Figures 2.4 to 2.7 show both spectral plots and waveforms). The spectrum of a sound is a 2D representation showing on the horizontal axis the frequency components and on the vertical axis the amplitude of sine waves of different frequencies that comprise the wave. Each spike on

FREQUENCY VERSUS TIME DOMAIN - COMPLEX WAVE (INHARMONIC)

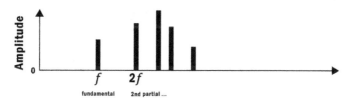

Figure 2.6 A complex wave.

FREQUENCY VERSUS TIME DOMAIN - NOISE

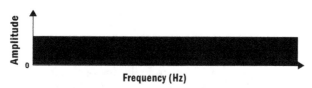

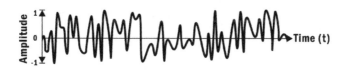

Figure 2.7 The flat spectrum and rough waveform of white noise.

a spectral plot corresponds to a sine wave. So in Figure 2.4, the spike in the spectral plot on the left corresponds to a single sine wave, shown on the right. The height of the spike is the amplitude of the sine wave.

2.3   More complex waves

Sounds in nature are more complex than the examples that we have seen so far. Figure 2.5 shows a more complex wave. The different spikes of energy seen in the spectral plot are called partials, with the lowest frequency being the first partial, the next higher the second partial, and so on. This is an example of a special class of sound in which the frequencies of the partials are integer multiples of the lowest, fundamental frequency. When this is the case, the partials above the fundamental are also called harmonics of the fundamental frequency, and the class of sound is called harmonic.

Harmonic sounds are periodic (their period is the same as its fundamental) and have a definite pitch. Perfectly harmonic sounds cannot be found in the real world and can be only synthetically generated by a computer; some musical instruments such as violins and flutes are designed to produce quasi-harmonic sounds. They have a clear pitch and can blend with other harmonic sounds in pleasing ways.

Sound Example 2.2: Illustrating the sine wave components making up a complex harmonic wave. A 200 Hz complex tone consisting of 20 harmonics is played. The lowest ten harmonics are removed and restored. Note that when nothing is changing, you hear a single tone, but on the transitions when harmonics switch on or off, the individual components can be heard.

Figure 2.6 shows another complex sound made up of five sine components. In this case, the partials are not integral multiples of the fundamental frequency. Consequently, the tone is inharmonic, and one does not call the partials harmonics. Sounds with this property are by far the most typical sounds in the everyday world. Note that in this simple example, the waveform does not repeat itself as obviously as the sine wave does and, in fact, may be periodic only at very low frequencies (one over the product of the component frequencies).

Sound Example 2.3: A complex inharmonic wave.

Note that the pitch is not well defined, and one would not consider the sound musical (in traditional terms, anyhow).

Noise is created by energy at different frequencies. Figure 2.7 shows the flat spectrum and rough waveform that characterizes white noise, which contains equal amounts of all frequencies. Not all noise is white; for instance, a noise might be band-limited, containing energy in a certain band of frequencies. Bandwidth refers to the range of frequencies involved in a tone or noise.

Sound Example 2.4 White noise: This is a sound that has an equal amplitude at all frequencies in the audible spectrum.

2.3.1 Sound, obstacles, bending, and shadows

Sound waves have the property that they will not bend around obstacles in their path whose size is greater than the sound's wavelength. For example, if there is a 1-meter-wide column between a person and a sound source, the column will cast a sound shadow, preventing from hearing all frequencies whose wavelength is less than 1 meter. (Well, almost – nothing is perfect, and in practice, one will hear some of these frequencies, but they will be greatly attenuated. This is because some of the cutoff frequencies will bounce off other objects and get to the ears by an indirect route.)

To find the frequency above which sounds will be cut off by a given obstacle, we need to only find the frequency whose wavelength is the same as the minimum dimension of the obstacle. Remembering that a wave's period is the inverse of its frequency, from Equation 2.2, this can be expressed as follows:

cutoff frequency = speed of sound/obstacle dimension

Therefore, we can calculate the cutoff frequency for our example of standing behind a 0.5-meter-wide column:

cutoff frequency = 334 / 0.5 = 668 Hz

As we shall see in later sections, sound shadows have an important role to play in sound localization (which partially relies on shadows cast by the head and outer ears, or pinnae).

Sound Example 2.5 (2.4 Revisited): Sound shadows: Replay the white noise of example 2.4. Hold up and then remove a book between your ear and the speaker. Try holding up objects of different sizes. Listen for the change in high frequencies. Notice that the larger the object, the lower the cutoff frequency.

2.3.2 Phase: its implication on sound and representations

Frequency domain representations of sound can be more easily correlated to perception than can time domain representations. For example, two sounds whose waveforms look similar may sound quite different. On the other hand, two waveforms that look quite different may sound similar or the same (see, for example, Risset and Wessel [1982]).

Figure 2.8 shows two waveforms that have the same spectra and sound identical. Nevertheless, their waveforms differ. In this example, the different waveforms result from a change in the phase relationship between partials. We tend not to perceive phase differences between the harmonics of periodic sounds (Cabot et al. 1976). The lesson to be learned here is one that (most) computer

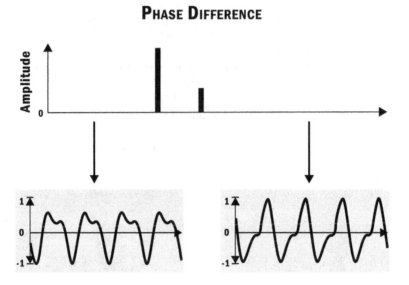

Figure 2.8 The same spectrum can give rise to very different waveforms, depending on the phase relations between partials (amplitude and decibels).

musicians learned a long time ago: specify sounds in the frequency domain, and resist the temptation to build a program that allows you to "draw" waveforms.

Humans are sensitive to an immense range of sound intensities – for instance, the most intense 2,000 Hz sound tolerable is about one trillion times as intense as the weakest that can be detected (Lindsay and Norman 1977). For this reason, intensity is commonly expressed in the logarithmic decibel scale, in which

$$dB = 10log(I / I_0) \qquad\qquad (2.3)$$

where I_0 is (usually) taken as the international standard reference level 0.0002 W/m2. Note that this implies (among other things) that two sounds separated by 10x dB have an intensity ratio of 10x.

Sound Example 2.6: The decibel scale: Broadband noise is reduced in 10 steps of 6 dB, 15 steps of 3 dB, and 20 steps of 1 dB. Demonstrations are repeated once.

Table 2.1 correlates sound pressure level, as measured in dB, with a number of real-world sounds.

Table 2.1 Correlation between SPL as expressed in dB and some real-world sounds

Sound Pressure Level (dB SPL)	Real-world sounds
	– 12" cannon 4 m in front and below the muzzle
220	– Threshold of pain
. . .	– Rock band or loud discotheque
140	– Hammering on steel, 1 m
130	– Subway station, express passing
120	– Electric power station, average factory
110	– Very loud home stereo
100	– Ordinary conversation, 1 m
90	– Department store, noisy office
80	– Quiet residential street
70	– Average residence
60	– Quiet whisper, 1.5 m
50	– Out of door minimum
40	– Threshold of hearing
30	
20	
10	
0	

Source: After Goldstein and Cacciamani (2021).

2.3.3 The inverse-square law

Consider sound as radiating an equal amount in all directions from a point in space. Thought of in this way, it can be seen that at any given distance, the energy emanating from the source is distributed uniformly over the surface of an imaginary sphere whose radius is determined by the distance. For a constant intensity at the source, the intensity at a distance from the source will diminish proportionally to the inverse of the area of the sphere having a radius equal to that distance. Generally stated: In a free field, sound intensity is inversely proportional to the square of the distance from the source.

This is known as the inverse-square law. It will be important later when we are interested in positioning sounds in space and want to give the illusion of distance. One important point to keep in mind, however, is that the sphere and uniform radiation on which the law is based is imaginary and is accurate only in idealized situations, namely a free field. In reality, sound hits the floor, walls, furniture, and so on. It may get absorbed by the surface, resulting in energy loss, or it may be reflected in a different direction, thereby creating another mini sound source that contributes to the overall intensity at another location. Like most laws, this one is better considered a guideline in practical terms.

BIPOLAR WAVES AND UNIPOLAR ADSR ENVELOPES

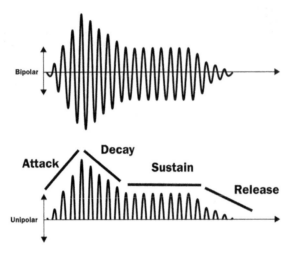

Figure 2.9 Attack, decay, sustain, and release (ADSR) of a sound. Top figure: the original waveform in the time domain. Bottom figure: The corresponding ADSR envelope.

2.3.3.1   *Simple variation: envelopes*

Virtually all natural sounds change over time. Perhaps the most obvious dimension of change is amplitude, for how else could a sound have a start and a finish? Typically, this change is not a simple switch on and then off. Amplitude is the term to describe the physical quantity, while loudness the perceived quantity. The loudness contour of most sounds is more complex. We can see this contour by looking at the outline of the graph of a sound's waveform. This can be seen in Figure 2.9 A, for example. If we traced the "silhouette" of the waveform, the result would be a sketch of the sound's envelope.[1] Using just the positive side, Figure 2.9 B shows the same waveform outlined by a representation of its envelope. Notice that the envelope is drawn as a straight-line approximation of what is actually a continuous curve. This is also the norm and will usually be adequate for our purposes, as demonstrated in studies of timbre and data compression by Grey (1978). Notice that the segments of the envelope are labeled attack, decay, sustain, and release (ADSR). These are common terms used for specifying envelopes with many synthesizers, although many more sophisticated systems permit much finer control.

Sound Example 2.7: Amplitude envelopes: A periodic complex tone of 440 Hz is played three times, each time with a different envelope. The example is presented twice.

A Time Varying Spectral Plot

Figure 2.10 A time-varying spectral plot of a complex sound.

2.3.3.2   Spectral variation over time

We have already seen that most sounds are made up of spectral components, or partials, of different frequencies. Typically, the relative amplitude of these partials does not remain constant throughout the duration of a sound. That is, it is usually incorrect to think of the envelope simply as a function that controls the scaling of a waveform's amplitude over time.

A more accurate picture of what happens can be obtained by thinking of a waveform in the frequency domain and then using a separate envelope to describe each partial. An example of this is shown in Figure 2.10. This type of representation is known as a time-varying spectral plot.

Since the lower frequencies usually have the higher amplitudes, they appear at the back of the plot so as to not obscure our view of the lower amplitude high frequencies plotted in the foreground. Notice that while each spectral component has its own envelope, we no longer have a graph of a single envelope describing the shape of the sound as a whole. As a first approximation, we could derive the overall envelope as the sum of the envelopes of each of the partials; however, in reality, the amplitudes do not sum linearly, especially in the higher frequencies where spectral components fall within about 1/3 of an octave of each other, where an octave is a series of eight notes occupying the interval between (and including) two notes, one having twice or half the frequency of vibration of the other. This has to do with the perceptual system and something called the critical band, discussed later in this chapter.

> *Sound Example 2.8: The effect of time-varying spectra on timbre: (a) The sound of a Hemony carillon bell, having a strike-note pitch of around 500 Hz (B4), is synthesized in eight steps by adding successive partials with their original frequency, phase, and temporal envelope. (b) The sound of a guitar tone with a fundamental frequency of 251 Hz is analyzed and resynthesized in a similar manner.*

2.3.4 *Helmholtz revisited*

The study of acoustics has been dominated for over a hundred years by the pioneering work of Helmholtz (Von Helmholtz 1912). One of his main theories, and one which is still widely taught, is that timbre can be explained solely in terms of spectra, independent of time. Subsequent work has demonstrated that his theories are inadequate and that the relative temporal change among partials is an important determinant of the timbre of a sound. In fact, these relative time-varying characteristics appear to be as important (and sometimes more so) as the frequencies of the partials actually present in the sound.

This is illustrated in the pioneering work of Risset and Wessel (see Risset and Wessel [1982]). They demonstrated that convincing brass sounds could be synthesized using spectral components that were foreign to natural brass sounds. What they found was that it was the relative rise and fall of energy in regions of the spectrum, rather than the specific components, that determined the brass-like character. Specifically, they showed that brass instruments are characterized by an increase in spectral content with frequency – that is, low-frequency partials build up faster than high ones, as is illustrated in Figure 2.11 top. A convincing trumpet sound can be synthesized by following this rule, even if the partials used are, for the most part, foreign to the actual spectrum of a trumpet. This illustrates two important observations relevant to the understanding and design of sound. First, the traditional account of timbre is inadequate in that it ignores variations in time which are crucial for perception. Second, independent and dynamic control of spectral components is critical for the effective exploitation of timbre.

RISSET

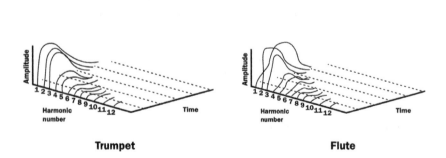

Trumpet **Flute**

Figure 2.11 Characterizing brass sounds and flute sounds by the distribution of spectral energy over time.

> *Sound Example 2.9: Time and timbre: Synthetic and recorded brass sounds are presented. The spectrum of the synthetic instruments differs from the natural ones; nevertheless, they all sound "natural." This is because of the overall behavior of the spectral components rather than what specific components make up the sound.*

2.3.5 Spectrograms

In light of the importance of the distribution of spectral energy in the perception of timbre, it is worth briefly introducing a graphical representation of sound in which this is highlighted. The representation is known as a spectrogram. An example is illustrated in Figure 2.12.

Rather than showing the amplitude envelopes of individual partials, a spectrogram shows the energy in bands of the audible range. The brighter the plot in each band, the more energy is there. This type of representation makes it very easy to get a sense of how the spectral energy is distributed over time.

2.3.6 Formants versus partials

In Figure 2.12, notice that there are two regions in the spectrum where there is pronounced energy. Many sounds can be characterized by the presence and location of similar bands of spectral activity. These bands, known as formants, are most frequently encountered in studies of phonemes of speech. However, they are characteristic of most sounds that are produced by mechanical means. Formants are important to our understanding of sound

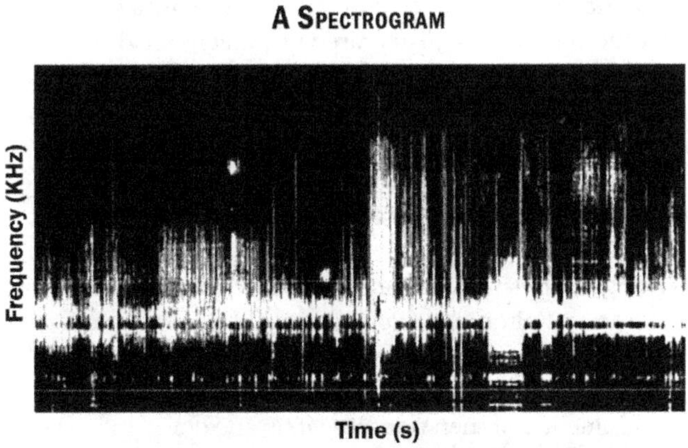

A SPECTROGRAM

Figure 2.12 A spectrogram.

and especially timbre. To understand them, we need to slightly modify the model of sound. We have been using a simplified model in which mechanical vibrations were transformed directly into atmospheric pressure variations (sound waves). Important to the understanding of formants is the introduction of the concept of resonance.

Think about an elastic band that is stretched between your fingers and then plucked. This is a good example of the simplified model that we have been using thus far. Now, if you hold one end of the same elastic against a matchbox, stretch it to the same tension and length, and pluck it exactly the same as before, the sound will be different. The reason is the same as why acoustic guitar strings are stretched over a hollow body rather than a flat plank: the body produces a resonator that modifies the spectrum of the vibrating string. These resonances occur in particular regions of the spectrum, and a large part of the craft of instrument design is determining the strength and frequency of these resonant frequencies.

Formants occur when partials of the primary vibration (for example, the guitar string) fall within these resonant regions and are accentuated relative to those that fall outside the resonant frequencies. We can illustrate this further with another example using our voice.

Pick a pitch that you are comfortable with, then say – and sustain – the sound "ee" as in "beet." Now, without changing the pitch or loudness of your voice, change to the sound "aw" as in "hot." What you are doing is changing the properties of the resonators of your vocal tract. What you are not doing is changing the spectrum of the sound wave leaving your vocal cords. But since the spectrum of the wave leaving your vocal cords must pass through the "resonator" of your mouth, certain spectral components get attenuated while others get accentuated – all depending on whether they fall within the resonant regions (determined by the tongue, lip, and jaw position).

The voice is interesting in that the resonant frequencies, and hence the formant frequencies, can be varied over time. Whereas this is also true for many electronic instruments, it is rare with mechanical instruments. The resonant frequencies of a violin are a function of the materials used and its shape. The same is true for other instruments, such as the piano or bassoon. Therefore, because they are rooted in the physical structure of the instrument, formant frequencies are fixed and do not vary with the frequency of the vibration that is exciting the system. (See, for example, Slawson [1968] for more on this.)

One consequence of this is that for a given instrument, the spectral properties of a note at one pitch will typically be different than those at another (since being at different pitches, different parts of the spectrum will fall within the resonant regions of the instrument). Therefore, we cannot just analyze one note of an instrument and then transpose it up and down and expect the effect to be one of all notes coming from the same instrument. This is illustrated dramatically in the next sound example.

Sound Example 2.10: Change in timbre with transposition: A three-octave scale on a bassoon is presented, followed by a three-octave scale of notes that are simple transpositions of the instrument's highest tone. This is how the bassoon would sound if all of its tones had the same relative spectrum.

Here is the summary thus far:

- Sounds are pressure variations that propagate as waves in the atmosphere.
- The waveform of a sound can be displayed in the time domain as time (horizontal axis) versus amplitude (vertical axis).
- The time for one cycle of a repetitive wave is called the period and is the inverse of the wave's frequency (the number of repetitions per second).
- Complex waves may be analyzed according to the sine waves that could be combined to produce them. The results may be displayed in the frequency domain on a spectral plot.
- When the frequencies of the partials of a complex sound are integer multiples of the sound's fundamental frequency, the sound is harmonic.
- Most complex waves are inharmonic. The individual frequency components of the wave are called partials.
- Noise contains energy at many different frequencies and is not periodic. Band-limited sounds contain a certain range of frequencies; the size of this range is its bandwidth.
- Intensity is commonly expressed using the logarithmic decibel scale, in which $dB = 10 \log (1/10)$.
- Sounds cannot bend around obstacles whose size is longer than their wavelength. Consequently, we have the existence of frequency-sensitive sound shadows.
- Inverse-square law: in a free field, sound intensity is inversely proportional to the square of the distance from the source.
- The overall amplitude variations of a tone are commonly referred to as the tone's attack, decay, sustain, and release.
- A more precise description of a sound's evolution over time is given by a time-varying spectral plot with the dimensions time, frequency, and amplitude.
- The physical properties of sound generators typically create resonant frequencies that accentuate partials that fall within them. The resulting regions of high spectral energy are known as formants. Formant frequencies are independent of the fundamental frequency and spectral makeup of the exciting vibrating body.

2.4 Digital filters

Before investigating the field of sound in space, it is important to learn a fundamental concept of digital signal processing (e.g., the concept of a filter).

According to the digital signal processing guru Julius O. Smith from Stanford University, *everything is a filter* (Smith 2000). In fact, a filter is any device that takes an input signal, performs some manipulations, and produces an output signal.

In order to understand the effect of a filter, it is important to calculate its *frequency response*. The frequency response shows the effect of a filter in a frequency versus amplitude axis. To calculate the frequency response is not a straightforward task. The frequency response is the representation of the filter in the frequency domain, while the impulse response is the representation of the filter in the time domain.

A low-pass filter reduces the amplitude of the high-frequency components of a sound, leaving the low frequencies unvaried. A parameter that specifies the effect of the low-pass filter is the cutoff frequency. Below the cutoff frequency, the input signal remains unchanged, while above the cutoff frequency, the high-frequency components are reduced. Figure 2.13 shows the frequency response of a low-pass filter.

In the time domain, digital filters are mathematically represented by expressing their difference equation. The difference equation represents the output of a filter at the current time $y(n)$ as a function of the input samples $x(n), x(n-1), \dots$ and the previous output samples $y(n-1), y(n-2) \dots$

As an example, the simplest low-pass filter that can be implemented has the following difference equation:

$$y(n) = 0.5x(n) + 0.5x(n-1) \tag{2.4}$$

This corresponds to calculating the output as the average of the input values at the current time and the previous time.

A LOW-PASS FILTER

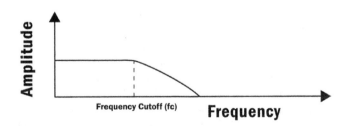

Figure 2.13 Frequency response of a low-pass filter.

A HIGH-PASS FILTER

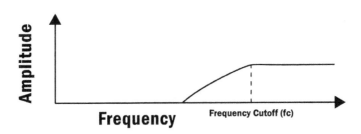

Figure 2.14 Frequency response of a high-pass filter.

A BAND-PASS FILTER

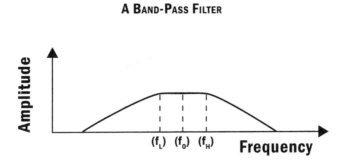

Figure 2.15 Frequency response of a band-pass filter.

Figure 2.14 shows the frequency response of a high-pass filter.

A band-pass filter keeps the frequency components of a signal around a certain bandwidth, removing the higher and lower frequencies outside the bandwidth. Two parameters specify a band-pass filter: the bandwidth (i.e., the width of the filter band) and the center frequency (i.e., the frequency at the middle of the band).

Such parameters are shown in Figure 2.15. A band-pass filter can be considered as the combination of a low-pass and a high-pass filter. Can you explain why? The band-pass filter reduces the frequencies that are above and below a certain frequency band, therefore acting as both a low-pass and a high-pass.

A band-reject filter removes the frequency components of a signal around a specified bandwidth (see Figure 2.16). As in the case of a band-pass filter, the parameters to control are the bandwidth (i.e., the width of the filter band) and the center frequency (i.e., the frequency at the middle of the band).

An all-pass filter is a filter that lets all frequencies pass without any change in amplitude. An obvious question would then be: what is the point of having

A BAND-REJECT FILTER

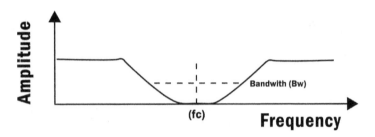

Figure 2.16 Frequency response of a band-reject filter.

A PHASOR EFFECT

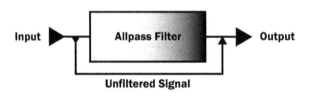

Figure 2.17 Block diagram of a phasor effect.

such a filter? An all-pass filter does not affect the amplitude of a sound but the phase. This means that, when applying an all-pass filter to a sound, different frequencies will have a different change in phase. All-pass filters can therefore be used to create robotic-like effects when applied to the human voice. As an example, all-pass filters are used to design phasors (see Figure 2.17), often used to give a "synthesized" or electronic effect to natural sounds, such as human speech. The voice of C-3PO from *Star Wars* was created by taking the actor's voice and treating it with a phasor.

As can be seen in Figure 2.17, in a phasor a signal is split, one portion is filtered using an all-pass filter to produce a phase shift, and then the filtered and unfiltered portion are summed together.

The different filters are indeed widely used to create several digital audio effects. There exists a vibrant community with an associate conference called DAFX (abbreviation of digital audio effects). This community runs the annual digital audio effects conference and has also published a useful book for more technical-minded researchers in digital audio processing (see Zölzer [2011]).

Here we summarize some effects that are interesting for audio designers. One typical effect is the bass-boost effect, which means to amplify the low-frequency content of a sound to enhance the bass. This effect can be achieved by designing a low-pass filter that extracts the low frequencies of the sound, enhancing their amplitude and summing them with the original sound.

A wah-wah effect is also known as parameteric equalization. This is a single band-pass filter whose center frequency can be controlled and varied anywhere in the frequency spectrum. The electronic version, which sweeps the peak response of a filter up and down in frequency to create the sound, was first heard in 1945 on a pedal steel guitar created by Leo Fender and in the early '60s on Vox amplifiers. An equalizer is a set of filters used to boost or attenuate certain frequency bands of a signal.

An equalizer (usually abbreviated as EQ) is described by specifying how many bands are used and their correspondent frequency range.

An equalizer can be easily built by using different band-pass filters in parallel, each tuned to a specific frequency band. Filters are also used to create spatial sound effects, as described in the following section.

2.5   Spatial hearing

The location of a sound is an important and potent cue that can be used when working with nonspeech audio cues. An attractive notion is to be able to distribute sounds in space (in one, two, or three dimensions) in order to get many of the same types of benefits that one achieved from the spatial distribution of graphical objects in the desktop metaphor of graphical user interfaces and window managers.

Much of our understanding of human sound localization is based on the classic duplex theory (Rayleigh 1907), which emphasizes the role of two primary cues to location, interaural differences in time of arrival, and interaural differences in intensity. The original proposal was that interaural intensity differences (IIDs) resulting from head-shadowing determine localization at high frequencies, while interaural time differences (ITDs) were thought to be important only for low frequencies (because of phase ambiguities occurring at frequencies greater than about 1,500 Hz). Binaural research, however, points to serious limitations with this approach. For example, it has become clear that ITDs in high-frequency sounds are used if the signals have relatively slow envelope modulations. The duplex theory also cannot account for the ability of people to localize sounds along the median plane where interaural cues are minimal (e.g., see Blauert [1983]). Furthermore, when subjects listen to sounds over headphones, they are usually perceived as being inside the head even though interaural temporal and intensity differences appropriate to an external source location are present (Plenge 1974). Many studies now suggest that these deficiencies of the duplex theory reflect the important contribution to localization of the direction-dependent filtering, which occurs when incoming sound waves interact with the outer ears, or pinnae. As sound propagates from a source (e.g., a loudspeaker) to a listener's ears, reflection and refraction effects tend to alter the sound in subtle ways, and the effect is dependent upon frequency. Such frequency-dependent effects, or filtering, also vary greatly with the direction of the sound source, and it is clear that listeners use such effects to discriminate one location from another. Experiments have shown that spectral shaping by the pinnae is highly direction-dependent (Shaw 1974), that the absence of pinna cues degrades localization accuracy (Butler and Humanski 1992), and that pinna cues are important for externalization, or the "outside the head" sensation (Plenge 1974).

Such data suggest that perceptually veridical localization over headphones may be possible if this spectral shaping by the pinnae and the interaural difference cues can be adequately reproduced. There may be many cumulative effects on the sound as it makes its way to the eardrum, but all of these effects can be coalesced into a single filtering operation, much like the effects of an equalizer in a stereo system. The exact nature of this filter can be measured by a simple experiment in which an impulse (a single, very short sound pulse or click) is produced by a loudspeaker at a particular location. The acoustic shaping by the two ears is then measured by recording the outputs of small probe microphones placed inside an individual's (or an artificial head's; e.g., the KEMAR [Gardner and Martin 1995] or Neumann heads) ear canals. If the measurement of the two ears occurs simultaneously, the responses, when taken together as a pair of filters, include estimates of the interaural differences as well. Thus, this technique allows one to measure all of the relevant spatial cues together for a given source location, for a given listener, and in a given room or environment.

Ludwig et al. (1990) and Cohen and Ludwig (1991), for example, have introduced and discussed the notion of audio windows to achieve these purposes. The use of spatial cues is also useful in collaborative work. If events are accompanied by sounds, the location of those sounds can, for example, provide the cue as to who initiated specific events. Through spatialization, distributed workers can occupy a shared acoustic ecology that provides many of the awareness generating prompts and cues that are found and exploited in the natural everyday world.

Figure 2.18 shows the aspects of sound localization that are important to take into account when designing a 3D auditory environment. There are four aspects of sound localization that we want to understand in order to make full use of available resources:

- The direction of the source, which is generally expressed in terms of its angular displacement, or azimuth, on the horizontal and median (vertical) plane
- The distance to the source
- The elevation of the source
- If the source is not stationary, its movement

SPATIAL HEARING

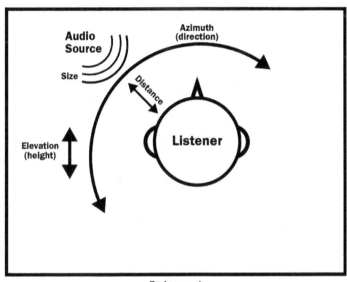

Environment

Figure 2.18 A schematic representation of a 3D sound environment, shown in a 2D plane.

Normally, azimuth and elevation are described in degrees, so 0 azimuth and elevation corresponds to a sound that is positioned directly in front of the listener.

The environment is mostly simulated in terms of reverberation and room effects. Unfortunately, achieving all of these benefits is easier said than done. Sound localization is a complex issue. What follows is a brief introduction of some of the issues and some pointers to where help may be found.

We first cover the acoustical properties of 3D sound and then examine perceptual qualities. A detailed discussion of spatial hearing is provided by Blauert (1997), with applications in multimedia and virtual reality presented in Begault and Trejo (2000).

In order to localize the angular position of a sound source in the horizontal plane, it is important to analyze the differences between the waveforms reaching the two ears.

2.5.0.1 *Interaural time difference (ITD)*

Consider a person as represented in Figure 2.19. The sound located in position A, at 0 azimuth, has the same distance from both ears. On the other hand, the

AZIMUTH DIFFERENCE

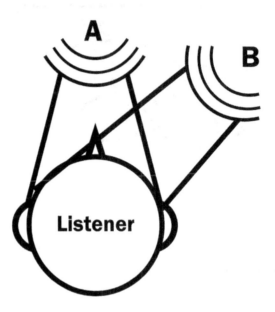

Figure 2.19 Sound A is located at 0 azimuth, while sound B is located on the right of the listener. So sound A will reach both ears at the same time, while sound B will reach first the right ear and then the left ear.

sound placed in position B reaches the right ear earlier than the left ear. This difference is at the basis of the ITD (e.g., the time difference it takes for a sound to reach one ear versus the other).

2.5.0.2   *Interaural intensity difference (IID)*

Related to the ITD is the IID: when a sound travels in space, it loses intensity. The further the sound has to travel, the more intensity it will lose. Therefore, the IID is defined as the difference in intensity between the sounds arriving at the two ears. ITD and IID together are some of the cues that contribute to the perception of lateralization. When the same sound source is delivered to both ears, through headphones, the listener perceives that the sound is placed inside the head. As ITD and IID change, the position of the sound source will also start to shift. ITD and IID also provide some ambiguities, and they cannot alone provide sound localization cues, as shown in Figure 2.20. The three sound sources in Figure 2.20 have the same IID and ITD but are physically placed in three different locations.

CONE OF CONFUSION

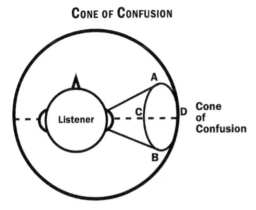

Figure 2.20 The cone of confusion.

2.5.1 *Head-related transfer functions (HRTF)*

Other important cues are what is called head-related transfer function (HRTF), defined as the spectral filtering of a sound source before it reaches the eardrum. This spectral filtering is caused primarily by the outer ear but also by the shape of a person's head and body. The use of HRTF spectral shaping is a key component in a 3D sound system, and it can be obtained by direct measurement or modeling.

Direct measurements are performed in a room without echo, called an anechoic chamber, where measurements are made using a so-called dummy head (a mannequin that has two microphones, one for each ear). It should be noted that the spatial cues provided by HRTFs, especially those derived from simple anechoic (free-field, dry, or echoless) environments, are not the only cues likely to be necessary to achieve veridical localization in a virtual display. Anechoic simulation is merely a first step, allowing a systematic study of the perceptual consequences of synthesizing spatial cues by using a less complex and, therefore, more tractable stimulus.

A dummy head is designed to replicate an average-sized human head. Depending on the manufacturer, it may have a nose and mouth too. Since a sound stimulus needs to be captured from several azimuths and elevations, the process of recording HRTFs is quite cumbersome. Moreover, this process provides a database of impulse responses that fit an average head, but they are not personalized to specific individuals.

Another approach consists of using signal processing techniques to reproduce the signal that represents the filtering effect of the ear. This solution does not require storing information in a database, and the algorithm can be adapted to simulate different ears' shapes and head sizes.

2.5.2 *3D sound distance and reverberation*

The inclusion of distance and environmental cues is essential in order to create a realistic 3D auditory environment. In the absence of other cues, the intensity of a sound source is the primary distance cue used by a listener. Generally, the inverse-square law is used, where the intensity is proportional to the square root of the distance. Another cue to simulate distance is the emphasis of low-frequency versus high-frequency content of the sound source (Von Békésy and Wever 1960). Reverberation is also an important cue for distance perception, where reverberation is the energy of the sound source that reaches the listener indirectly by reflecting from surfaces within the surrounding space.

Reverberation simulation is what provides a sense of place. Several algorithms for simulating reverberation are described, for example, by Gardner (2002). Most of the pioneering reverberation algorithms are based on a combination of different filters.

Figure 2.21 shows the impulse response of a room. The impulse response of a room literally represents the response of a room to an impulse, which means the signal obtained by having an impulse as input and recording the corresponding response of the room. Such response is obtained by recording a loud impulsive noise. For example, typical ways of recording the impulse response are by popping a balloon or shooting a gun in a room and recording the resulting sound. The impulse response is usually characterized by early reflections, which are waves that reach the ear of the listener earlier in time, and late reverberations, which are more spatially diffused and result from many subsequent reflections

IMPULSE RESPONSE

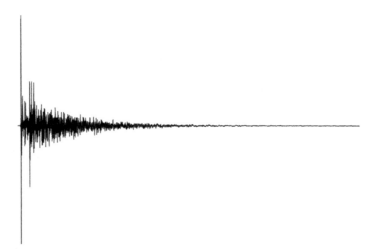

Figure 2.21 An example of an impulse response, in this case recorded in a church. Notice the early reflections followed by late reverberation.

from surface to surface. The impulse response can be used as the filter. This means that by calculating the convolution of the impulse response with different signals (or by multiplying their frequency response), we can simulate sounds played in different rooms.

Spatial sound and room acoustics are active fields of research with dedicated books, and here we have offered only a small taste. One good starting reference is the book by Begault and Trejo (2000).

2.6   Psychoacoustics

Up to now, we have been primarily discussing the physics or acoustics of sound. However, our body does not take these stimuli from the physical world and just linearly maps them into the perceptual. The mapping between stimulus and percept is complicated by nonlinearities and interactions and bounded by the limitations of our sensory and cognitive capability.

In this section, we look at these mappings and interactions, building upon the basic understanding of acoustics developed in the previous section. We outline fundamental topics of psychoacoustics that are important for designing audio interfaces, discuss each topic briefly in turn, and explore some of the design implications of each. We begin with two concepts that are prerequisites for what follows: just noticeable difference (JND) and critical band.

2.6.1   *Just noticeable difference (JND)*

Just noticeable difference (JND) is the minimum physical difference in a stimulus that a person can detect. In the auditory domain, we consider JND in frequency – that is, the minimum difference in frequency between two sounds in such a way that a person can distinguish such sounds as different. The same concept exists for amplitude.

2.6.2   *Critical bands*

Critical bands are frequency regions within which sound energies interact. They seem to be explicable in terms of the vibratory response of the basilar membrane. Simplified, frequencies that stimulate the same hair within the basilar membrane typically fall within the same critical band. Critical bands are roughly a third of an octave wide. For a center frequency above about 500 Hz, they are 20–30 % wider. Below 500 Hz, they are narrower. Critical bands around a given center frequency f (both in Hz) can be approximated by the following equation (Zwicker and Terhardt 1980):

$$CB = 25 + 75(1 + 1.4f^2)0.69 \tag{2.5}$$

Some aspects of masking can be explained by critical bands. Detecting a pure tone that is masked by a band-pass filtered noise centered around its frequency becomes more difficult as the bandwidth is increased up to a critical value (corresponding to a critical band) when further increases do not affect detection. Critical bands may help explain consonance and dissonance. Broadly speaking, sounds within a critical bandwidth sound rough; those without do not. For audio designers, the implications are the following: multiple sounds interact differently depending on their frequency separation. Knowing the nature of these interactions is crucial for designing systems in which more than one sound may be heard at once.

2.6.3 Pitch

Pitch is the sensation most directly associated with the physical property of frequency. The pitch of a sine tone is a function of its measured frequency. The pitch of a harmonic tone is a function of its fundamental frequency. The pitch of an inharmonic tone or noise is a function of its amplitude-weighted average frequency (brightness). The JND for pitch discrimination is about 1/30 of a critical band.

The functional relationship between pitch and frequency is not a linear one but rather logarithmic. Doubling the frequency nominally raises the pitch of a sound by an octave. Thus, in terms of pitch, the difference between 110 Hz and 220 Hz is the same as that between 440 Hz and 880 Hz. This is illustrated in Figure 2.22. We say that the function is nominal, however, since other factors besides frequency affect pitch, such as those discussed in the next paragraph. Pitch is also affected by loudness. The pitch of sine tones under about 1,000 Hz decreases as the sounds get louder; the pitch of sine tones over about 1,000 Hz increases as the sounds get louder.

Pitch is also affected by timbre, a perceptual parameter that will be described later in this chapter. Bright sounds (those with a relatively great amount of high-frequency energy) sound higher than dull ones with the same fundamental

FREQUENCY AND PITCH

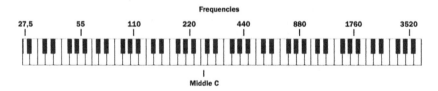

Figure 2.22 The relationship of frequency to musical pitch. The frequency corresponding to the nominal fundamental frequency of each A on the piano keyboard is shown. Note that each octave between successive As corresponds to a doubling of frequency, not a fixed number of hertz.

THE PITCH HELIX

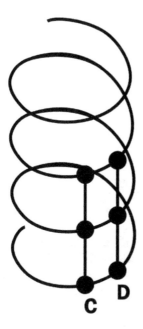

Figure 2.23 The pitch helix, or spiral. Pitch height increases as one goes along the spiral. The closer two points on the spiral, the closer their pitch height. The vertical lines indicate notes of the same chroma – in this case, Cs and Ds. Because of the perceptual similarity of notes having the same chroma, despite large differences in pitch height, pitch height alone should not be used in mapping data to pitch.

frequency. Pitch is not a single perceptual dimension. That is, unlike a ruler, as one goes further and further along, one does not necessarily get further and further from where one started. For example, perceptually, two notes separated by an octave (12 semitones) will often be judged closer in pitch than two notes separated by just one semitone. There are two properties of pitch at play here. The first is pitch height, which is how high or low a sound is. The second is pitch chroma, or pitch class, which is the note type (such as A, B, or C#). We can discuss these two concepts of pitch using three notes as an example: A440, the A# a semitone above it, and A880, the octave above it. In terms of pitch height, the A# is closer to A440 by 11 semitones. However, in terms of chroma, the A880 is closer. Pitch height and chroma can be visually represented together as a helix, as shown in Figure 2.23. Here, the relationship between C and D is shown. Pitch height is along the spiral. Pitch chroma is represented by the vertical lines linking notes of the same pitch class.

Most people are bad at making absolute pitch judgments. The ability to do so, known as perfect pitch, is rare and cannot be taught reliably. However, people have varying degrees of ability to make relative pitch judgments, especially with tones that fit on the musical scale. This skill varies with musical ability and can be taught reasonably reliably. People's ability to hear high-pitched sounds, especially soft ones, drops off as they get older.

2.6.4   Pitches, intervals, scales, and ratios

From what we have read, we now know that the relationship between frequency and pitch is not linear and that musical intervals are expressed as frequency ratios rather than fixed values. For example, an octave above frequency f is 2f, while an octave below is f/2.

But what about musical intervals besides the octave? Here we fall into a bit of a black hole. For a detailed guide, the reader is referred to Chapter 8 of Backus (1977), for example.

In what follows, we will introduce a few terms that the reader may encounter and try to give a quick introduction to the issues.

Western music divides the octave into twelve steps. In the perfect world, the interval between each step would be the same. Rather than expressing the intervals as a ratio, a linear scale is often encountered. In this case, the octave is said to consist of 1,200 cents, and each semitone represents an interval of 100 cents. Since the time of J. S. Bach, most pianos and other musical instruments have been tuned such that their notes, or intervals, fall as close as possible to this uniform-sized semitone. This is known as the tempered scale.

Nature, however, is not quite so perfect. We can try to generate the notes of the Western scale from the pitches of natural harmonics. We start with a note of frequency f. The first harmonic, 2f, gives us the octave above. The second harmonic, 3f, gives us a new note: the fifth, or dominant of the pitch associated with f. If f corresponds to the note C4 (C in the fourth octave), then 2f corresponds to C5 and 3f corresponds to G5, and G5:C5 = 3:2. In general, the fifth above any note is 3/2 times the frequency of that note. Going around what is known as the circle of fifths, we should be able to generate all 12 pitches in the scale using this interval (since as we go clockwise around the circle, each successive pitch is separated by a fifth).

Without working through all of the arithmetic, suffice it to say that by the time we get all the way around the circle, the fifth above F does not have a power-of-2 relationship with C. That is, using the 3:2 ratio, we don't really get a circle. So the tempered scale and uniform semitone are "artificial" and result from adjusting the ratios found in nature in order to "close" the circle of fifths. The result makes diatonic music possible but removes us from the world of simple ratios.

For designers, the logarithmic relation between the musical scale and frequency should be used if an equal-interval scale of pitch is desired. Pitch encodings, especially musically based, can be used effectively. The absolute encoding of data as pitch is to be avoided if absolute judgments are to be made. It is important to be aware of the myriad of interactions between pitch and other attributes of sound when using pitch, particularly if the aim is to convey orthogonal data dimensions using attributes of sound. Similarly, if pitch is used to represent magnitude, it is important to be aware of the cyclic nature of musical tones.

Finally, most pitch cues should be kept in the middle of the audible range. That way, they will be reproducible on even poor quality equipment and be audible by most people.

2.6.5 Loudness

Loudness is the sensation most directly associated with the physical property of sound intensity, where sound intensity is proportional to the sound pressure level squared. Roughly speaking, loudness (L) relates to intensity (I) according to the power law

$$L = kI^0.3 \qquad\qquad (2.6)$$

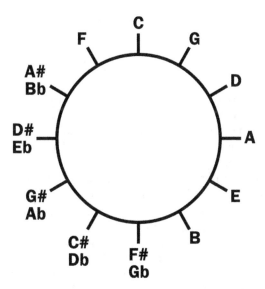

Figure 2.24 The circle of fifths. All 12 notes of the Western scale can be generated from a start note and the interval of a fifth (seven semitones). Each new note is a fifth above the previous one. If we use the ratio of 3:2 for a fifth, however, the note that we get after 12 steps does not have an exact octave relationship with the start note.

REGULAR RHYTHM

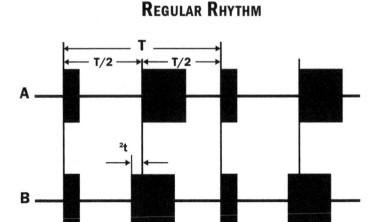

Figure 2.25 The equal-loudness contours for sine waves, after Fletcher and Munson (1933).

Source: From Roederer (2012, p. 83).

where k is a proportionality constant and loudness is measured in sones (an international standard defines the loudness of a 1,000 Hz tone at 40 dB as 1 sone) and intensity as decibels. This relationship means that a 10 dB increase in intensity results in a doubling of loudness. However, loudness depends on frequency. In general, tones at a given amplitude with frequencies between about 1,000 and 5,000 Hz are perceived as louder than those that are higher or lower. The frequency versus loudness function can be found in the form of equal-loudness contours. The equal-loudness contours for sine waves, also known as the Fletcher-Munson curves, are illustrated in Figure 2.25 (Fletcher and Munson 1933), depicted for sine waves. As an example, a sine wave at 1,000 Hz and 5 dB in amplitude is perceived as loud as a sine wave at 100 Hz and 40 dB in amplitude.

These curves establish, for example, that a tone at 60 dB is not as loud at 100 Hz as it is at 500 Hz. Not surprisingly, the frequency content of speech, which is approximatively between 100 Hz and 7 kHz, is within the part of the curve that shows maximum sensibility.

Moreover, loudness is affected by bandwidth. Within a critical band, the energy is summed; outside of a critical band, loudness is summed. Sounds with large bandwidth are louder than those with a narrow bandwidth, even if they have the same amplitude. Loudness also depends on duration. For sounds shorter than about a second, loudness increases with duration. For example, for each halving in duration, the intensity of noise bursts below 200 milliseconds must be increased by about 3 dB in order to maintain constant loudness (Scharf and Houtsma 1986). However, for sounds longer than a second, loudness remains constant. People are very bad at making absolute judgments about loudness; our ability to make absolute judgments of loudness is limited to a scale of about three to five different levels. As previously mentioned, loudness is affected by the location of the sound source with respect to the listener due to the inverse-square law and the effect of any obstacles that may be creating sound shadows.

For designers, as with pitch, if loudness is to be used to encode data, the proper function must be used to translate amplitude to loudness. Also, the interactions between loudness and frequency, bandwidth, and timbre should also be recognized, particularly if several of these variables are to be manipulated at once. Finally, remember that users are certain to adjust and misadjust playback loudness. Any data encoded by loudness must take this into account and be tolerant of a large margin of error. Alternatively, calibration procedures to help the end user set levels appropriate for their environment must be provided.

2.6.6   Duration, attack time, and rhythm

For most sounds, perceived duration corresponds pretty well to physical duration. The just noticeable difference (JND) for perceiving changes in the duration between two sounds is a change of about 10% for sounds longer than 50 milliseconds and proportional to the square root of the duration for sounds of less than 50 milliseconds (see Scharf and Buus [1986, p. 14.62]). This JND is independent of the level and the spectral bandwidth of the signal. However, duration affects rhythm. For instance, if two notes of equal duration alternate so that their onsets occur every 4 time unit, we hear a regular rhythm. If the duration of one is changed to be 3/4 the duration of the other, however, our perception changes. Even though the onsets are spaced equally, we don't hear it that way. Instead, the duration gives the long one extra weight that perceptually pulls the beat off-center (see Terhardt [1978]).

The perceived onset of a sound depends on the slope of its attack. People don't hear sounds, as starting until they have built up a certain amount of energy. Hence, in an orchestra, the gong player must anticipate an entry and start playing before other sustained instruments, such as the trumpets (Terhardt 1978; Wessel 1979; Vos and Rasch 1981). This is illustrated in Figure 2.26.

2.6.6.1   Implications for design

Once again, though physical dimensions of sounds can be specified independently, their perceived qualities may interact. In particular, care should be taken if duration and attack are to be manipulated independently. Likewise, rhythm involves more than the spacing of onset times, and manipulating rhythm separately from the durations of component sounds may be difficult.

SPECTRAL FUSION

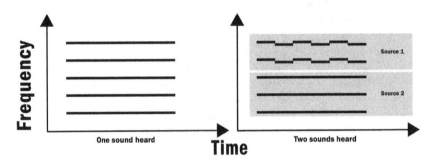

Figure 2.26 Two streams of sounds are shown, A and B. Each consists of a short sound
followed by a longer sound. All sounds have rectangular envelopes (i.e.,
sharp onsets and offsets). In A, the onsets of the sounds are equally spaced.
Consequently, one would expect a regular rhythm to be perceived if the
pattern repeats. However, this is not true due to the difference in length
of the two sounds. In order for the two sounds to repeat such that the long
sound is perceived to fall midway between the onsets of the short sounds,
the longer sound must start early by an experimentally determined value
Δt, as shown in B (after Terhardt 1978).

2.6.7   *Microvariation and spectral fusion*

We are seldom in an environment where we are exposed to only one sound
source. In a concert, for example, several instruments may sound at once; in
driving a car, there is the sound of the motor, the radio, the turn signals, and
the passenger speaking. Often the partials of the different sounds overlap.
How then do we know to which sound source a particular partial belongs?
For example, does a particular time-varying spectral component belong to the
clarinet or the oboe? The acoustic cues which enable us to make these judgments are largely a result of the time-varying nature of the sounds. In addition
to the comparatively large-scale amplitude changes described by envelopes, the
spectral components of virtually all natural sounds also have microvariations
in both pitch and amplitude. Vibrato and tremolo are two examples of such
microvariation.

Perhaps the most important cue in deciding whether two partials belong
to the same sound is the degree of coherence in their respective variation.
When the variation of spectral components is coherent, they are normally
judged to be derived from the same sound source. This process is known as
spectral fusion. This phenomenon is illustrated in Figure 2.27. Part A of the
figure represents several partials sounding simultaneous. There is no variation
in the frequency of the partials. They are, therefore, coherent. Consequently,
they are fused together perceptually and heard as a single complex sound.

A. One Sound is heard

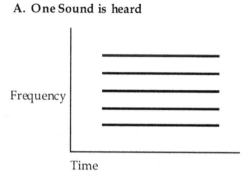

B. Two sounds are heard

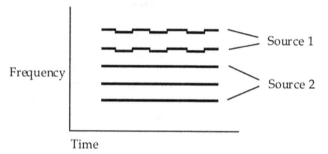

Figure 2.27 Coherence of variations results in spectral fusion and grouping of partials by source.

In part B of the figure, coherent microvariations (in this case vibrato) have been introduced on two of the partials. The partials now cluster into two groups, according to coherence: those with vibrato and those without. What will be heard are two distinct sounds from two different sources.

An understanding of spectral fusion is particularly important to those concerned with synthesizing nonspeech sounds. Two sounds meant to be distinguished may fuse into one complex sound if no microvariations are present. At best, the distinction of sources is made more difficult. In order to avoid this, special care must be taken to introduce the appropriate cues when sounds are to be distinguished. Conversely, manipulating these same cues gives us the means to merge two sounds that would otherwise be separate.

2.6.8   Timbre

Timbre, or tone color, is defined as "that attribute of auditory sensation in terms of which a listener can judge that two sounds similarly presented and having the same loudness and pitch are dissimilar" (American National Standards

Institute 1973). Given the negative nature of this definition, it is perhaps not surprising that timbre has been called "the psychoacoustician's multidimensional wastebasket category" (McAdams and Bregman 1979).

Timbre is influenced by the spectrum of a sound, and changing the partials of a sound will generally have the effect of changing its timbre. To the extent that a sound's waveform is determined by its spectral components, there is a relationship between a sound's waveform and its timbre.

However, this is not a very useful notion for at least two reasons. First, the spectrum of virtually all sounds in nature is not static, so it makes little sense to talk about the waveform of a violin, for example. Second, it has been shown that properties of harmonics' dynamic behavior can be far more important to timbre than the actual harmonics themselves.

As an example, some pioneering work by Risset and Wessel (1982) explored musical timbre by using computer-generated sounds. Back in 1969, Risset performed studies on trumpet tones, discovering the importance of time-varying characteristics of the spectra in order to obtain realistic simulations. Specifically, he observed how the spectrum varies with the frequency, maintaining a mostly invariant spectral envelope. Moreover, the attack's characteristics were discovered to be extremely important in order to create a realistic simulation, especially for longer sustained brass simulations. This pioneering research, as well as the multitude of research on timbre which followed, shows how the original theories of Helmholtz about spectrum and timbre are incomplete, to say the least. Timbre is clearly multidimensional, but the dimensions are still only partially known. Back in 1977, Grey (1977) proposed three dimensions of timbre using multidimensional scaling. Their physical correlates were (1) spectral energy distribution (brightness), (2) the relative amount of high-frequency energy in the attack, and (3) the degree to which amplitude functions of partials are synchronous (Grey 1977).

Although timbre research has been motivated recently by advances in computer music, many computer musicians are turning to physical modeling to understand and control sound. This move leads to research on everyday listening.

2.6.8.1   *Implications for design*

Given the range of audible differences that are referred to as timbre, there is obviously great potential to vary timbre to encode information. But given how little is known about what the perceptual dimensions of timbre might be, using timbre is also a tricky undertaking. Certainly, systems that use more than one manipulation of timbre at a time should be founded on good theory or, better, should be tested experimentally.

2.6.9   *Masking*

The loudness of a sound is context-dependent. Sounds may mask each other, as when conversations in a noisy car become impossible. Masking depends on loudness; in general, a loud sound masks a soft sound. Masking also depends on frequency. In general, sounds mask higher frequencies more than lower ones. Sounds within a critical band mask each other more than those more than a critical bandwidth apart. Sounds can be masked by other sounds that come before or after them; the masking sound does not have to be played at the same time as the masked sound. Masking can be predicted with great accuracy if the characteristics of ambient environmental noise are known (see Patterson [1982] for a good example of sound design to avoid masking in a noisy environment). Moreover, complex tones are more difficult to mask than pure tones.

2.6.9.1 Implications for design

Masking refers to context effects on hearing. Obviously, an audio cue will be useless if it is masked. One can reduce the probability of a sound being masked by increasing the complexity of its spectrum. Of course, this needs to be done with care since this could have the drawback of increasing the chance that the tone may become a masker rather than a maskee – a situation that is equally undesirable. A way to reduce the probability of one signal masking another is to avoid sustained signals. In cases where the cue must be sustained over time, use repeating short sounds rather than a long one. The intent of this approach is to leave "space" where otherwise masked sounds can be heard. Remember, however, that there must be enough space to ensure that forward and backward masking can't hide intended signals. There is a great deal of literature about masking; see in particular Boff and Lincoln (1988).

2.6.10 Auditory streaming

Auditory streaming refers to the tendency for separate sounds to be assigned to perceptual "streams," which correspond to different sources of sound. Streaming takes place both in grouping sequential sounds and in "fusing" partials in the perception of complex timbres. Figure 2.28 shows an example of streaming. In A, notes that are relatively close in frequency are alternated slowly. In this case, one perceptual stream is heard. In B, notes that are relatively far apart in frequency are alternated rapidly. In this case, two streams are heard: one of repeating low notes and one of repeating high notes. Comparing rhythms is much more difficult between streams than within. Overall, streaming is determined by frequency separation, tempo (the faster the tempo, the stronger the effect), timbre, and common fate. This last element, common fate, is the tendency of components to share similar temporal or frequency patterns.

For designers, understanding streaming is crucial in developing good auditory cues, be they sequential or simultaneous. In particular, if sequences of sounds break into undesirable streams or fail to be heard as separate streams, the intended message may be lost. For more information on streaming, see, for example, Bregman (1994) and McAdams and Bregman (1979).

STREAMING

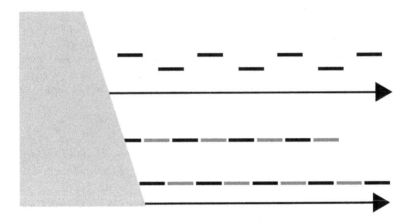

Figure 2.28 A typical example of streaming.

2.6.11   *Sounds with variations*

Sounds that include variations are the most noticeable and the most informative. Most simply, all sounds involve changes in air pressure; if such changes are not large enough or fast enough, we won't hear anything. But even if we can hear a sound, what we are most sensitive to are changes, transitions, or transients. Sounds that do not change quickly fade into the perceptual background.

Since changes convey information, we tend to seek and attend to informative stimuli. Static sounds are moved to the background. Sensitivity to change holds at all levels. Steady-state tones are less noticeable than changing ones (think of the rapid changes of sirens); steady rhythms – which involve transients – are less noticeable than changing ones (think of the steady "tick tick" of a clock).

Consider sitting in a restaurant when the air conditioner goes off. Two things become apparent: First, it may be that only when it goes off that you will become aware that it was ever on. This is even more surprising given the second observation that it was incredibly loud when it was on, and yet you "didn't hear it." It was constant, carried no information, so you pushed it into the background of your consciousness.

Consider walking down a street and hearing somebody walking behind you. Soon you will ignore the sounds, even though they contain many transients. But they will rapidly return to your attention should the person start running.

For designers, audio monitors can be designed so that in normal circumstances they produce relatively steady sounds which fade into the background. Changes associated with abnormalities can be signaled by sudden changes in the sounds that will attract attention. Why use the steady-state part at all? Think again about the air conditioning example. If somebody asked you "Is the air conditioning on?" you could shift your attention and give the answer. The point is that auditory displays can be designed so that information is constantly available but not obtrusive except in times of rapid and important change.

2.6.12 Psychoacoustic illusions

In this section, we will introduce some popular auditory illusions that have been discovered using computer-generated sounds.

2.6.12.1 Infinite rising in pitch

This effect is one of the most known auditory illusions and was first demonstrated by Shepard (see Shepard [1964]) and is therefore usually known as Shepard tones. His demonstration involved a chromatic scale (i.e., discrete notes rising stepwise at constant intervals of a semitone. This effect is the audio equivalent to the rotating "candy cane," like a barber's pole: the pitch of the sound seems to rise (or fall) continuously. Like the barber's pole, the effect works by introducing spectral components in at one end and out at the other. Risset later demonstrated the same effect that more directly followed the barbershop pole. Rather than going up or down in discrete steps, the pitch changes were continuous, constituting the perceived effect of an infinite glissando, either up or down (see Risset [1969]).

The mechanism underlying the effect is illustrated in Figure 2.29. It consists of a set of coherent sine waves, each separated by an octave. The entire set of waves is raised or lowered in pitch over time. The loudness of the sine waves varies, depending on their pitch. The amplitude/frequency function is a bell

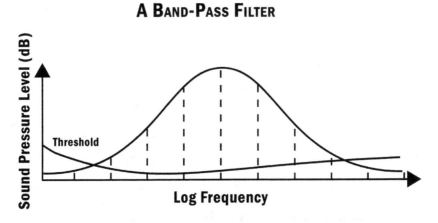

Figure 2.29 Shepard tones – the illusion of an infinite rising or descending pitch.

curve. Tones are loudest in the middle of the audible range and softest at the extremes. Consequently, tones fade in and out gradually at the extremes. Since they are octaves (therefore harmonic) and coherent (therefore fuse spectrally), the overall effect is of a single rising or falling complex tone.

Sound Example 2.11: Infinite glissando – a psychoacoustic illusion: Three examples are provided. An upward gliss, a downward gliss, and one that glisses in both directions.

2.6.12.2   Infinite accelerando/deccelerando

Furthermore, in 1974, a researcher at Bell Labs, Kenneth Knowlton, demonstrated that the technique underlying Shepard tones could also be applied to tempo/rhythm. The result was the illusion of an infinite accelerando of a beat, such as a drum (see Risset [1986]).

Sound Example 2.12: Infinite accelerando and deccelerando psychoacoustic illusion: First, we hear the accelerando, then a deccelerando.

2.6.12.3   Implications for design

The use of the techniques pioneered by Shepard (as applied to pitch, tempo, or both) has the potential to provide effective feedback as to the direction and rate of some background processes, especially when one does not know how long the process will take. That is, since the effect is infinite, the feedback will be effective no matter how long the process takes, always continuing to rise or fall without ever falling outside of the limits of perception.

2.7   Perception of 3D sound

Until now, we have examined the auditory perception of sounds without any particular cues regarding space. Perceiving sounds in space is also determined by several cues, such as head movements. An important source for localization is given by our head cues. Several studies have shown how allowing a listener to move the head improves sound localization (see Wallach [1940] and Begault and Trejo [2000]).

The Doppler effect is an effect whereby the perceived pitch of a sound source changes due to its relative motion toward or away from the listener. This is an effect that we hear every day, such as when a car or train passes us: the pitch goes up as the sound source approaches and goes down as it moves away. It is

DOPPLER EFFECT

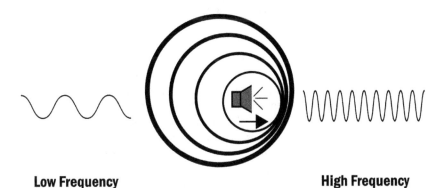

Low Frequency   **High Frequency**

Figure 2.30 The Doppler effect. A sound source of fixed frequency moves from A to B at 1/2 the speed of sound. A sound wave emitted at m will arrive in 1/2 the time of one that was emitted at A, thereby raising the perceived pitch by an octave.

an important effect to understand if one wants to be able to simulate moving sound sources.

Why does the pitch change? As we already know, the pitch that you perceive a sound is primarily determined by the frequency at which successive waves reach one's ear. The shorter the interval between waves, the higher the pitch, and vice versa. Consider the case illustrated in Figure 2.30.

Assume that a sound source is moving from point A to point B at half of the speed of sound. If a sound wave was initiated at point A, then by the time it reached point B, the source would have traveled halfway from A to B (to point m). Since it only has half as far to travel, a second wave initiated at m would reach B in half the time that it would have had the source remained stationary at its original position, A. The effect of the early arrival would be a rise in the perceived pitch of the sound by an octave (since the period between successive waves has been halved).

Conversely, if the sound is moving away from the listener, the pitch goes down since the interval between successive waves is lengthened due to the added distance that the wave must travel compared to a stationary source. The effective period of the sound wave is 3/2 that of the stationary case (remember, we are assuming that the source is traveling at 1/2 the speed of sound), so the sound will be perceived a fifth lower than it would if it were stationary. More formally, the frequency, f^1, at which a moving source of frequency f will be perceived, can be stated as

$$f^1 = f\left(\frac{c}{(c + rv_s)}\right) \tag{2.7}$$

where c is the speed of sound, r is the unit vector in radial direction, and v_s is the velocity of the sound source. Note that while we have described the effect in terms of the source moving and a stationary listener, a comparable effect occurs if the source is stationary and the listener is moving. The next formula takes into account the motion of both the source and the listener. Beware, however. Unlike the previous equation, we have simplified the math by making the assumption that the vector of motion is on the line intersecting the source and listener.

Note also that, as seen in the previous example, for an object moving at a constant speed, the magnitude of the pitch shift in approaching the listener is greater than that in moving away. In moving away, a negative value must be specified for velocity. As an exercise, verify the previous example by calculating the frequency of a source of A 440 Hz moving toward and away from a stationary listener at half the speed of sound. Use either the previous formula or the following one (Aesthetic Research Centre of Canada et al. 1978):

$$f^t = f_s \left(\frac{x(v - v_o)}{(v - v_s)} \right) \tag{2.8}$$

where: v is the velocity of the sound in the medium, v_o is the velocity of the observer relative to the medium, v_s is the velocity of the source relative to the medium, and f_s is the frequency of the source while stationary. The net implication of all of this is that the frequency of simulated moving sounds must be shifted in accordance with the Doppler effect in order for motion to or away from the listener to be realistic. Examples of how this can be accomplished can be found in the works of Chowning (1971) and Bosi (1990), for example.

2.7.1   Precedence/Hass effect

The precedence or Hass effect shows the importance of the listener's position when creating a phantom source between two real sources. When a sound is followed by another sound separated by a sufficiently short time delay which is below the listener's echo threshold, listeners perceive a single auditory event. The perceived spatial location is dominated by the location of the first-arriving sound (Haas 1949). The position of the virtual source will depend on the relative loudness of the sounds presented by each speaker. Figure 2.31 illustrates the case of placing a phantom midway between real sources.

The precedence effect is lost if the listener is closer to one speaker than the other. If not equidistant, the sound image will be localized to the closest speaker only (although both speakers will contribute to loudness). When listening to a stereo, if you hear sounds from the far speaker when sitting close to the other, you are hearing two channel effects, not stereo (i.e., the sound you hear from the far speaker is not being presented from the near speaker).

STEREOPHONY

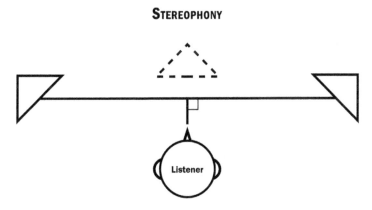

Figure 2.31 Stereophony – creating a phantom speaker using two real speakers.

2.7.2 *Binaural rendering*

If the problems of the precedence effect are due to both ears hearing the sounds from both speakers, then an alternative approach is to get around this by using headphones. Such binaural presentation works well in terms of being able to place sounds at specified angles relative to the ears. However, while the azimuth may be correct, there are often front/back ambiguities, and perception and rendering of elevation are still challenging.

One of the primary strategies for localization is head rotation. Since headphones are attached to the head, they rotate too. This means that a head tracker is needed in order to measure the rotation. The head-tracked position and orientation are combined with a real-time adaptive presentation of the sounds. One of the first examples of this system was the Convolvotron (see Wenzel et al. [1988]).

2.7.2.1 *The cocktail party effect*

The cocktail party effect is the phenomenon of the brain's ability to focus one's auditory attention on a particular stimulus while filtering out a range of other stimuli. Spatial sound enhances stream segregation by allowing auditory localization. The cocktail party effect refers to a phenomenon described in the literature (Cherry 1953; Arons 1992) on binaural hearing in which sound source intelligibility is shown to improve when listening dichotically (with two ears) compared to monotically (with one ear). Thus, at a party with many simultaneous conversations, a mingler can still follow any particular exchange by filtering according to one's position, the speaker's voice, or the subject matter.

Listeners have the ability to segregate different stimuli into different streams and subsequently decide which streams are most pertinent to them. This effect is what allows most people to "tune into" a single voice and "tune out" all others. It may also describe a similar phenomenon that occurs when one may immediately detect words of importance originating from unattended stimuli – for instance, hearing one's name among a wide range of auditory input.

For designers, accounting for 3D sound cues and paying attention to specific elements of a scene or event has recently become an essential element, especially given the recent developments in virtual, augmented, and mixed realities. 3D sound offers full surrounding experiences that are not possible with vision, given the limited field of view. With 3D sound, we can capture the attention of the user to specific locations. This topic will be treated in more depth in Chapter 9.

2.8   Hearing versus listening

As described in the previous examples, hearing can be considered as the ability to perceive mechanical vibrations as sound. It differs from listening, as it does not involve an attentive focus. We can hear sounds without the specific intention of doing so. Listening is an activity we carry out. It can bring our attention toward unnoticed sounds.

In one of the most important works on the phenomenology of sound, the composer Pierre Schaeffer describes four types of experiences of sound (Chion 1983). We can perceive sound, we can listen to it, and we can hear it and understand through it. Schaeffer's description unfolds the complexity of hearing and listening as processes that relate together perception, sound, consciousness, and meaning.

Michel Chion drew upon Schaffer's typologies to identify objective and subjective relationships with sound and their relative modes of listening (Chion 1994). He calls them causal, semantic, and reduced listening. Causal listening involves the listener focusing the understanding on which source produces the sound. When the source is known – for example, because we can see it – casual listening can help, for example, determine if a container is full or empty depending on the sound it produces. Semantic listening refers to a code or a language to interpret a message. In semantic listening, the purpose of a listener is to understand the meaning that a series of sounds can represent. Reduced listening is the mode in which a listener focuses on the acoustic attributes of sound itself, independently of its cause or meaning. Reduced listening has the power of opening up our ears and sharpening the power of listening. Pierre Schaeffer also proposed the concept of reduced listening. For both Schaeffer and Chion, reduced listening can be considered as a specific way in which we listen to sound, looking for its acoustic, spectro-morphological, and musically relevant characteristics. This is a form of analytical listening based on categorizations of the acoustic phenomenon, commonly used in specialized practices such as music theory, composition, and psychoacoustics. Listening for intentional reduction is useful for music composers who may use everyday sounds in their compositions. This is particularly relevant for cases in which the sound is not reproduced by its natural sound source, such as in acousmatic sounds, and technologically mediated reproduction of sounds, such as a digital sound played back by a computer. Reduced listening is a very strong intentional mode of listening that focuses on defining characteristics of sound, which require substantial effort in terms of concentration, as well as the skill of the listener to build categories in which a sonic phenomenon can be differentiated.

Understanding listening for Chion is instrumental in manipulating what is felt like a very embodied tie by the perceiver between the image seen and the sound heard. According to Chion, action-sound relationships can be continuously manipulated as they need to be believable and meaningful and not necessarily realistic.

The meaning-making power of listening is, therefore, a useful process for understanding the design of novel interactions mediated by sound. The link between our moving body, sounding, and ability to hear is another factor to consider when we analyze listening. In the book *Le Son*, Michel Chion (1985) describes ergoaudition, a modality in which listening reveals our sense of agency in the production of sound as a direct consequence of our own bodily actions. For example, we may be suddenly aware of our footsteps on a creaking wooden floor. By hearing sounds we produce with our actions, we become aware of our sounding potential, which can lead us to move differently. For example, we can walk slower if we want to avoid being loud and disturbing another person that may be in the same space as us.

2.9 Annoying sounds

So far, we have learned about the relationship between the physical parameters of a sound and the way it is perceived. But what makes a sound annoying? Having this knowledge is certainly helpful when designing auditory interfaces. We focus on some knowledge regarding everyday sounds. Much of the motivation for studying annoying sounds comes from industry. Manufacturers have long had an interest in understanding what makes sounds aversive so as to avoid these properties in products that emit noise (electric saws, refrigerators, cars, trains, etc.), and studies on this topic date back many decades.

When people are asked to rate the annoyingness of large sets of real-world sounds, considerable agreement is usually observed across listeners (Cardozo and Van Lieshout 1981). In addition to overall loudness, two properties that have substantial influence are sharpness and roughness (Terhardt and Stoll 1981). Sharpness describes the proportion of energy at high frequencies, with sharper sounds (those with more high-frequency energy) generally found to be less pleasant. Frequencies in the range of 2–4 kHz contribute the most to annoyingness (Kumar et al. 2008). This range is high in absolute terms but well below the upper limit of what is audible to a human listener with normal hearing. Screech-like sounds, much like fingernails on a blackboard, lose some of their annoying characteristics when frequencies in the 2–4 kHz range are filtered out but not when frequencies above this range are removed (Halpern et al. 1986). Roughness is the perceptual correlate of fluctuations in energy that occur over time, analogous to the fluctuations in surface depth that determine the roughness of an object to the touch. Fluctuations at rates between approximatively 20 Hz and 200 Hz are those that determine roughness (Terhardt 1974); for lower values, the fluctuations can be heard individually rather than contributing to the overall timbre. As a rule of thumb, the rougher a sound, the less pleasant it tends to be. The annoying effects of sharpness may be rooted in the frequency sensitivity of the ear, which peaks in the range of 2–4 kHz. The ear canal has a resonance in this range, boosting sound levels of these frequencies by as much as 30 dB (Chesky and Henoch 1999). Exposure to noise in this frequency range is thus most likely to damage the ear. The aversive response to these frequencies could therefore be because they sound the loudest and are potentially the most dangerous to listen to. Notably, most highly unpleasant sounds are much less aversive at low volume. It is less clear why roughness is unpleasant, as it does not obviously pose any danger to the auditory system. It is also unclear at present whether the reaction to roughness and other sound properties is universal. In Western music, rough sounds are thought to be unpleasant (Von Helmholtz 1912; McDermott et al. 2010). In some cultures, however, roughness is a staple of musical expression, and its aesthetic interpretation may be different than in the Western world (Vassilakis 2005). Even in Western music, rough sounds have become common in some subgenres, such as electronic and computer music. Associations between sounds and the events in the world that cause them also clearly play some role in whether we experience a sound as pleasant or unpleasant. In a large internet-based experiment, the sound rated most awful out of a large set was that of someone vomiting (Cox 2008). It is likely that this is mostly due to our association given to vomiting rather than the sound itself. The same study found that seeing the image of fingernails on a chalkboard or that of a dentist while listening to the corresponding sound yielded a worse rating for the sound (Cox 2008). This is an example of multimodal interaction, and we will see more of them in Chapter 8. Visual input can also render sounds less annoying. For example, white noise is deemed less objectionable when accompanied by a picture of a waterfall that suggests a natural sound source (Abe et al. 1999). In the field of auditory interfaces, Bonebright and Nees (2007) found that high-pitched interface sounds can be considered particularly annoying.

2.10   Pleasant sounds

Obviously, not all sounds are annoying, and it is particularly interesting in the context of auditory interfaces to understand how to design a sound that is pleasant. Indeed, many people find natural environmental soundscapes (ocean waves, leaves, wind, rainfall, etc.) to be relaxing and pleasant, to the point that recordings of such sounds are marketed to aid sleep and relaxation.

Why are these sounds enjoyable? Very little research has addressed the pleasantness of environmental sounds, but emotional associations with relaxing circumstances surely play some role. Such sounds also typically lack the acoustic properties described previously that are found in many annoying sounds. The sounds of oceans, rain, wind, and so on usually have more energy at low frequencies than at high (Voss and Clarke 1975) and feature slow temporal modulations (Attias and Schreiner 1997; Singh and Theunissen 2003) rather than prominent modulations in the roughness range. It is also interesting that the perception of many natural sound textures, such as water sounds, can be explained in relatively simple terms with generic statistics of the early auditory system (McDermott et al. 2009), though a relationship between this sort of simplicity and pleasantness remains conjecture at present. In general, very little research has addressed the role of aesthetics in auditory display design, and many questions remain regarding how to make aesthetically pleasing interface sounds. Regardless of the approach, evaluation of aesthetics needs to be longitudinal since preferences can evolve, and acceptance can increase or decrease as the user becomes more familiar with the interface.

2.11 Embodied sound and music cognition

So far, we have considered individuals as mere listeners (e.g., as minds that receive input); however, it is also interesting to examine the embodied way of understanding and experiencing sound and music that considers a listener in a closed interacting loop with her or his environment, being it a musical instrument or any sonic interface.

Sound is something that the listener can interact with, using sensorimotor, cognitive, and emotional abilities that optimize the interaction; it can be seen as an expression of the embodied mind (Leman et al. 2008; Leman 2016).

It was only until quite recently that embodied music cognition was explicitly proposed as a paradigm for music research (Leman et al. 2008), and there are several reasons for that. One is that new technologies became available that have enabled the recording of body movements. Motion-capture technologies and sensors are becoming now ubiquitous and easily accessible by researchers and practitioners who are interested in investigating how to track motion and gestures. Broadly speaking, musical gesture has been defined as "human body movement that goes along with music" (Jensenius and Wanderley 2010). In music, we often see people making sound-accompanying gestures, such as moving their bodies, shaking their heads, gesticulating with their arms, and so on to the music; we also see people making sound-producing gestures, such as playing air drums, air guitar, or air piano, when listening to music. Studies of people with different levels of expertise playing air piano, ranging from novices with no musical training to professional musicians, suggest that associations of sound with sound-producing gestures are common and also quite robust even for novices (Godøy et al. 2005).

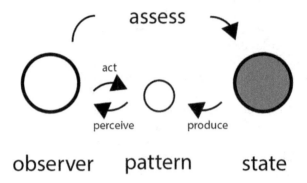

Figure 2.32 An action-prediction model that can be used in embodied sound design.

The embodied music cognition paradigm has therefore expanded its research field from cognition in perception to cognition in interaction. In fact, during the last decade, research in embodied music cognition has been strongly motivated by a demand for new tools in view of the interactive possibilities offered by digital media technology. These embodied cognition theories are supported by recent results in neuroscience. Studies on auditory-motor interactions in the perception and production of music have brought evidence of a strong coupling between action and perception (Haueisen and Knösche 2001; Zatorre et al. 2007). The interaction between auditory and motor systems is of particular interest because each action in a performance produces sound, which influences each subsequent action, leading to remarkable sensorimotor interplay. The notion of action-perception coupling is therefore central to the design of interactive systems where technology mediates our bodily interaction with sound.

A model of assessment is shown in Figure 2.32, adapted from (Lesaffre et al. 2017). The inferred action-state refines a prediction model for future assessments of moving sonic patterns.

A model of assessment. The observer interacts with a pattern (sound) and generates an estimate about the state of being that might have produced the observed pattern. An enactive assessment would imply that the assumed state is an action-state, which the observer connects with their own repertoire of action experiences.

Research in embodied music and sound cognition focuses on enactive aspects of sound perception, describing how gestural and bodily movement can be used to articulate descriptions of sound.

HCI researchers have also begun to consider interaction in terms of embodiment at the beginning of the 21st century (Dourish 2004). Dourish argued that the shift toward embodied perspectives in HCI was driven by the gradual expansion of the range of human skills and abilities that can be incorporated into interaction with computers. Increasingly since then, digital artifacts reveal affordances through the actions we perform on and with them, and the manipulation of these objects demands multiple senses so that sound is now becoming an inescapable component of interaction design. In interaction and sound discourses, the acousmatic notion of a sound object is replaced by the embodied notion of a sounding object (Rocchesso and Fontana 2003).

As humans, we inhabit an enacted world, and we experience sounds that are the products of our own actions, actions of other living creatures, or physical processes of various kinds. In most everyday situations, sounds can be associated with the actions that produced them or with the actions taken in response. Embodied interaction with sound and music supports an ongoing meaning formation process, in which actions allow for continuous refinement of the prediction model. Ongoing here means that assessments are, in fact, changing, on account of changing musical configurations, changing interaction patterns (due to attention, movement), and changing contexts (in concert, at home, during functional or aesthetic listening).

Rolf Godøy argues for a motor-mimetic theory of sound perception (Godøy 2003) in which he claims that perceiving sound is closely linked with mentally simulating the gestures that we believe have been made in the production of the sound itself. Godoy's work is inspired by electroacoustic composer Pierre Schaeffer and his theories of reduced listening (Chion 1983). Godøy investigated the link between gestures and raw sonorous objects, arguing for an intimate, corporeal, and felt link between energy aspects and morphologies of both gestures and sound. These sound objects are embodied as co-articulated gestural-sonic objects (Godøy 2010) and based on chunks of perceptual auditory groupings from psychoacoustics (Bregman 1994).

The gestural tracing of a sound can provide both kinesthetic and associative, extra-auditory information. By rendering sound as movement, we can study the relationship between the temporal aspect of sound and what we identify as action. This gestural rendering helps us to highlight not only matters of bodily response to sound. It also offers us ways in which we can try to frame bodily enaction as a form of communicating a visual impression of a sound heard.

We can see this as a form of embodied listening. As we have seen earlier, Godøy and Leman focus on the evoked corporeal response of musical stimuli and listening, focusing on imitational aspects of spectro-morphological and time-based profiles of sound in one case, or gestural association with playing a musical instrument or conducting music in the other. In addition to their accounts of embodied listening, listeners may draw upon other non-sonic elements of the associative process with sound, such as those rooted in their cultural baggage or in their memory. This can form a repertoire of action-sound relationships, gestures, and movements, conscious and unconscious, that may go beyond pure musical or sonic aspects instead of drawing upon other experiential aspects.

In embodied listening, we use the body as part of the listening process, as a way to relate to both the temporal pattern-based aspects of sound and to its symbolic everyday dimension, which affords our bodily participation in the sonorous event. In the work of Caramiaux et al. (2014), the concept of embodied listening is used as a way to design gestural-sound mappings. The authors claim that by looking at action-sound relationships arising from analyzing different listening modes, such as causal, based on sound-source, and acoustic, based on sound features, designers can implement instantaneous, temporal, and metaphorical mappings, which are intuitive for the users. Embodied listening refers to action-sound relationships that are revealed through the bodily movement of the listener, such as gestural rendering of sound. Studying nonmusical sounds, Caramiaux et al. (2014) showed that the gestures performed by participants while listening to environmental sounds depended on the level at which they were able to identify the sound source. Their experiment studied embodied listening – gestures invoked in the act of listening to sound. Gestures were performed in response to a sound stimulus and did not involve interactive control of sound production. The sound stimuli were either causal sounds, in which the action that has produced the sound is clearly identified, or transformed versions of the same sounds, in which the sound source could no longer be identified (noncausal sounds). Results showed that gestures associated with causal sounds mimicked the action causing the sound, whereas gesture associated with noncausal sound follows the sound's acoustic contours. This study helped to enhance the understanding of the link between sound perception and embodiment.

In the context of embodied music cognition, action-sound relationships rendered as gestures and trajectories have been studied merely through laboratory experiments with participants. Different techniques can be applied. Sound-tracing (Godøy 2010) consists of asking listeners to draw on a digital tablet what they felt as gestures corresponding to the musical excerpts they heard. This technique has been extended to study free movements (Nymoen et al. 2013) by asking participants to produce spontaneous gestures according to the musical and/or sound stimuli they listen to in the experiment. Sound-tracing provides researchers with ways to collect and analyze data on embodied links between sound and motion from the perspective of listeners.

Within interaction design, two subfields that do embrace the embodied perspective are haptics (Gillespie and O'Modhrain 2011) and tangible interfaces (Hornecker 2011) and will be considered in Chapters 7 and 8.

2.12   Conclusions

This chapter has reviewed the main concepts related to physical and perceptual parameters of audio, concluding with an overview of the latest developments in embodied music cognition and its relationship to interactive sound design. As this chapter has outlined, auditory display design requires a strong understanding not only of the acoustics of sound but also of how sound is perceived by the end users and what the implications are for audio designers.

There is a clear trend toward studying embodied music interaction in ecological settings, such as real listening, dancing, and music contexts. Ecological settings have a major advantage over the research laboratory because they allow for the study of human embodied interaction "in the wild." This is of particular relevance to the idea that the human brain (as a co-controller of interaction) works differently under a brain scanner (when lying still) than it does "in the wild" (when involved with actions). However, in comparison with laboratory conditions, the ecological approach requires clever experimental design in order to control for added variables. Alongside this emphasis on ecological settings, there is an agenda to simulate ecological settings in the laboratory and, even better, to bring the laboratory to the ecological setting. Such trends will be analyzed in the following chapters.

Note

1 Actually, what we get by tracing the waveform's outline is the sound's amplitude envelope, not that of its loudness. While amplitude and loudness are related, they are not the same, as our discussion of psychoacoustics will explain. However, it is the concept of an envelope that is important at this stage. Since the envelope is always symmetrical on either side of the x axis, we normally draw only the positive side. In specifying envelopes to sound synthesis equipment, for example, this is virtually always the case.

3 Sonification

3.1 Introduction

In 1989 William Buxton coined the term "sonification" at a tutorial of the CHI conference:

> *The use of sound for data representation*[, being] *the auditory counterpart of data visualization.* The definition of sonification was refined and adopted by the community in 1997, as the use of nonspeech audio to convey information. More specifically, sonification is the transformation of data relations into perceived relations in an acoustic signal for the purposes of facilitating communication or interpretation.

Sonification has been defined as a subtype of auditory displays that uses nonspeech audio to represent information. One of the earliest uses of nonspeech audio in the interface was the representation of complex data. Even with sophisticated analysis, exploring such data to find meaningful patterns is still often a problem requiring human intervention.

Consider the graph in Figure 3.1 (and listen to Sound Example 3.1). It is easy to identify examples 1, 3, 4, and 7 as one set (*Iris setosa*), examples 2 and 5 as a second set (*Iris versicolor*), and examples 6, 8, and 9 as a third set (*Iris virginica*).

Representing complex data in sounds might be considered the acoustic equivalent of scientific visualization. Typically, representing scientific data as nonspeech audio involves mapping the parameters of the data to the parameters of sound. In the previous example, the sepal length was mapped to pitch, the sepal width to volume, the petal length to duration, and the petal width to the fundamental waveshape (a variation between a pure sine and a square waveform); the petal width, therefore, represents the timbre dimension. The acoustic properties of each sound are thus shaped by the values of the parameters of the underlying data.

3.2 History

One of the earliest and most successful examples of sonification is the Geiger counter, invented in 1908. A Geiger counter has a tube of low-pressure gas;

DOI: 10.4324/9781003260202-3

DATA SONIFICATION

	S-length	S-width	P-length	P-width
1	1.34	5.32	4.31	8.014
2	7.34	2.87	2.45	12.349
3	4.67	9.04	9.99	1.57

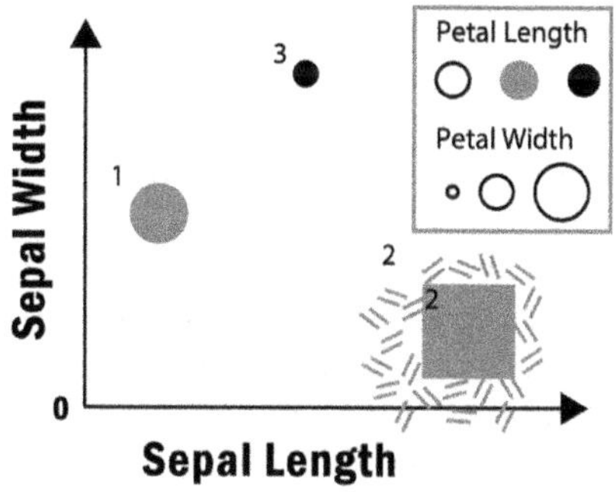

Figure 3.1 It is difficult to distinguish the three sets of data by looking only at the numeric data. In both graphical and aural representations, the three sets are easily differentiated.

each particle detected produces a pulse of current when it ionizes the gas, producing an audio click. The original version was only capable of detecting alpha particles. The first use of an auditory Geiger counter was reported in 1917 when a sensitive telephone was incorporated into the electrical circuit in order to listen to the audification of electrical impulses (Kovaric 1917).

A scientific version of representing data in sound was presented by S. D. Speeth in 1961 (see Speeth [1961]). Speeth was particularly interested in distinguishing underground explosions from natural earthquakes. Seismograms were digitized at a sampling rate of ten samples per second and then time compressed to 1,000, 2,000, 4,000, and 8,000 samples per second. These samples were read through a digital-to-analog converter and written on magnetic tape for audio playback. Listeners were quite successful in separating the explosions from the earthquakes.

One of the first examples of the use of sonification in a composition dates to 1970. The American composer Charles Dodge wrote a piece entitled "The Earth's Magnetic Field" (Thieberger and Dodge 1995). In this composition, the sounds correspond to the magnetic activity of the Earth in the year 1961. Dodge and colleagues used the Kp index for magnetic activity. A new value for the index is calculated every three hours and may take any of 28 distinct values. The musical interpretation is a correlation between the succession of indices and pitches over four octaves.

In the early 1970s, Max Mathews and colleagues (Chambers et al. 1974) used both graphics and sound to present up to five dimensions of data. Two variables provided a visual x-y scatter plot, while frequency, timbre, and amplitude modulation provided a corresponding note of three dimensions for each point. A user interactively selected a sequence of points to hear. Thus, the user sees the entire scatter plot while hearing a sequence of sounds. Using examples of actual scientific data, Mathews and colleagues demonstrated that auditory representations reveal structure in the data.

Mathews proposed a number of aural dimensions: loudness, pitch, vibrato, rate of modulation, aspects of timbre, and tempo. While these parameters are suited for discrete or continuous variables, Mathews also was interested in the use of chords, stereo, and localization for discrete events. He suggested that eye-tracking devices might be useful in integrating the visual and aural representations of sounds so that what one hears is what one sees. Mathews identified several problems for data sonification: The range of most of the sound dimensions is relatively small, thereby limiting the range of the data values represented. Sounds provide a gestalt of the data; other methods of analysis are necessary for quantitative results. Graphics have the advantage of offering a simultaneous view of all the data, while sound is inherently a stream of events.

In 1980 Yeung, a chemist, also recognized that sound could be used in addressing human pattern recognition in data analysis (Yeung 1980). He was concerned that sound dimensions are based on quantitative standards, continuity in scaling, independence, resolution, and relative ease in perception. The nine parameters he chose were pitch (two dimensions, one in the 100–1,000 Hz range and the other in the 1,000–10,000 Hz range), loudness (in increments of 3 dB), amplitude damping, direction (as determined by three variable values to locate a position in a cube thus requiring six loudspeakers, at the top, bottom, front, back, left, and right of the listener), duration/repetition, and rest (the time between repeats of the entire sequence).

Yeung felt that it would be possible to use at least these nine dimensions in sound and perhaps as many as 20. Yeung took a data set of elemental concentrations of ten metals in 63 samples from four sites and mapped seven of the ten variables to his primary sound parameters (neglecting the 3D location information). Four analysts heard 40 samples from the four data sets and were subsequently able to achieve 90% to 100% correct classification after one or two training sessions.

In all cases of early work of representing data in sounds, scientists were concerned with the human ability to find patterns in a complex set of data. They were interested in making use of the fact that we easily distinguish a variety of sounds and that this gestalt listening could be applied to data exploration. Furthermore, Speeth, Mathews, and colleagues and Yeung were concerned about verifying their results and ran experiments to show that the sound did yield appropriate and useful information relative to the data being represented. Their methods involved mapping the values of the data itself to various parameters of sounds. They raised issues about the perceptual abilities of the human ear, the need for a variety of data representation methods, and the necessity for user interaction with the data presentation.

In 1992, the International Community for Auditory Display (ICAD) was founded by Gregory Kramer as a forum for research on auditory display, which includes data sonification. ICAD has since become a home for researchers from many different disciplines interested in the use of sound to convey information through its conference and peer-reviewed proceedings.

There have been many explorations and examples of sonifications. Medical applications of sonification have included heart rate monitoring (Ballora et al. 2004), knee-joint signals (Krishnan et al. 2001), and EEG data (Väljamäe et al. 2013), which will be examined as a case study in more depth. Moreover, weather data (Childs and Pulkki 2003; Flowers et al. 2001) and financial and stock market data have been widely explored (Neuhoff et al. 2002).

Sonification has also been used in data analysis and exploration tasks. For example, a report on sonification commissioned by the National Science Foundation describes a problem during the Voyager 2 space mission while the spacecraft was traversing through the rings of Saturn. Visual displays were not helpful in identifying the problem. When the data were played using sound, a rapid-fire pattern was detected whenever the spacecraft was passing through an area with a higher concentration of dust. The machine gun sound heard after the data were played was linked to high-speed collisions with micrometeoroids (Barrass and Kramer 1999). In this case, visual display techniques have failed to provide insightful information, whereas the sonification helped with identifying the origin of the problem.

In 2013, Dubus and Bresin presented a review of mapping strategies for sonification (Dubus and Bresin 2013). The review resulted from studies in the field of sonification documented in 179 scientific publications representing 60 projects. Five high-level categories of sound parameters were identified: pitch-related, timbral, loudness-related, spatial, and temporal. The measures used in the classification were the frequency of use of mapping; moreover, the kind of sonification technique used was also examined. Results showed that pitch was the most used dimension in sonification, used in 86.7% of the analyzed projects; this was followed by loudness (73.3%), spatialization (51.7%), duration (40%), brightness (23.3%), timbre (20%), tempo (16.7%), and spectral power (15.0%). Spatial auditory dimensions are almost exclusively used to sonify kinematic physical quantities. An important sonification technique called model-based sonification (Hermann and Ritter 1999) will be described in the following section.

3.3   Model-based sonification (MBS)

Model-based sonification (MBS) is a sonification technique that takes a particular look at how acoustic responses are generated in response to the user's actions and offers a framework to govern how these insights can be carried over to data sonification. MBS refers to all concrete sonification techniques that make use of dynamic models, which mathematically describe the evolution of a system in time, parameterize and configure them during initialization with the available data, and offer interaction/excitation modes to the user as the interface to actively query sonic responses, which depend systematically upon the temporal evolution model (Hermann and Ritter 2005). MBS has been demonstrated to be effective in a number of situations, including in being able to intuitively perceive the complexity or dimensionality of a data set (Hermann and Ritter 2004), a problem that had been previously explored using parameter-mapping sonification (Bly 1994).

In the following sections, we will examine some sonification examples in more detail.

3.4 Case studies

Studying the representation of data in sounds explores not only the accessibility of complex data but also the forms of audio representations. Five pieces of work will illustrate several characteristics of sonification research, from the origins to more modern examples. One of the early studies was the dissertation work of Bly (1982), who undertook to verify that sounds could yield useful information about the underlying data. At the same time, Mezrich et al. (1984) focused on time-varying data and the potential for integrating sound and graphics to promote pattern recognition. Smith et al. (1990) created a workstation environment for exploratory data analysis using scientific visualization and sonification. (Lunney and Morrison 1981) concentrated on applying the methods for the visually impaired.

3.4.1 *Case study 1: presenting information in sound*

Bly was interested in the problems of portraying multidimensional data for exploratory data analysis. Although a variety of graphical methods existed for data representation (Everitt 1978; Tukey 1970), the analyst was nevertheless limited to the number of dimensions that can be perceived visually and to the constraints of a visual display such as focused visual attention. Bly's work made two contributions to the study of sonification: one is that she tried a variety of data types and mappings, and two is that she conducted an experiment to show that the sound representation did, in fact, yield useful information for exploratory analysis.

Bly attacked three types of data: discrete multidimensional samples, logarithmic data, and time-varying data. With sets of discrete data samples, the particular problem Bly addressed was that of discriminant analysis. Given known samples from each of the three sets, can an analyst correctly classify an unknown sample? Bly represented each data sample as a single note of up to six characteristics: pitch, volume, duration, waveshape, attack, and harmonic. The pitch was selected from the 128 musical notes ranging over four octaves. The volume was dependent on the equipment available and ranged across 12 levels ("very soft" to "very loud"). The duration of a single note varied in 5-millisecond steps from 50 milliseconds to 1,050 milliseconds. For timbre, a sine wave with 128 samples between −1.0 and 1.0 was the base parameter. For each of the original 128 values, one was randomly selected and modified until a completely random waveshape resulted. This provided 128 waveshape variations. The attack envelope was varied in fifteen increments between a gradual attack (slope of 45 degrees) and a constant attack. Finally, an odd harmonic (the fifth) was chosen and varied in waveshape as the fundamental. Bly recognized but ignored the problems of psychoacoustics in the hopes of gaining some basic results with respect to the usefulness of a straightforward application of sound to data.

She first applied her technique to the Fisher iris data as described in the introduction to this chapter. Representing the data aurally, Bly found the three species of iris flowers to group as accurately as with most graphical methods (nearly all listeners could classify all but one or two samples correctly). Similarly, spectra data was encoded into sounds. A few individuals were given 20 known samples from each of four sets and then asked to classify twenty unknown samples. The results were quite successful and compared favorably to a similar classification test using Chernoff's faces as a graphical representation (Chernoff 1973).

In representing logarithmic data, Bly was motivated by the logarithmic relationship between frequency and pitch and by the frequent difficulty in reading logarithmic data more generally. Like Speeth, Bly took advantage of seismic records of earthquakes. However, she was interested in finding patterns within the earthquake data itself and in representing logarithmic data generally. Given the longitude, latitude, depth, magnitude, and start time for a series of quakes, Bly encoded the magnitude (the exponential variable) in pure frequency while displaying the location. A magnitude of 0.0 mapped to 5,120 Hz; 8.0 mapped to 20.8 Hz. Depth was not used, but patterns and extremely large events were easily observable, suggesting that sound could be used to highlight features that are most relevant to seismologists.

More interesting, perhaps, was an attempt to play logarithmic plots musically. Frequently a 2D logarithmic plot could not be easily distinguished from another, but audio representations of the same data were distinguishable. The plots consisted of scatter points and the corresponding best fit line of the following form:

$$y = Ae^{Bx}$$

By varying the values of A and B, different plots were obtained, which appeared visually quite similar. A chirp designated a sound plot in which the x-value was encoded as time and the y-value provided the frequency. A warble designated a sound plot in which the slope (y/x) provided the frequency base (thus, a linear plot has a constant warble). Listening to the plots made them much more distinct than the graphs alone.

For time-varying data, Bly took information from battlefield simulations. These simulations were run with different starting parameters and then analyzed based on the results of the battle. However, the length of the battle and the amount of data collected over time made it difficult for the analyst to gain any appreciation for the differences that occurred in the process of the battle itself. Therefore, Bly created battle songs for the simulations. The intuition was that similar battles would create similar songs so that an analyst could quickly find those battles that differed substantially from the norm. An analyst could subsequently attend to a more careful examination of the distinguished battles.

To validate the notion of sonification for exploratory data analysis, Bly ran a series of experiments. The data sets were discrete data samples of six dimensions generated in well-defined ways. Subjects listened to a few sounds from each of the two sets and then decided for each subsequent sound whether it belonged in set 1 or in set 2. The training samples and test samples were chosen randomly but did not overlap. The study consisted of three phases: One, the data was translated, scaled, and correlated to ensure that users appropriately recognized the differences in data sets. Two, the subjects performed a discriminant analysis task on 6D data sets. Three, different mappings and training further substantiated the results.

In phase 1, a set of data was transformed to create a second, related set of data. In this way, the expectation was that as the data sets were further apart (a greater transformation), participants could more easily determine into which set a sound sample belonged. The second set of data was created from the first set by translating, scaling, or correlating the data values. As expected, subjects were able to identify an increasing number of samples as the translation factor increased and the data sets became more widely separated. Similarly, as the scaling factor increased, the ability to discriminate between two sets increased. However, for some value of increased scaling, the ability to discriminate became more difficult (although the sets were even further "apart"). Overall the scaled data was more difficult to distinguish but notice that set 1 essentially lies within set 2. In the final experiment of phase 1, the data in set 1 were strongly correlated, and those in set 2 were a random mix of samples with no correlation. Subjects did not perform particularly well on the correlation differences. Note that in none of the cases were subjects given information about how the data sets differed.

Despite some mixed results, phase 1 did indicate that participants obtained useful information about data from aural representation. The goal of phase 2 was to determine if sound could add information to a graphical method of data presentation. In this case, the two sets of data were generated so that they were only distinct in space. That is, data was obtained from a normal random deviate generator and then separated into two sets such that a sample belonged to set 2 if and only if the following applies:

$$x_{22} + x_{32} + x_{42} + x_{52} + x_{62} <= 1.52 \text{ OR}$$
$$x_{12} + x_{32} + x_{42} + x_{52} + x_{62} <= 1.52 \text{ OR}$$
$$x_{12} + x_2 + x_{42} + x_{52} + x_{62} <= 1.52$$

Thus, at least five of the six variables in each sample of set 2 had a value less than 1.5, and at most one of the variables, x1, x2, or x3, could have a value greater than 1.5. In a complete positive and negative space, set 2 lies somewhat within set 1, and a projection plot onto any two axes has overlap.

Each sample was represented by a note consisting of pitch, volume, duration, waveshape, attack, and harmonic, as described earlier. For the experiment, the mapping was as follows:

x1 → *waveshape*
x2 → *overtone waveshape*
x3 → *pitch*
x4 → *envelope*
x5 → *duration*
x6 → *volume*

The sounds in set 2 were generally shorter and softer than set 1 sounds because variables x4, x5, and x6 were always each less than 1.5. If a set 2 note were buzzy (random waveshape), then it was low in pitch since both x1 and x3 couldn't both be large. Similarly, if it were high in pitch, then it was a more pure tone. For the visual display, 2D plots were generated of the data. A particular sample was indicated by highlighting that point.

Seventy-five subjects participated in phase 2, 25 in each of three groups. The first group had only an aural representation of the data, the second group had only a visual representation of the data, and the third group had both aural and visual representation. With sound only, the first group correctly identified 64.5% of the samples, the second group with graphics only identified 62% correctly, and the third group using both sound and graphics identified 69% of the samples. All the results verified significantly better discrimination between sets than if the subjects were responding by chance. In particular, the identification with both sound and graphics was significantly better than with either sound or graphics alone.

In phase 3, the same data was used as in phase 2; however, the mapping was changed. From discriminant analysis calculations on the data, it was determined that the importance of the contribution of each variable could be ranked as x2, x1, x3, x6, x4, and x5. Subjectively listening to the sound variables suggested a ranking of pitch, duration, waveshape, volume, envelope, and overtone. These rankings determined a new mapping (x2: pitch, x1: duration, x3: waveshape, x6: volume, x4: envelope, and x5: overtone). The results did not indicate a significant difference with this change in mapping.

Another aspect of phase 3 was to provide additional training. A set of subjects who had participated in phase 2 again performed the discriminant analysis task. This time, they were given examples and explanations of the data differences in phase 1 to acquaint them with ways sounds might differ based on data values. They could listen to each of the six dimensions varying alone, they were allowed to listen to the training samples at any time throughout the experiment, and they could listen to the training samples in any order. The average number of correct responses was 73.8%, compared to 64.5% originally for sound-only representation. Unfortunately, there was an experimental flaw, and training samples were not deleted from the larger set of test items. This potential repetition of samples could contribute to better performance.

Bly's work confirmed her hypothesis that sound offers useful information for multivariate data presentation. In addition, she offered a number of early explorations of various data types and possible sonifications. The weaknesses of the work indicate a number of issues for further study. The interdependencies among the sound parameters (the psychoacoustics) cannot be ignored. The question of which sound parameters to use and how to map the data to these parameters is very much open. The integration of more sophisticated graphical displays deserves attention. Furthermore, this work gives very little indication of the effects of learning and what types of data are best suited for sound encoding.

Sound Example 3.3: Illustrate Bly's work with experimental 6D data.

3.4.2   Case study 2: dynamic representation of multivariate time series data

While Bly's work demonstrated that multidimensional data samples can be usefully represented in sound, the work of Mezrich et al. (1984) took a systematic approach to the design of animated graphics with audio representation. They were interested in finding patterns in time-varying data. Using economic indicators, they mapped the data to musical notes so that each indicator has its own melody over time. The resulting data presentation takes advantage of the listener's ability to pick out similar sequences of notes to locate trends in the data.

Typically, time-series data is depicted graphically as a 2D plot, the horizontal dimension being time. Multiple variables are overlaid, stacked, or even displayed on separate axes so that seeing correlations in the data is difficult. Even more difficult is the problem of finding patterns in the data as a whole. The usual statistical methods often just reduce the multiple variables to a single composite index. Mezrich and colleagues hoped to use audio and graphical animation to provide insight into dynamic information while preserving all the information available. Their goal was to facilitate global pattern recognition to allow an analyst to find relationships among variables. They did not intend to portray precise quantitative data or to replace traditional graphs as one means of data representation.

Mezrich and colleagues explored their ideas using seven economic indicators descriptive of the cyclic state of the economy. For each of the seven indicators

SONIFICATION MAPPING

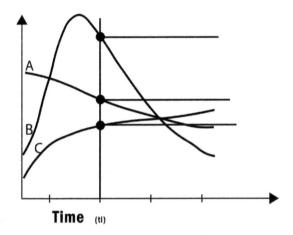

Time (ti)

Figure 3.2 At a time, *ti*, the value for each economic indicator determines the length of the vertical line pair and the pitch of the corresponding note.

or variables, they assigned both a note and a vertical line pair. At any point in time, the pitch of the note was determined by the value of the economic indicator at that time; all other characteristics of the note, such as loudness, were held constant. Similarly, the height and position of the vertical line were also dependent on the value of the variable. For small values, the note had a low pitch, and the corresponding vertical line pair was short and near the center of the graphical display. For large values, the note had a high pitch, and the corresponding vertical line pair was tall and positioned at the edges of the display. Each of the seven economic indicators was assigned a different color for the respective line pair. The seven corresponding notes did not differ except in pitch as determined by the values of economic indicators. Figure 3.2 illustrates the mapping from economic data to notes.

An analyst could play a single variable over a period of time, listening to the notes rise and fall while watching the pair of lines come forward and retreat. A combination of variables provided an animation of line pairs and a tune of the corresponding pitches or voices. A combination of variables could be explored for correlations among the indicators; time slices could be explored for patterns of behavior.

There are few, if any, experimental methods for measuring the amount of insight a data representation provides. In order to test the usefulness of their approach, Mezrich and colleagues set up a series of experiments to determine a user's ability to discern correlations among variables. The experiment was designed to measure how easy it is to perceive a relationship among a set of variables – that is, how easily a correlation among a set of variables can be perceived. Using four variables or dimensions, the experiment compared three graphical techniques (overlaid, stacked, and separated graphs) and the dynamic technique. The experiment measured the threshold correlation for each of these four techniques. Six subjects were tested on all experimental conditions with the order of representation balanced across subjects. Subjects recognized correlations more readily with the dynamic presentation than with most graphical representations. The partial exception, overlaid graphs, appears to be related to series length, suggesting that temporal effects or data magnitude are important.

In a subsequent study (Frysinger 1988), Frysinger explored the issue of correlations in overlaid graphs as well as other issues raised by Mezrich and colleagues. He conducted an investigation of auditory/visual representations of multivariate time-series data to determine the sensitivity of the previous results of Mezrich and colleagues to time-series dimensionality and signal detection tasks, as well as to determine the degree to which an auditory display was enhanced by a simultaneous visual display. Two forced-choice experiments were conducted in which subjects were to determine which of the two data sets was correlated (Task 1) or contained a perturbed version of a previously trained data set (Task 2).

A modified up/down procedure was used to estimate the psychophysical threshold of signal recognition for each of three display types: overlaid visual line graphs, a dynamic auditory/visual representation, and an auditory-only representation. This threshold was taken as a measure of display effectiveness. Subjects' data interpretation performance was found to depend upon the detection task. For correlation detection, time-series dimensionality was a significant variable in display performance, and the combined auditory/visual display proved superior to the auditory-only display. For trained-pattern detection, dimensionality was apparently not a factor, and the performance of the auditory/visual display was essentially the same as the auditory-only display.

These results illustrate the futility of attempting to characterize the properties of auditory data representation independent of the data analysis task.

The work of Mezrich et al. (1984) was important both in terms of the presentation offered, an integration of animated graphics and sound for time-varying data, and in the experimental data to test their approach. They also discovered informally that mapping the frequencies to the chromatic scale was more effective than using pure frequencies. Furthermore, they offered a system that was user-tailorable. The real-time interactive capabilities provided an important opportunity to highlight or tease out patterns in the data that might convey information.

Sound Example 3.3: Illustrate Mezrich's work with a pattern and then the pattern repeated but embedded in a larger context.

3.4.3 Case study 3: stereophonic and surface sound generation

The third type of data, to be distinguished from discrete samples and time-varying data, is that of a space of coherent, or inherently visual, data such as a surface or solid. Although the data might be sampled at discrete points in the space, those data points have a meaningful relationship as one moves among them in the space. Such data occurs, for example, in brain scans, solid volume measurements, and geographic tracking data. Smith et al. (1990) had been tackling the problem of designing a workstation for scientific perceptualization, providing specifically for inherently coherent or visual databases. One particular domain of data has been magnetic resonance imaging scans of a cross-section of a human brain. The typical resolution of these scans is 256×256, with eight bits of information per pixel. Note that each of the 256×256 pixels can be considered as a data sample of eight dimensions. However, unlike the discrete samples in Bly's domain, these samples are related in the x,y space. Thus, one is interested not only in examining the individual data points but also in examining the relationships among neighboring points. It is important to note, however, that their techniques may certainly be used for inherently nonvisual databases (such as Bly's samples) in which the user specifies the x- and y-axis parameters.

As with other work on scientific data representation using nonspeech audio, Smith and colleagues are interested in capitalizing on multiple domains of human perceptual capabilities and in finding new paradigms for exploratory data analysis. Their work is further motivated by the desire to design and build a workstation environment that allows the exploration of multivariate data interactively and with a multitude of data sets. A third goal is to provide support for experimentation in the use of iconographic displays. The Exvis (Exploratory Visualization) project underlying their work is aimed at providing a visualization (we might say perceptualization) workstation that supports these goals.

Exvis data is represented both graphically and aurally as icons. Each data point (or pixel) has an x,y position on a graph. At each point, the variables at that point are displayed as a graphical icon of an unlimited number of dimensions, typically at most 20. The graphical icons are stick-figure icons consisting of a body and some number of limbs (typically four) arranged in some topological configuration. (Limbs are restricted to being attached only to the ends of the body or to the ends of other limbs, and only two attachments can be made at any point.) Each limb has length, width, angle, and color. Thus, a five-limb icon can represent 20 data dimensions. In addition, each icon has an associated auditory icon/note consisting of five dimensions or sound characteristics: pitch, loudness, waveshape (as determined by the depth of frequency modulation), rate of attack, and rate of decay. Note that the mapping of the data values to the graphical and auditory dimensions may be independent or redundant. The premise is that interesting gradients and contours in the auditory or visual texture of an iconographic display reflect structures in the underlying data.?

Also, an analyst may choose to use only the visual representation, only the aural representation, or both.

The sonification is entirely interactive in that the auditory data presentation is triggered by the mouse position within the graphical display. For example, if one selects the point illustrated in Sound Example 3.3, one might hear the note. In addition to listening to the samples as discrete notes, an analyst can play a sequence by sweeping along a line in the space. Depending on the rate of attack and decay of the various notes, the auditory sound becomes a texture of sounds, just as the graphical display is a texture of icons. The sound texture varies depending on the speed and direction in which the user moves the cursor. Up to eight voices are used in sequence so that each sound icon or note is unique. The repertoire of sounds includes but is not limited to musical tones, bells, and even apparently random noise. Although changeable, the vibrato, tremolo, and ratio of carrier frequency to modulation frequency are held constant for a given display or sound representation. Ongoing work includes a focus on using left/right stereo and distance (created by reverberation) to offer clusters of auditory icons. Within a cluster or region, the sounds may be heard simultaneously with or independently of other sounds in that region. The ordering of the presentation of the sounds in the region is a user-defined ordering, such as left-to-right/top-to-bottom. Another scheme for activating the sounds of several icons as a cluster is to use *sound paintbrushes* that specify an area of the display.

A pilot study was run to test the hypothesis that sound attributes, in addition to visual attributes, would improve the performance of subjects in classifying regional patches. The data set was 4D with two regions, A and B, specified for the experiment. Regions A and B had a single point of intersection. Test subjects were shown representative samples from A and B and were then shown a display consisting of 16 different patches of icons. The task was to determine for each of these patches whether it belonged to Region A or to Region B. Each patch was created from a data set clustered around a point selected at random from Region A or Region B. A patch from Region A and a patch from Region B might have a non-empty intersection. Two dimensions of the data were mapped to the visual icon (one-limb icons with variable length and variable angle) and two to auditory attributes. Eight subjects performed the task twice, once using only the visual texture of the patches and once using both the auditory and visual attributes. For each task, the screen was created anew.

As with the work of Bly and Mezrich and colleagues, Smith and colleagues used the chromatic scale for determining sound pitch.

Sound Example 3.3: Various notes highlighted on a graph visually and a sequence/sweep, also shown on the graph.

3.4.4 Case study 4: auditory presentation of experimental data

Another major area of early work is the use of sonification for those who are visually impaired. Lunney and Morrison attacked problems similar to those of Bly, Mezrich, and Smith's multidimensional data representation for exploratory analysis, but with the need to represent the entire work in the aural domain (Lunney and Morrison 1981). Lunney and Morrison were interested in the presentation of infrared spectra, both because it is complex data (multidimensional) and because it is an important tool in the identification of organic compounds. Their goal was to provide improved access to data for visually impaired scientists and students. Their techniques were intended to allow the identification and classification of samples and the recognition of similarities and differences in data patterns.

To obtain infrared spectra, scientists use spectrophotometry to measure the absorption of light by a given sample. For each wavelength, the spectrophotometer detects the intensity of the light passing through the sample. Typically a graph is created in which the intensity of the transmitted light is plotted as a function of the wavelength. The method is particularly important in the identification of organic (carbon-containing) compounds because almost every organic compound has a unique spectrum. To translate a visual spectrum to one in the aural domain, the continuous infrared spectrum is considered a set of discrete events. That is, each absorption peak in the spectrum is replaced by a vertical line having location (frequency) and height (intensity). Thus, a single spectrum consists of some number of ordered pairs of values. The frequency of each peak (the location) is mapped to pitch and the intensity to time durations. Lunney and Morrison presented the resulting set of notes in three different ways. One, the spectrum was represented by a "tune" consisting of the notes played in order of decreasing frequency. Since peak frequencies are mapped to pitch, the "tune" was monotonically decreasing. In the second set, the notes were played in order of decreasing intensities. In this case, all notes in the sequence were played with the same duration so that only the order in the "tune" indicated the relative value of the intensity of the peak. This representation was mostly like a "spectral melody." Finally, the six peaks with the greatest intensities were played together as a chord.

To present a chemical infrared spectrum, the first pattern (or tune) was played twice, then the second was played three times, and finally, the chord was played. In general, the second pattern was heard as a somewhat syncopated piece with multiple parts. Because the pitch sequence was unconnected, the perception was often of one part taking a rest while another part entered. The chords were most often dissonant. Each of these can be listened to in Sound Example 3.4.

Sound Example 3.4: Listen to three or four different spectra.

Lunney and Morrison ran informal tests in which there were very few failures in matching identical patterns. The chords themselves allowed rapid screening and matching; a scientist could easily listen to known compounds until the match was found for the unknown. Also, the perceived syncopation in the second part of the sound sequence added an element of rhythmic interest, making the recognition task somewhat less dependent on pitch discrimination. The method can be applied to any continuous x,y function, such as chromatograms or nuclear magnetic resonance spectra.

This work was interesting not only because it was motivated by eliminating the visual representation totally but also because it used a combination of melodies and chords to present the data. Rather than offering graphics and sounds, they offered different perceptions within the aural representation. Also, the data analysis problem differed somewhat in that the scientist was not looking primarily for patterns in the data but rather for recognition of known data. Thus, memory played a particularly important role in this work. Lunney and Morrison suggested that the sequences of notes are more memorable than single chords. Yet for quick comparisons, the chords provided a useful tool.

Lunney and colleagues also used speech output, sometimes in combination with simple tone-varying representations, to give data information to visually impaired scientists. They developed their own hierarchy of auditory variables (Lunney and Morrison 1990): pitch, duration, attack, waveform, loudness, and decay rate. However, they noted that attack and waveform interact so strongly that it is not advisable to use them to represent independent variables. Also, as seen in Chapter 2 with the Fletcher-Muson curves, loudness is affected by frequency, so it is most useful when used to distinguish among notes of the same frequency. Their experience is that the decay rate is almost useless in conveying data information.

3.4.5   Case study 5: sonification of EEG data

An interesting and relatively more recent area of research is the sonification of electroencephalogram (EEG) data. EEG data are a particularly interesting type of data for the application of sonification since they consist of multiple time series. Moreover, this kind of multi-channel data contains a lot of noise, which complicates automatic pattern detection so that an exploratory analysis can make great profit from the high-developed human auditory skills in signal/noise separation (Hermann et al. 2002).

In the work of Hermann et al. (2002), three sonifications are developed, which provide a means for the fast inspection of short-time Fourier transform spectra from EEG measurements. Spectral mapping sonification allows frequency-selective browsing of EEG data. It represents a technique to monitor EEG data spectrally resolved and allows the comparison of data variations in different channels. This sonification is concerned with allowing the user to follow the spectral activation within the brain.

Distance matrix sonification allows the following of the time-variant distance matrix of the spectral vectors. This sonification allows the observation of the synchronization of different brain areas as a function of time.

The third approach, called differential sonification, allows the summary of the results of a comparison of data for one subject under two conditions in an auditory scan through the brain. It allows the comparison of data recorded for one subject under different conditions in order to accelerate the detection of interesting channels and frequency bands along which the conditions may cause systematic differences.

For primary data screening, data audification allows the detection of outliers and rhythmical and pitched patterns in the raw signals. Spectral mapping sonification allows the researcher to bring in listening skills to investigate frequency-specific patterns of different EEG channels. Besides that, the data are monitored at a high time resolution. Distance matrix sonification transforms the data into a sound that allows the detection of long-range couplings of brain regions with high temporal resolution.

3.5 Discussion

The five case studies were chosen because they represent a variety of data analysis problems and a range of techniques for presenting that data in sound. Several other researchers have been exploring sonification in equally interesting and provocative ways. Mansur provided an early notion of "sound graphs" to convey x,y data to visually impaired scientists (Mansur et al. 1985). The pitch varied continuously as a function of the changes in the y-axis. His goal was to offer a "holistic" view of the curve (a typical graph only lasted a few seconds) and an independence in exploring typically visual data. Mansur produced 13 training graphs and 22 testing graphs for the identification of linear slopes, curve classification (linear or exponential), monotonicity, convergence, and symmetry. His subjects were able to answer the questions with 79–95% accuracy. Mansur raises the issue of linear data being mapped to frequencies that are inherently logarithmic. One approach of his was to increase the frequency in a logarithmic fashion.

Work at the National Center for Supercomputing Applications offers a number of data visualization problems and aural representations (Scaletti and Craig 1991). The work is focused on combining data-driven sound with data visualizations to elucidate the data further. The general method is to map streams of time-varying data to parameters of sound. Examples include the movements of two pendulums to illustrate the behavior of a Duffing oscillator, forest fire suppression and its effect on decreasing forest diversification, and models of simulations, such as air pollution and the human arterial system. A significant aspect of the work is the implementation and use of a set of tools for data sonification. This provides a strong base for examining many different data sets with various aural mappings.

Airflow turbulence is a rich data set for exploring sound representation (Blattner et al. 1992) with interesting comparisons to the time-varying economic data of Mezrich and colleagues. Blattner and colleagues characterize fluids as continuous sounds and then vary parameters based on the fluid vicosity, density, temperature, speed of motion, direction of motion, the vortices (size, velocity, and density), and the energy dissipation. Although they have not produced sonification of the data, they do offer a rationale for mappings to sound parameters and the suggested mappings themselves. Unlike the fairly straightforward mapping of Mezrich and colleagues, where separate voices represent several data parameters, Blattner and colleagues propose the creation of complex sounds utilizing not only frequency changes but waveforms, frequency relations, and tempo of the various component sounds. The introduction and dissipation of the vortices pose a combination of exploratory pattern recognition and event notification. A type of data not directly considered thus far is that of process flow. In previous examples of time-varying data, we have been concerned with detecting patterns in the data. In the case of process flow, sound can offer both an ongoing awareness of the status of the process and a notification of particular events. Program control or computational processes is an example of the process flow used as a basis for sonification (Sonnenwald et al. 1990; Francioni et al. 1991). Sonnenwald's work was concerned with simulation and the execution cycle for parallel computation.

In the work of Francioni et al. (1991), three different mappings showed ways that sonification can contribute to information about program execution in distributed memory parallel programs. They used trace data consisting of event identifications, time, processor, message type, and message length. For issues of load balance in the parallel programs, each processor was mapped to a frequency that became louder as idle time increased. They followed the program flow-of-control by assigning a specific timbre to each processor and then using a note or pitch for each event. Finally, the process communication tracked send events and receive events by incorporating stereo to aid in the movement from send states to receive states. In all cases, Francioni et al. (1991) found that they gained useful insights into the program execution, that they could obtain several different perspectives with a single pressing of the trace data, and that they could easily synchronize the aural and visual representations. Their various representation schemes are noteworthy for depending on the information needed rather than on an obvious mapping of data to sound. For example, in considering the load balance, the load on each machine might have been mapped to a pitch. However, they were more concerned with the idle time and thus not only mapped idle time per processor to a note but also increased the loudness to draw attention to lengthy idle times.

Although several of the research projects consider the use of sound itself as opposed to considering only the data analysis problem, the work at NASA in developing the Convolvotron was significant in pushing the hardware to support sonification (Foster and Wenzel 1992) in the early days. The Convolvotron provided externalized 3D cues over headphones in real-time digitally. Up to four moving or static sources could be simulated as localized sounds in space. Several types of sonifications had been explored, such as computational fluid dynamics. Here the fuel flow around a liquid oxygen post of the main shuttle engine was visualized with a fly-through model. Auditory representations of various particles tracked the interactions of those particles with the shuttle engine.

3.6   Issues

The early work was exciting in verifying that sonification has potential for multivariate data representation. However, despite a growing interest in sonification, little has been done beyond the demonstration of the concept. No compelling evidence exists to indicate that sonification is more than an interesting twist on visualization. It is imperative that the community of research and development scientists in auditory data representation (1) show beyond doubt at least one example in which sonification yields information in exploratory data analysis beyond other methods, (2) provide tools and environments for other workers in the field, and (3) issue guidelines for mapping data to sound parameters.

The remainder of this chapter outlines three areas of work that are informed by the studies to date and that offer difficult questions for further research. The three areas of work are represented by ten research problems. These address the issues of going beyond a demonstration of the concept of sonification to (1) a better understanding of multivariate data, (2) the representation of that data in sound, and (3) the evaluation of the representation. Though the problems clearly have a relationship to one another, progress on each will offer valuable insights on which to build a theory and framework of sonification.

3.7   Issues of data

Understanding the nature of multivariate data is key to exploring and understanding sonification of that data. Here are two issues that attack the types of multivariate data and how those data types relate to sound.

Sonification Problem 1. What implications does the data type have for the type of sonification?

Scientific multivariate data may be loosely described as discrete events, as time-varying, or as continuous over some space. Discrete events have no inherent ordering. Time-varying data is such that samples occur in time sequence. Generally, continuous data can be described by a function. Somewhat similarly, sounds may be thought of as single notes, chords, or sequences of notes (tunes). A note is made up of sound characteristics such as frequency, amplitude, waveshape, and so on. A chord is several frequencies or voices sounded together. A tune is a sequence of notes or chords. Given a sample $s = (x1, x2, x3, \ldots, xn)$, the sample s could be a note as $x1$ to xn are mapped to the note characteristics, a chord as $x1$ to xn are mapped to different frequencies, or a tune as $x1$ to xn are mapped one at a time to successive notes.

Table 3.1 Examples of sonifications from the early literature

	Discrete	*Time-varying*	*Continuous*
Single note	Bly, 6D		
	Kramer, 9D		
	Grinstein, 5D		
	Rabenhorst, 2D		
	Michigan State, 2D		
CHORD			
TUNE	Lunney		
(one sample sequence)			
TUNE			
(sequence of samples)		Mezrich	
		Francioni	
		Sonnenwald	

An approach to understanding more about the relationship of the data type to the sonification method is to find a framework for the multivariate data and sound categories. Table 3.1 attempts to classify the work described in this chapter into such categories. In the work to date, discrete samples have been represented by notes, by chords, or by tunes. Time-varying data have been represented as tunes by varying pitch only or by complex notes or chords. Data continuous in n-space has been represented as discrete events with a visual attachment for the location in space. It would be useful to the field of sonification to have a more complete space of data types and implications.

Sonification Problem 2. What data is appropriate for hearing directly?

The issue here is to distinguish between aural representations that involve mapping data parameters to sound characteristics or directly presenting the raw data as sound. Several researchers have used data directly as an aural signal. For example, seismic signals can be heard by shifting the raw data to the audible frequency spectrum.

The approach presented in this chapter focuses on n-dimensional measurements of the data, which are then mapped into sounds. The relationship between these two approaches and a systematic understanding of the implications of each would benefit the understanding of multivariate data and sonification.

3.7.1   *Issues of sound parameters*

Perhaps the most crucial aspect of sonification is the mapping of data values to sound parameters. The following five issues present a range of problems, from straightforward relationships among sound components to user navigation in the aural space.

Sonification Problem 3. What constitutes a useful mapping of data to sound?

Taking a systematic look at mappings requires not only deciding which data parameter to represent by which sound parameter but also the relationship among the data parameters (are they independent or dependent variables and if dependent, what is the relationship) and the relationship among sound parameters (see the psychoacoustics discussion in Chapter 2). As in Problem 1, an approach to this issue might be to begin finding a framework for the possible data parameter relationships, the available sound parameters, the relationships among those sound parameters, and the perceived changes as sound parameters vary.

Sonification Problem 4. Where am I?

One of the disadvantages of using sounds for data representation is its temporary nature. While it may be relatively easy to know how one sound differs from another when they're presented in sequence, it's very difficult to remember any baseline over time. With the possible exception of those with perfect pitch, most listeners need guideposts or reference tones. Two possible approaches might be to provide a constant underlying tone or to provide a baseline tone before each other tone.

Sonification Problem 5. How do parameters of sound relate to mathematical or data parameters?

As yet, there has been no systematic calibration of sound parameters and data (mathematical) parameters. Though we talk about the value of psychophysics, there has been no attempt to relate such findings to mathematical parameters. Such an understanding of the relationship between aural and mathematical structures is imperative for sonification.

One approach would be to start with a good list of psychophysics/psychoacoustics results and a good list of mathematical relationships, then suggest ways that one would expect mathematical relationships to be heard in aural parameters, then test the resulting hypotheses, and then issue a set of guidelines so that given data that varies in some known way, a particular set of sound parameters would be an accurate representation.

A related problem is that most sonification to date does not take advantage of statistical methods of data analysis. Statistical methods offer two primary benefits. One, they can often reduce the data to a simpler data set. Two, they can often find relationships among the data that can be exploited in the sound parameters. The value of the first goes without saying, and no excuse can be offered for not investigating statistical methods before applying sonification techniques. The value of the second requires an understanding of sound parameters, as suggested by Problem 1. Using statistical methods to find relationships in the data is the first step in mapping the data to sounds. Those relationships in the data then become the basis for determining which sound parameters will be most effective in representing the data.

Sonification Problem 6. How does the audio space meet the graphics space?

Just as it is important to understand the relationship between parameters of sounds and parameters of mathematical data, it is important to understand the relationship between sounds and graphics. One needs to ensure that patterns available in the graphics space are consistent in the aural space. More interestingly, consider the integration or merger of the two. How do sound parameters vary relative to graphics parameters? If one maps a dimension in a graphical way and another in an aural way, do the two vary appropriately? Approaching this issue is much like approaching the mapping problem generally but with the addition of visual parameters. The field of scientific visualization offers a basis for study. Problems 1, 3, 5, 8, 9, and 10 suggest particularly relevant issues to consider.

Sonification Problem 7. Where is an ideal environment for sonification?

Given a set of multivariate data, there must be a computing environment to support the exploration. This environment must provide tools for statistical analysis, for mapping data dimensions to sound parameters, and perhaps for using graphics and audio together. To date, the sonification community does not have shared tools for this purpose, and every research lab has its own preferences in strategies and software tools.

3.7.2 Issues of evaluation

Underlying all the issues for sonification is a need to evaluate the usefulness and the information provided by the sonification techniques. Three problems offer pointers to evaluations that need to be considered.

Sonification Problem 8. How do we know if we're making progress?

Not only should evaluations be included in sonification. There is also a lack of common methodologies. These issues have been addressed in evaluations in other fields of computing applications and depend on the application of psychology and social science.

Sonification Problem 9. Can we hear anything that we can't see?

A central evaluation for sonification is whether or not it is a contributor to scientific perceptualization. The strong motivation for the value of sonification is the fact that more dimensions and/or different data types may be represented in sounds than in visual displays. If so, it should be possible to find patterns or characteristics in data with sonification that have not been found with standard statistical or graphical methods. Can information, in fact, be uncovered using sonification that has not been uncovered otherwise? Two approaches to this problem are (1) systematic data generation that creates patterns that can't be detected otherwise and (2) close collaboration with a scientific exploration of multivariate data. Two types of data seem particularly suited for sonification: time-varying and highly dimensional data. Tackling this problem in close collaboration with scientists using such data offers an opportunity to push sonification techniques.

Sonification Problem 10. How annoying are sounds?

User interface issues for the data exploration are important in ensuring that users have good listening capabilities without hindering colleagues and that the sounds generated are acceptable.

Certainly, earphones provide a means of listening to data. The sounds themselves may be influenced by cultural as well as psychoacoustical features. Several researchers have suggested anecdotally that they have used only frequencies in the musical scale because sounds based on general frequencies were difficult to hear and distinguish.

3.8 Conclusions

Overall, theoretical accounts of human interactions with sonification and other nonspeech auditory display designs have been slow to develop, in part due to the highly interdisciplinary nature of the field (Nees and Walker 2007). A number of authors have taken steps toward elaborating sonification theory, including de Campo's sonification design space map (De Campo 2007); Frauenberger, Stockman, and Bourguet's audio design survey (Frauenberger et al. 2007); and Nees and Walker's model of auditory graph comprehension (Nees and Walker 2007). Despite these recent advances in the field, concrete and specific sonification design guidelines that are grounded in literature and theory are still not generally available.

Defining the boundaries of sonification is still a hot topic, with some researchers expressing the need to have a somewhat stricter, systematic definition (Hermann 2008), whereas others are willing to step over the border to data-driven music (Vogt 2010). As for any kind of auditory display, the use of sound as a medium for communicating information makes it well suited for time-related tasks such as monitoring or synchronization.

4 Earcons

4.1 Introduction

Although scientific data representation has led the way in studies of nonspeech audio interfaces, the use of nonspeech audio for more general information is also being explored. In data representation, all the examples so far have depended on the parameters of sound to represent the data information. We call this a reference to the sound source. Similarly, one can easily imagine informational cues being encoded in parameters of sound. There are many examples in the everyday world – the ticking of a clock, for example. In general, these audio cues don't tell the listener so much about the source of the sound as about the fact that some event is taking place to which the listener might want to give attention.

An early example of using audio cues in interfaces was again scientific data. Note that the data values were not encoded in sound but rather the events surrounding the data. In 1975, Lee and Riviello used audio cues in a film portraying a two-step laser isotope separation process. Their work was about representing the values of the data variables in sounds but about using an audio interface to draw attention to isotope excitation and attraction. A gas of mixed U-235 and U-238 was exposed to a laser that excited the U-235. A beep corresponded to each isotope excitation. Subsequently, a second laser ionized those isotopes in the excited state so that they were attracted to a negative plate. For each ionization, a tone was heard that lasted until the ionized isotope reached the negative plate. If more than one isotope was ionized, then more than one tone was heard. Graphics displayed the motion of all isotopes. An isotope raised to an excited state was enlarged; an ionized isotope immediately fell toward the negative plate. However, the many events occurring on display often distracted the observer's attention away from other critical events. The audio cues were valuable in drawing the observer's attention to the isotope excitation and the subsequent ionization. Furthermore, the observer heard sequences of events without having to scan the display for rapidly changing situations.

Blattner et al. (1989) introduced the concept of earcon to define nonverbal audio messages that are used in HCIs to provide information to the user about some computer object, operation, or interaction. These messages are called

DOI: 10.4324/9781003260202-4

motives (e.g., a brief succession of pitches arranged in such a way as to produce a tonal pattern sufficiently distinct to allow it to function as an individual recognizable entity). Earcons are the audio counterpart to graphical icons in that they aim to present concise information using sound. Examples of earcons include a ping to indicate the arrival of a new text message, a short sound (e.g., a chord) to indicate computer startup or shutdown, or a ding to inform a driver their seatbelt is not fastened. Earcons are sound symbols, and as is the case with most symbols, these must be learned since there is no intuitive relationship between the symbol and the meaning.

In the early literature on auditory displays, earcons were abstract/musical signals opposed to auditory icons (Gaver 1986), where natural/everyday sounds are used in order to build auditory interfaces (see Chapter 5).

While in the current literature, the distinction between auditory icons and earcons is obsolete, and modern auditory interfaces mix elements of the two. Nonetheless, for historical validity, we keep the description separate.

Because earcons are designed based on elements of sound, the dimensions inherent to sound and the way they are manipulated play an important role in how well an earcon represents its significate. The fundamental dimensions of sound include pitch, loudness, spatial location, duration, and timbre. These dimensions have been studied and used by many in determining how earcons should be designed and which parameters are more and less important.

Absolute pitches are often of little use unless most of the population has perfect pitch. However, people are quite sensitive to intervals or relative pitches since a large portion of the population can carry a tune. Therefore, if two pitches are sequentially organized, most people will be able to judge a simple relationship between the notes (e.g., the first tone is higher than the second tone). The pitches in a motive are usually chosen from a tonal scale and occupy a narrow frequency range, within one octave (Blattner et al. 1989).

Related to pitch, the register of an earcon can be a meaningful parameter in conveying information. Register refers to the position of the motif along with the frequency range. The meaning of an earcon can change depending on the register in which it is presented (Brewster et al. 1995). For example, when representing temperature, high pitches can be used for high temperatures, while low pitches would be used for cooler temperatures.

In earcon design, loudness is considered to be a less useful parameter because listeners are not very good at making absolute judgments on loudness. The overall volume of a device may affect the way in which the loudness of individual notes is perceived. Depending on the frequency of the tone, discrete changes in loudness can also be difficult to perceive. However, a sharp change of loudness (over a short amount of time) may be effective in signaling an event.

The spatial location of an earcon can be a very informative parameter. Not only does spatial separation allow multiple sounds to be presented simultaneously while being well segregated from one another (Bregman 1994), but the location itself can be an information-carrying parameter. For example, when representing files on a computer using earcons, the spatial location of the sound can be correlated to where the file is located. As previously discussed, timbre is the most complex characteristic of sound, involving the spectral content, amplitude envelope, and transient attack of a sound. It is the characteristic of sound that allows us to distinguish a flute from a piano when they are playing the same note at the same loudness level. Different timbres are easily recognizable and can be a significant component of earcons when conveying information.

Rhythm is the most prominent characteristic of a motive in an earcon. It is a very powerful tool. Blattner et al. (1989) describe rhythm, or the timing and weighting of notes, as the most crucial feature of music that takes precedence over melody when it comes to creating motifs. In fact, even when spectral and pitch differences are large, earcons can be confused when a similar rhythm is used (Patterson 1982). Patterson's research also indicates that sounds that are too short (less than 0.0825 seconds) may go unnoticed unless the earcon contains only one or two notes. As far as the length is concerned, earcons are short. They are sufficiently long to convey information but no longer typically two to four notes. Their short length makes them easy to learn, recognize, and remember.

Blattner and colleagues identify four kinds of earcons:

- One-element earcons. One-element earcons are the simplest type and can be used to communicate only one bit of information. These earcons may be only a single pitch or have rhythmic qualities. The one-element earcon, unlike the other three types, cannot be further decomposed to yield more information.
- Compound earcons. Compound earcons are formed by concatenating any other form of earcon together to form more meaningful messages. They can be understood as the analogy of forming a sentence out of words, where one-element earcons represent words and compound earcons represent phrases. For example, three one-element earcons representing *save*, *open*, and *file* can form compound earcons by being played after each other to form earcons for the *open* and *save* operations (Brewster et al. 1994).
- Hierarchical earcons. Hierarchical earcons are constructed around a grammar, where each earcon is a node in a tree, and each node inherits all of the properties of the nodes above it in the tree. Hence, an unpitched rhythm might represent an error; the next level will alter the pitch of that rhythm to represent the type of error and so on. This is summarized in Figure 4.1, taken from Blattner et al. (1989).
- Transformational earcons. Transformational earcons are similar to hierarchical earcons in that they are constructed around grammar. This has the advantage that instead of having to learn each individual earcon, such as with compound earcons, it is only necessary to learn the rules by which earcons are constructed in order to understand them. In the

EARCON HIERARCHY

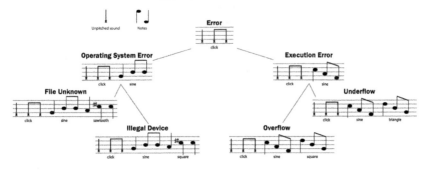

Figure 4.1 An overview of the grammar used to construct a set of hierarchical earcons representing computer error messages.

Source: Adapted from Blattner et al. (1989).

transformational earcon type, each auditory parameter, such as timbre, pitch, rhythm, and so on, can be transformed or modified to change the meaning of an earcon. Hence, with this type of earcon each attribute of the data can be mapped to an individual auditory parameter. The common grammar is a strength of earcons as less learning is required. Rather than having to learn a large number of arbitrary mappings and sounds, as with one-element earcons, it is only necessary to understand the grammar and the small number of different timbres, melodies, or registers used in the grammar to understand the earcons.

A number of studies have tested the effectiveness of compound earcons, focusing on applications where visual displays are not possible. Brewster et al. (1996) used hierarchical earcons to provide navigational cues through a menu hierarchy, similarly to a hierarchy in a book menu, for example. Hierarchical earcons use sound parameters, such as timbre, pitch, register, and intensity. Each level in the hierarchy inherits the structure from the higher level and then changes it. For example, earcons from level one to level two inherited their continuous sound, but the instrument, pitch, and location along the left/right stereo axis were changed. A four-level hierarchy with a total of 27 nodes was used. During a short training session, the compound earcons representing the hierarchy were played. The hypothesis of the authors was that listeners would learn the earcon rules during the training and apply these to elements in the hierarchy, even if they hadn't heard them before. The goal of this experiment was to test the knowledge of earcons by asking listeners to select where the element representing the earcon fit into the hierarchy. Results showed that 81.5% of earcons were identified correctly. Errors indicated that the nodes from the lowest level in the hierarchy had the worst recall, suggesting that hierarchical earcons may have trouble representing hierarchies with a large number of levels.

In 1998, Brewster (1998) presented a new structured approach to auditory display, defining composing rules and a hierarchical organization of musical parameters (timbre, rhythm, register, etc.) in order to represent hierarchical organizations of computer files and folders. Typical applications of this work are telephone-based interfaces (TBIs), where navigation is a problem because the visual display is small or absent. As already mentioned, the main idea is to define a set of sound-design/composing rules for very simple musical atoms, the earcons, with the characteristics of being easily distinguishable one from the other.

The three experiments described in the paper explore different aspects of the earcons. The first one is more abstract and aims at defining easily recognizable and distinguishable earcons. The second one addresses the very concrete problem of lo-fi situations, where monophony of signals and limited bandwidth are strong limitations. In the same experiment, a fundamental aspect of musical memory is considered: the navigation test was carried out right after the training and repeated after one week. As far as retention is concerned, very good results were achieved: there was no significant difference between the performances right after the training and after one week.

On the contrary, in some cases, the listeners were even more skilled in recognizing the earcons one week later than immediately after the training. An interesting feedback coming from the experiments was that the listeners developed mnemonic strategies based on the identification of the earcons with something external as, for example, geometric shapes (triangles, squares and so on). This could be a good cue for earcon sound design. The third experiment was a bit more artificial: the idea was to identify a sound (timbre + register) with numbers and to represent hierarchies in a book-like style (chapter, sections, subsections) by means of sounding numbers. In general, these experiments show how problematic the design of earcons is, when many hierarchical levels are involved or when many items are present: one needs to think about very articulated or even polyphonic earcons, challenging the listening skills of the user. In any case, situations that do not present very complex navigation requirements can build upon earcons a robust and extensible method for representing hierarchies. Brewster also suggested some design guidelines for earcons, summarized as follows:

- Use musical instrument timbres to differentiate between earcons or groups of earcons as people can recognize and differentiate between timbres relatively easily.
- Do not use pitch or register on their own to differentiate between earcons when users need to make absolute judgments concerning what the earcon is representing.
- If register must be used on its own, then there should be a difference of two or three octaves between earcons.
- If pitch is used, it should not be lower than 125 Hz and not higher than 5 kHz to avoid the masking of the earcon by other sounds and be easily within the hearing range of most users.

- If rhythm is used to distinguish between earcons, make the rhythms as different from each other as possible by putting different numbers of notes in each earcon.
- Intensity (loudness) should not be used to distinguish between earcons as many users find this annoying.
- Keep earcons short in order not to slow down the user's interaction with the system.
- Two earcons may be played at the same time to speed up the interaction.

4.2   Case studies

As in scientific data perceptualization, the use of audio as interface cues is being explored in a variety of areas. Three case studies point to techniques and issues in auditory interfaces. First, Blattner and others have looked at a wide range of applications for sound in workstation environments with a particular focus on providing a basis for determining a set of sounds and the relationships among those sounds. Edwards, like Lunney and Morrison, is concerned with using sound to aid the visually handicapped in their use of computer workstations. Finally, somebody has taken seriously the notion of an experiment to test the effectiveness/use of audio cues.

4.2.1   Case study 1: alarms and warning systems

Alarms and warnings are by far the most common nonspeech audio messages and perhaps the only kind of auditory displays that have been thoroughly studied. Audio alarms range from ambulance sirens to computer error beeps, from stall alarms on aircraft to foghorns, from car horns to buzzers on clothes dryers. What all these uses of sound have in common is that they are meant to override ongoing processing and attract attention to themselves. In contrast, one of the largest challenges to auditory interfaces is to design sounds that can inform users without distracting them.

There is a danger that alarm systems can be too alarming. This is a problem with many existing systems. There is a great deal we can learn by examining audio alarms and warnings. First, the design of traditional alarms reflects the kinds of psychoacoustic principles we discussed in Chapter 2. Second, some of the problems with existing systems of alarms can help make us aware of the kinds of traps we should avoid in designing our own auditory interfaces. A milestone publication summarizing several contributions to auditory alarms is the book edited by Stanton and Edworthy (2019).

4.2.2   Alarms as applied psychoacoustics

Most of the principles of psychoacoustics we discussed in Chapter 2 can be found reflected in the design of auditory alerts. For instance, think of the loud electronic drone that is used as a fire alarm in many buildings. Why is it so loud? Obviously, this is so you can hear it in any part of the building, despite any ongoing activities. Very loud sounds like these are likely to be immune to masking by virtually any other sound. In fact, they are so loud that they prevent very effective communication, which is good in that it convinces people to suspend their activities even if it is just another fire drill, but bad if it prevents conversations necessary to deal with the problem. Notice that many fire alarms do not change much in pitch or amplitude. Why is this? Apparently, the mere fact of a very loud sound is enough to alert people in office environments.

But think of the rising and falling pitch of the typical siren. Again, sirens tend to be very loud, and again this is to overcome possible masking noises. Why do they rise and fall? Because changing sounds tend to attract attention to a much higher degree than static sounds. In fact, many police cars now have a rather wide repertory of different sirens (one can count ten distinct police alert sounds in New York City police cars), ranging from the traditional rising and falling pitch to the "do-dah, do-dah" more familiar to Europeans to a sound like a massively overamplified cricket. Why all the different kinds of sounds? Two reasons. First, changing sounds further reduces the possibility that an alert will be masked by other noise (like a loud car audio system) since different sirens have different spectra. Second, and probably more important, changing sound patterns alert listeners even more than one repetitively changing pattern. Switching among different sirens introduces attention, getting changes at a higher level than the variation of sound in any single siren.

In a very different domain, consider the low booming sound made by a foghorn. Why is this sound so different from the high-pitched wailing of a siren? Well, there are several reasons. Perhaps the most important is that foghorns must be audible for long distances so that sailors far out to sea can use them for navigational purposes. Low-frequency sounds lose much less energy as they propagate in the air than high-frequency sounds do, which is why you hear the bass *thump-thump* of your neighbor's stereo much more than you do the highs.

In addition, the sounds made by foghorns must not be obscured by obstacles, such as a hill or point of land. As discussed in Chapter 2, sounds whose wavelengths are shorter than the width of an obstacle (i.e., high-frequency sounds) are greatly attenuated behind it; the zone in which these sounds are muffled is called the shadow zone (see Figure 4.2). If a sound should be heard behind a hill, then its wavelength should be as long as possible; it should be a very-low-frequency sound.

Auditory alarms and warnings have evolved over long periods of time to attract and hold attention. Listening to them and considering the ways they are constructed can be quite valuable in understanding basic psychoacoustic principles such as those discussed in Chapter 2.

SPREAD OF FREQUENCIES

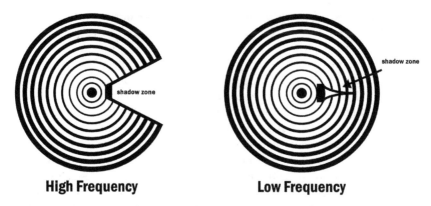

High Frequency **Low Frequency**

Figure 4.2 High-frequency sounds are greatly attenuated behind obstacles whose width is greater than the wavelength of the sounds; the area of attenuation is called the sound shadow (A). Sounds that have a long wavelength relative to the width of an obstacle cast relatively small sound shadows. This is one reason why foghorns make very low-pitched sounds (B).

4.2.3 *Problems with traditional alarms and convergences with audio interfaces*

At the most basic level, alarms are supposed to instantly draw attention to themselves, thus indicating that something is wrong with whatever triggered them. To be effective, an alarm must not be masked by ambient sounds and must not fade into the perceptual background.

Now creating a sound that draws attention and is not easily ignored is a simple task, such as asking any parent of a two-year-old. But there is a fundamental problem with the idea of an alarm as simply a loud, penetrating sound. Alarms usually signal emergencies, and the ability to communicate during an emergency is crucial. On the one hand, alarms must be heard; on the other hand, they must not prevent communication. As Patterson points out, most alarm designers opt for the better-safe-than-sorry approach of extreme loudness. His aim has been to develop alarms that permit communication but that will not be masked. He uses several techniques to achieve this goal. First, he tailors the alarm's acoustic properties to the environments in which they will be used so that they will not be masked even when played at fairly low levels. Second, alarms are not continuous but rather are presented in bursts with silence in between. Finally, the relative urgency of the bursts varies over the time course of the alarm so that the initial burst has fairly high urgency, following bursts are more subdued, and a high-urgency burst is played if the problem is not corrected.

It may seem that in developing auditory interfaces, problems of exces-sive loudness will not be relevant. After all, most of us are quite aware that auditory interfaces should not be annoying, and so they should probably be fairly quiet. But this leads us to the exact converse of the problem facing alarm designers: how can we create auditory interfaces that are quiet enough to be unobtrusive without making them so quiet that they can't be heard? Patterson's approach to predicting how masking will affect hearing thresh-olds at different frequencies suggests that the answer to this question can be systematically approached. Another problem with the idea of alarms being loud, attention-attracting sounds comes when an environment has several different alarms. Most of us are used to hearing (at most) one alarm in a given context: a siren as we drive, perhaps a fire alarm at work, and of course, the error beeps made by our computer. Given that context constrains what we expect an alarm to indicate, many sounds can suffice in these situations. So it is that though the proliferation of error beeps may be annoying, their functionality is pretty much unimpaired. Similarly, if we hear a new kind of siren while driving, we may marvel at its novelty, but we still know to pull to the side of the road.

But there are many environments in which many alarms may be present simultaneously. For instance, in the Three Mile Island power plant crisis, the operators had to contend with over 60 different auditory warning systems (Sanders and McCormick 1998). English hospital workers must contend with 33 possible warning sounds (Patterson 1989). Most of these alarms are not designed with other possible alarms in mind but instead are introduced to the environment with new equipment. In too many cases, one alarm (a repetitive beep, for instance) sounds pretty much the same as another (a slightly different repetitive beep). The problem, clearly, is in distinguishing between different alarms so that the particular problem can be recognized.

To give an idea of what this problem is like, think of being in a hallway near a series of offices, having a discussion with fellow workers. Suddenly a phone rings, and what happens? All the people with an office nearby disap-pear. The problem is that in such an environment, all phones tend to sound the same, so it is not clear what a particular phone ring means. And so it is with many complex environments with multiple alarms. In an emergency, it is important that alarms be distinguishable. Note that when we start to be concerned about the ability to recognize the meanings of alarms, we are beginning to address issues that are obviously important for informative audio interfaces. Clearly, if one wants to convey several different messages using sounds, they should not be confusing, whether the messages concern emergency states or multidimensional data. Examining the ways developers of multiple alarms have addressed this problem can be very informative to developers of audio interfaces.

Work on alarms has converged with that on auditory interfaces even more than this, as the relative importance of different warnings is considered. For instance, Patterson (1989) distinguished three kinds of hospital warnings:

emergency, cautionary, and information available. What are information warnings but earcons, or auditory icons, or auditory cues?

It should be clear that work on auditory warnings converges with the research we are presenting here. Moreover, because such work is done from a different starting point, the contrasts between alarms and audio cues can be quite informative. For instance, whereas Patterson is concerned with characterizing the perceived urgency of sounds, we might rather want to understand how to make sounds less urgent and more unobtrusive. Alarms are meant to be instantly recognizable to listeners, while perhaps audio cues should work more like the sounds our cars make; general users, like Sunday drivers, might not know what all the sounds mean, but they know when something is wrong; and expert users, like mechanics, could have much more information available to them. In any case, it should be clear from this case study that alarms are not simply loud annoying sounds meant to attract attention.

4.2.4 Case study 2: concurrent earcons

The work presented by McGookin and Brewster (2004) faces the problem of concurrent earcon presentation. Two experiments are illustrated, which are also exemplary for their use of statistical analysis and workload measures, representing likely the first empirical study of concurrent earcons. In the first experiment, the goal is to see how recognition of earcons and their parameters gets worse as the number of concurrent earcons increases. The main hypothesis of the experiment was that varying the number of concurrently presented earcons would significantly alter the proportion of presented earcons, which could be successfully identified.

In the second experiment, new design solutions are tested in their ability to increase the earcon robustness against concurrent presentation. It turns out that using multiple timbres or staggering the onsets will improve attribute identification. As a final practical result of the experiments, four guidelines for designing robust concurrent earcons are given.

The first guideline states that increasing the number of concurrently presented earcons significantly reduces the proportion of the earcons that can be successfully identified. Increasing the number of earcons concurrently presented can reduce correct identification from 70% to 30%.

The second guideline states that it may be beneficial to ensure that inharmonic intervals are used between earcons concurrently presented in different registers. This is likely to reduce the impact on register identification when the number of concurrently presented earcons is increased. The third guideline states that when timbre is used to encode a data parameter, each concurrently presented earcon should have a different timbre.

The guidelines of Brewster et al. (1995) should be used to select timbres to encode different values of a data parameter, but if two earcons with the same timbre encoded value are to be concurrently presented, each should use a different musical timbre from the same instrument group.

4.2.5   Case study 3: earcons for visually impaired users

A third area where earcons have been applied is to increase access to user interfaces and computer-based data for people who are blind or visually impaired.

Alty and Rigas (1998) developed the Audiograph system, which was designed to allow blind and visually impaired users to access graphical diagrams. Their system made extensive use of earcons to indicate operations that had been performed by the users, such as expanding or contracting a shape or undoing a previously carried out operation. They incorporated more iconic mappings into their earcon set. As an example, the expanded earcon was constructed from a melody that aurally appeared to expand, while the contract earcon was aurally contracting. The undo earcon was created by playing a motive with an error and then playing the motive without the error.

In the work of Alty and Rigas (1998), it is described how at first hearing users were confused by the design, but after an explanation, they understood it and had no further trouble recognizing it. To communicate information, pixels were sonified as the user moved over them. Two timbres were used to represent the x and y axes, with increasing pitch used to represent distance from the origin.

By using this method, blind participants were able to successfully draw the shapes that were presented. A closely related system has been developed by Murphy et al. (2007) to allow blind and visually impaired users to obtain a spatial overview of a web page. Using a force-feedback mouse, auditory information, including earcons, was presented as the user moved over on-screen elements.

Another important area is in the browsing and manipulation of algebraic equations. When presented through synthetic speech, mathematical equations might become ambiguous and confusing due to the time taken to present the equation. Stevens et al. (1997) considered how earcons could be used to provide a quick overview of the expressions and provide context during a more detailed analysis.

Their algebra earcons, rather than trying to provide information about the content of the algebraic expression, provided structural information. For example, the number of terms, subterms, and the type of each sub-expression were communicated through the earcons. Rhythm was used to denote the number of terms in each expression, with one note per term. Superscripts (such as x^2) were played with an increase in pitch, and sub-expressions were played in a slightly lower register. Operands such as + and = were played with a different timbre. In this way, the earcons formed an overview of how the equation was structured and aided the user in understanding it. They found that listeners were able to identify the structure of mathematical equations with high accuracy for both simple and more complex expressions.

4.3   Conclusions

This chapter introduced the concept of earcons and presented several examples where earcons have been adopted in user interfaces. Earcons can be of benefit in a wide range of applications, from simple augmentations of desktop widgets to sophisticated auditory interfaces for social media browsing. However, they must be well designed, and users must be trained in their use, at least to some extent.

For all the applications described, the issues revolve around the perception of the sounds, the information the various sounds convey, and what information is best presented in the different sounds. However, most of the work has concentrated on applying sounds and on the use and effectiveness of sounds in relation to visual displays.

5   Everyday listening

5.1   Introduction

Traditional approaches to acoustics and psychoacoustics have provided a number of valuable ways to understand audition, as we have discussed in Chapter 2.
Moreover, the vocabulary they offer for describing sound and hearing can be
applied in explorations of multidimensional data and in creating musical messages, as discussed in Chapters 3 and 4. Nonetheless, such approaches often
seem inadequate to describe our everyday experiences of listening to the world
around us. In this chapter, we introduce an alternative perspective from which
listening can be understood. In the next chapter, we show how this approach
can be applied, leading to novel methods for using sounds at the interface.

To understand the shortcomings of traditional approaches to audition, listen
to a few nonspeech, nonmusical sounds (such as Sound Example 5.1) and try to
describe them in psychoacoustic terms. For each sound, ask yourself: What is its
pitch? Its loudness? How would you describe its timbre? Is it discrete, rhythmic,
or continuous? Do these dimensions even make sense?

> Sound Example 5.1: Environmental sounds are difficult to describe in psycho-
> acoustical terms – easy to describe in terms of their sources. These sounds – or
> more exactly, the experiences they evoke – are good examples of everyday
> listening.

Many sounds prove difficult to describe using the kind of vocabulary suggested by traditional approaches to psychoacoustics. What is the pitch of
crumpled paper or the loudness of a passing airplane? Is the timbre of splashing water rough or smooth? Are the sounds made by a breaking bottle discrete,
repetitive, or continuous? Many of the dimensions that seem simple to apply
to musical sounds become much more troublesome when we try to apply them
to the sounds we hear in our everyday lives.

The problem goes beyond ease of description. Certainly, one can describe
such sounds fully, even if the descriptions may have daunting complexity.

DOI: 10.4324/9781003260202-5

Consider, for example, Sound Example 5.2. We might describe this sound as a repetitive (though not quite regular) series of band-limited noises, each with a fairly sharp attack and quick decay. We might produce a spectrum of the sound, note its temporal progression, perform experiments in which people match its perceived pitch with that of a standard, or ask people to describe it along dimensions such as sharp/dull or smooth/rough. But is the result of this sort of analysis really an adequate description of the sound?

Now listen to the sounds again, and instead of trying to produce a psycho-acoustical description of the sounds, simply ask yourself: what do I hear? The task should be much easier now – you hear a plane flying by, a bouncing ball, and so forth. In the case of Sound Example 5.2, one does not hear band-limited noises and so forth; you simply hear somebody climbing a flight of concrete steps, turning on the landing, and climbing another flight. The point is a simple one: psychoacoustics allows us to describe and understand sound in enormous detail, but there is more to listening than sounds alone.

Sound Example 5.2: An example of everyday sound.

5.2 Musical and everyday listening

Hearing the pitch of a sound or its loudness is an example of musical listening. But we often hear events rather than sounds. Listening to airplanes, water, birds, and footsteps are examples of everyday listening. This is a different sort of experience than that described by traditional psychoacoustics. Instead of being concerned with our ability to perceive attributes of sounds themselves – their frequency, spectral content, amplitude, and so on – everyday listening is a matter of listening to the attributes of events in the world – the speed of a passing automobile, the force of a slammed door, whether a person is walking up or downstairs.

5.2.1 *Musical and everyday listening are experiences*

Note that the distinction between everyday and musical listening is between experiences, not sounds. It is possible to listen to any sound either in terms of its attributes per se or in terms of the event that creates it. For instance, while listening to a string quartet, we might be concerned with the interplay of pitches, the juxtaposed timbres, or the intricacies of the rhythm – the patterns of sensation the sounds themselves evoke. This is an example of musical listening. Alternatively, we might listen to other sound sources in the same environment, such as a person coughing or the rustling of the audience. In this case, we are concerned with identifying the sources of sounds and properties of those sources. This is an example of everyday listening.

On the other hand, while walking down a city street, we are likely to listen to the sources of sounds: Is that car heading our way? How close is that guy walking behind us? Most of our experience of hearing the day-to-day world is one of everyday listening: we are concerned with knowledge about the events going on around us, what is important to avoid, and what might offer possibilities for action. But occasionally, we might listen to the world as we do music – to the humming pitch of a ventilator punctuated by a syncopated birdcall, to the interplay and harmony of the sounds around us. This may seem an unusual experience to many of us. But hearing the everyday world as music is one way to understand what John Cage, for instance, was attempting in his compositions. In presenting traffic sounds in a concert setting, he is trying to evoke an experience of musical listening to nonmusical sounds. The distinction between everyday and musical listening is fundamentally one between experiences, not sounds.

Nonetheless, some sounds seem more likely to evoke one experience than another. The tones made by many musical instruments, for instance, convey relatively little information about their source. Instead, their most salient features are their pitch, their duration, and so on. Hearing such sounds seems to throw the listener into an experience of musical listening. Other sounds, though, are difficult to listen to musically. It may be possible to hear the time-varying pitch of a breaking bottle, for instance, but the source of the sound seems much more compelling. So we may talk about everyday and musical sounds, but we must be careful. For it is not the type of sound we are interested in but the type of experience; not the sound's attributes but whether the attributes of interest are those of the sound or those of the source (this will become important in considering applications of everyday listening).

5.3   The psychology of everyday listening

The experience of everyday listening, if taken seriously, has the potential to produce a radically new explanatory framework for understanding sound and listening. Such a framework would allow us to understand listening and manipulate sounds along dimensions of sources rather than sounds. So, for example, we might imagine psychoacoustics concerned with measuring people's ability to hear the forces involved in events or a synthesizer that allowed us to specify whether a sound source was wood or metal.

Understanding sound in terms of everyday listening complements the account offered by traditional psychoacoustics. Clearly, the psychoacoustical phenomena we have discussed are valid whether we are talking about everyday or musical listening: a loud sound will mask a soft one, whether I am concerned with the soft one having a certain pitch or with the size of its source. But a new framework may alter some of the questions about sound and hearing we consider important. It certainly should allow us to refer more directly to attributes of everyday listening than does our present understanding of psychoacoustics.

Research on everyday listening has allowed us to discover several properties of everyday sounds both from the perceptual point of view and from the simulation's perspective.

5.3.1   *Knowledge about everyday listening*

Historically, studies of acoustics and psychoacoustics have been guided largely by a concern with understanding music and the sounds produced by musical instruments. From the ancient Greeks' discovery that doubling the length of a vibrating string halves its pitch, through to Helmholtz's studies of the harmonic structure of musical sounds, and even to present-day studies of computer music, the major thrust of disciplines concerned with nonspeech audio has been mostly to use musical sounds and to understand musical listening.

But an account of hearing based on the sounds and perceptions of musical instruments often seems biased and difficult to generalize. Musical sounds are not representative of the range of sounds we normally hear. Most musical sounds are quasi-harmonic; most everyday sounds sound inharmonic or noisy. Musical sounds tend to have a smooth, relatively simple temporal evolution; everyday sounds tend to be much more complex. Musical sounds seem to reveal little about their sources; everyday sounds often provide a great deal of information about theirs. Finally, musical instruments afford changes of the sounds along relatively uninformative musical dimensions, such as pitch or loudness; everyday events involve many more kinds of changes – changes that are often musically useless but pragmatically important. Our current knowledge about sound and hearing has been deeply influenced by the study of a rather idiosyncratic subset of sounds and sources. It is interesting to turn to a wider variety of sounds and sources in driving a study of everyday listening.

Theoretically, studies of everyday listening have been constrained by the supposed primitives of sound and by sensation-based theories of perception. Physical descriptions of sound are dominated by those suggested by the Fourier transform: frequency, amplitude, duration, and so on. Psychoacoustics has traditionally taken these dimensions as the physical primitives that correspond to elemental sensations. The end result, then, is acoustics and psychoacoustics that emphasize physical and perceptual dimensions best suited for describing music.

Traditional explanations of psychophysics take these primitive physical dimensions as their elemental stimuli and use them to motivate the identification of corresponding elemental sensations. From this perspective, more complex perceptions must depend on the integration of elemental sensations.

5.4   The ecological approach to perception

Taking everyday listening seriously as a domain for studies of acoustics and psychoacoustics suggests that we may broaden the range of physical parameters and perceptual experiences to be considered. For instance, we might add new perceptual dimensions, such as size or force, to the attributes of psychoacoustics and understand them in terms of their acoustic covariates. Such an endeavor implies that traditional psychoacoustics needs to be stretched in two ways: first, the perceptual dimensions we need to study concern those of sources as well as sounds, and second, we must be willing to treat apparently complex acoustic variables as elemental.

This approach is guided and inspired by the ecological approach to perception developed by Gibson (1979). The ecological perspective counters many of the assumptions of traditional accounts of perception. According to the ecological approach, perception is usually of complex events and entities in the everyday world. Moreover, it is direct, unmediated by inference or memory. According to this perspective, elemental stimuli for perception do not necessarily correspond to primitive physical dimensions but may instead be specified by complex invariants of supposedly primitive features. Thus, complex perceptions rely on complex stimuli (or perceptual information), not on the integration of sensations. From this point of view, there is rich and varied information in the world, both because our descriptions are no longer limited to primitive physical dimensions and because exploration of the world – as opposed to passive stimulation – becomes an important component of perception. Thus, according to the ecological account, the study of perception should be aimed at uncovering perceptual information and the ecologically relevant dimensions of perception.

5.4.1   Developing an ecological account of listening

The ecological account for audition started with the pioneering work of Gibson, who made some preliminary observations about listening but did not develop them to a great degree. Follow-up studies of listening were based on the ecological perspective (e.g., Warren and Verbrugge 1984; Vanderveer 1980; Gaver and Norman 1988); these will be discussed later in this chapter. However, though such studies have proven informative on their own and lent support to the idea that such an approach might be fruitful, a comprehensive account of everyday listening has yet to emerge. One of the purposes of this chapter, then, is to point the way to such an explanatory framework, both to help us understand everyday listening and in order to facilitate the creation of systems that analyze, synthesize, and manipulate sound in this way.

What might such a framework look like? It must answer two simple but fundamental questions. First, in expanding upon traditional accounts of elemental sensations, we must develop an account of ecologically relevant perceptual entities: the dimensions and features of sources that we actually obtain through listening. Thus, our first question is: what do we hear? Similarly, in expanding traditional accounts of the primitive physical features of sound, we must seek to find the acoustic properties of sounds that convey information about the things we hear. This involves the development of an ecological acoustics, one that describes the attributes of sounds that both provide information about sources and that are perceptually available. Thus, our second question is: how do we hear it?

In the rest of this chapter, we explore these two questions with the aim of developing an account of everyday listening that will complement and extend traditional psychophysics and will allow us to create and manipulate sounds along dimensions relevant to everyday listening.

5.5   What do we hear?

In trying to characterize what we hear, our concern is to develop a list of dimensions and features of everyday listening that are relatively simple and general. Just as we can capture a great deal of the sensory qualities of sounds with descriptions of their pitch, duration, loudness, and so forth, we would like to find an equally simple set of descriptive dimensions and features that characterize everyday listening. And just as qualities such as pitch and loudness apply generally to most musical sounds, we would like our dimensions and features to apply to broad ranges of everyday sounds. What sort of descriptions will do? Listen again to the Sound Example 5.2, and think about how you might describe what you hear. What sorts of dimensions might be useful in describing the sounds and the variations among them? Are there features that seem to apply generally and which have descriptive power?

The vast range of everyday sounds make simple descriptions of them difficult. Consider for instance, an excerpt from the table of contents of a sound-effects database. This is a domain in which descriptions of everyday sounds have developed out of necessity. The first thing to notice is that the number of distinctive sounds listed is quite large. The world of everyday sounds is immense.

Notice that the sounds are organized to some extent. Most are organized by the context in which they are likely to be heard: at the airport, in the kitchen, and so on. This may be useful for finding a desired sound, but it seems a poor basis on which to build a description of what we hear – the categories are not mutually exclusive; we can easily imagine hearing the same event in an airport and a kitchen. Nor do the category names constrain the kinds of sounds very much. We might expect to hear anything from running water to a small appliance in a kitchen, with the only unifying feature being their supposedly typical environment. Domain-based descriptions of sound-producing events seem unlikely to provide an adequate description of the attributes of everyday listening.

More interesting, however, are the suggestions for a hierarchical description of sounds in the table of contents. For instance, *automobiles* might be a superordinate category, with *sports car* and *Model T* as subordinates. The list also suggests some dimensions (e.g., big door, door closes slowly) and features (e.g., metal door, wooden door). A framework based on these sorts of entities – hierarchies, features, and dimensions – seems a more promising approach than one based on context. Superordinate categories based on types of events (as opposed to contexts) provide useful clues about the sorts of sounds that might be subordinate, while features and dimensions are a useful way of describing the differences among members of a particular category. Such a framework is more likely to be generative, to delineate a space of possible sounds.

We might consider two methods for building a description of everyday sounds that is both hierarchical and based on dimensions and features. The first is to consider the dimensions and features of sound-producing events that cause reliable and audible differences in sounds. The second is simply to ask people what they hear and to analyze their answers for commonly used descriptors. We will discuss each of these approaches in turn and end with an initial set of parameters that seem widely applicable to a number of everyday sounds.

5.6   The physics of sound-producing events

In this section, we describe the physics of sound-producing events in a qualitative way. The purpose here is not to provide an exact account of mechanical physics but instead to provide an initial orientation toward the relevant attributes of sound-producing events, such as the following:

- Closing a door
- Scraping fingernails over a blackboard
- Water dropping into a pool
- Wind whistling through wires
- An exploding balloon
- A resonating tuning fork

It will become clear that these events share a number of common features, the most general being that all are caused by interacting materials. But there are substantial differences in the physics of closing a door, water dropping into a pool, and an exploding balloon, for instance. Most fundamentally, these events fall into three categories: those in which sounds are produced by vibrating objects, those in which sounds are produced by changes in the surface of a body of liquid, and those in which sounds are directly introduced into the atmosphere by aerodynamic causes. Here I first describe vibrating objects in some detail and then use that discussion to illuminate liquid and aerodynamic sounds.

5.7   Vibrating objects

Sound waves are formed when a pressure variation is introduced into the atmosphere. One common source of pressure waves is vibrating objects. This class of events includes hitting books and scraping fingernails, as well as footsteps, closing doors, and breaking glass (several vibrating object sounds can be heard in Sound Example 5.1). An example of a vibrating object is shown in Figure 5.1.

Sound Examples in Chapter 5 show several examples of the sounds made by vibrating objects.

OBJECT VIBRATION

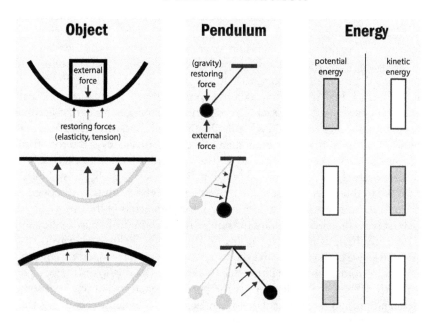

Figure 5.1 When an object is deformed by an external force, internal restoring forces cause a buildup of potential energy (A). When the external force is removed, the object's potential energy is transformed into kinetic energy, and it swings through its original position (B). The object continues to vibrate until the initial input of energy is lost to damping (C).

Objects vibrate when a force is exerted upon and then removed from a system that is otherwise at equilibrium. This input of energy deforms the sounding object from its original configuration; the forces that resist this deformation result in the buildup of potential energy in the new configuration. When the deforming force is removed, the object starts to return to its original shape due to various restoring forces acting with the potential energy stored by the deformation. This results in the movement of the object toward its initial configuration. But when it reaches this initial position, the potential energy has been converted to kinetic energy, and the object moves through the resting configuration. Just as a pendulum swings back and forth once it is set in motion, the repeated translation from potential energy to kinetic energy and back again causes the object to move through its resting configuration repeatedly: it vibrates.

If no energy were lost in this translation, the vibration would go on forever, and the world would be a very noisy and shaky place. But energy is lost for various reasons, collectively referred to as damping. So the object moves until all the initial energy responsible for its deformation has been lost, and it returns to its old (or finds a new) equilibrium configuration.

A number of parameters of the physical system affect how it vibrates. These attributes are grouped in terms of object properties in Table 5.1. It is also useful to consider two domains of vibration separately in discussing these parameters and separate those that affect the frequency domain from those that affect the temporal domain. Some source attributes have substantial effects on the sounding object's initial return from deformation and thus influence the frequencies of its subsequent vibrations. Other attributes produce effects that become apparent only after repeated cycles of vibration, and thus, their influences may be said to exist in the temporal domain. Of course, frequency is the reciprocal of time, so these domains are not physically different but rather the result of different representations. But the two domains are separable both psychologically when things repeat fast enough; they are perceived as pitch, otherwise as changes in other attributes and in terms of the parameters of the event.

Four types of source attributes influence vibrations in the frequency domain. These are the restoring forces acting on the object, the object's density, the size and shape of the object, and the manner in which it is supported. For solid objects, restoring forces are either due to elasticity (hardness) or tension. The strength of these forces determines the potential energy resulting from some deformation, and the inertia of the system depends on its density; both together determine how quickly it will return from its deformed state and the frequency of its vibrations. The size and shape of the system constrain its vibrational patterns, as does the manner in which it is supported.

Three types of source attributes influence vibrations in the temporal domain: the first is the type of interaction that causes it to vibrate, the second is the damping that causes it to stop vibrating, and the third is the internal structure.

Table 5.1 Attributes of a sound source and effect on the resulting sound

Source attributes	Effects on the sound wave
Interaction	
Type	Amplitude function, spectrum
Force	Amplitude, bandwidth
Material	
Restoring force	Frequency
Density	Frequency
Damping	Amplitude and frequency
Homogeneity	Complex effects on amplitude and frequency
Configuration	
Shape	Frequency, spectral pattern
Size	Frequency, bandwidth
Resonating cavities	Spectral pattern

A basic division can be made between interactions that are discrete and those that are continuous. For instance, hitting is a discrete interaction, while scraping is continuous. The style of interaction usually has very obvious effects on the sounds produced. Damping has various causes, including internal heat transfer, plasticity, and external absorption of energy (including by the air as sound). Finally, the internal structure of the vibrating material makes many complex effects on the sound it produces, particularly in the temporal domain.

Note that, in general, attributes of the object (e.g., the strength of restoring forces, density, size) tend to influence the sounds in the frequency domain, while attributes of the interaction (e.g., its type and force) tend to influence the temporal domain. While this correspondence is by no means perfect, for instance, the force of interaction can affect a sound's bandwidth in the frequency domain, and the damping of a material is a strong determinant of the sound's temporal behavior, it is good enough to lend some support to the hypothesis of Vanderveer (1980), which states that the interactions affect the temporal domain of sounds and the objects affect the frequency domain.

Vibrating objects, as described previously, include many common sources of sounds, such as hitting or dropping books, scraping blackboards, clattering silverware, closing doors, and so on. In addition, this level of description can serve as a foundation for describing other more complicated events. For instance, crumpling paper makes sounds for similar reasons as a hit book. But when the paper is deformed, it doesn't return to its initial configuration but instead bends and creases along the lines of stress. The sounds made are a result of both the sudden folds and the vibrating surfaces between them. Though new source attributes may come into play in such an event, those listed in Table 5.1 remain important. In general, it may be expected that these attributes are salient in determining the sounds produced by all events involving vibrating objects.

5.7.1 Aerodynamic sounds

The properties of aerodynamic events are somewhat different than those describing vibrating objects. Where vibrating objects introduce pressure waves due to the interaction of a vibrating surface with the atmosphere, aerodynamic sounds are caused by the direct introduction and modification of atmospheric pressure differences from some source.

> *Sound Example: Several examples of aerodynamic sounds.*

The simplest aerodynamic sound is exemplified by an exploding balloon (Figure 5.2 A). When a balloon bursts, a mass of high-pressure gas is released into the surrounding atmosphere. This sudden pressure variation propagates

OBJECT VIBRATION

A. Explosion

B. Airflow

Figure 5.2 Aerodynamic sounds involve abrupt changes in air pressure, as when a balloon explodes (A) or wind rushes past a cylinder (B). When an object falls into a liquid (A), it forms a resonant cavity with a characteristic frequency (B), which changes as more liquid is pushed aside (C). Finally, the liquid's pressure causes the cavity to close in on the cavity (D) until the object is completely immersed.

as a wave that may be heard if the pressure differences that reach the ear are large enough and if they change at an appropriate rate. In such events, sound is directly caused by sudden pressure variations in the air, not by the effects of a vibrating surface. Most of the information conveyed by explosions seem to be carried by the frequency bandwidth of the sound and seem likely to concern the size or force of the explosion. High-frequency components indicate the suddenness of the pressure change near the source; low-frequency components the amount of gas involved (and thus the duration of the initial pressure release). So one can hear large, sudden explosions or smaller, less abrupt bursting noises.

The sudden change in pressure caused by a bursting balloon or explosive is analogous to a discrete interaction (such as a hit) that causes an object to vibrate. Other aerodynamic sounds are caused by more continuous events, such as the hissing of a leaky pipe or the rush of wind from a fan. These events also make sounds due to the introduction of pressure variations in the atmosphere.

The attributes of the specific sources of pressure variations seem likely to produce the most salient effects on these sounds. That is, the sounds produced by leaky pipes are determined by the pressure within the pipe and variations in this pressure caused by turbulence. The sounds made by wind rushing from a fan are affected by the speed and size of the fan and thus the volume of air it moves. Although the gases involved also affect the sounds, listeners are likely to be relatively insensitive to this information. In general, we expect aerodynamic sounds to be made by air (or in more ecological terms, our auditory system is attuned to a world in which air is by far the most common gas). That this is so can be seen by considering why the sound of someone talking after inhaling helium is so humorous. The heightened pitch of the voice is perfectly predictable due to the lower density of the gas but quite unexpected on the basis of experience.

Another sort of aerodynamic event involves situations in which changes in pressure themselves impart energy to objects, causing their vibrations. For example, when wind passes around a wire, eddies form on alternating sides, and the variations of pressure on each side cause the wire to vibrate (Figure 5.2 B). The frequencies of vibration thus produced depend on the wind speed, size, and tension of the wire. This is the principle used in creating Aeolian harps. In addition, sound itself may impart energy to objects, as when its minute pressure variations match the frequency of a tuning fork, causing it to ring through sympathetic vibration. Such sounds are not purely aerodynamic but perhaps better thought of as hybrids of aerodynamic and vibrating object sounds.

5.7.2   *Liquid sounds*

Sound-producing events involving liquids (e.g., dripping and splashing) are like those of vibrating objects in that they depend on an initial deformation that is then resisted. But it seems that the resulting vibration of the liquid does not directly affect the air in audible ways. Instead, sounds are affected by the formation and change of resonant cavities on the surface of the liquid.

This can be seen most clearly in considering how an object dropping into liquid makes a sound, as shown in Figure 5.3. As the object hits the liquid, it pushes it aside, forming a resonant cavity with a characteristic frequency. The cavity grows as the object pushes more liquid aside, and thus, the resonant frequency decreases. But the liquid's pressure causes it to close in on the cavity, and ultimately the object is immersed. The sound caused by such an event is likely to be influenced by many factors, particularly the mass, size, and speed of the object and the viscosity of the liquid, all of which influence the evolution of the resonating cavity.

More complex splashing sounds also seem to produce their sounds as changing cavities are formed, which resonate, amplify, and modify the sounds made by impacts of liquid on itself and other objects. Again, the properties of interacting objects and the liquid itself are likely to affect the sounds. In most cases, liquid sounds are probably heard as involving water, just as most aerodynamic sounds are probably heard as involving air. Still, the liquid's viscosity may produce effects on the sounds that are both salient and known by listeners.

Drop Impact

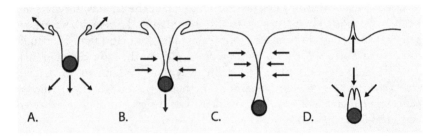

Figure 5.3 A hierarchical description of simple sonic events.

After all, it seems easy to tell whether a liquid gurgling out of a bottle is water or a thicker syrup or oil. Such sounds seem to be related to one another as liquid sounds because of common, high-level characteristics of their evolution in time.

Though the physical attributes of aerodynamic and liquid sounds are not the same as those of vibrating objects, they do share common features. Aerodynamic sounds seem to be influenced largely by the interactions that create atmospheric pressure differences, so that explosions, hisses, and fan noises all depend to a great degree on their causes. Liquid sounds also depend on the properties of their causal interactions, such as the size and speed of an object falling into liquid. They are also influenced by attributes of the liquid, such as its pressure (a restoring force) and viscosity (analogous to density). Most generally, all such sources involve the interaction of materials.

5.7.3 *Temporally complex events*

Although all sound-producing events seem to involve vibrating objects, aerodynamic, or liquid interactions, many also depend on complex patternings of the simple events described previously. So footsteps consist of temporal patterns of hitting sounds, and door slams require the squeak of scraping hinges, the whoosh of displaced air, and the hitting of the door on the frame. Though the previous discussion may point to a useful framework for understanding the attributes of single sounds, it does not address those of more complex events.

Traditional physical accounts of sound-producing events do not address these sorts of complex events, but there are undoubtedly higher-level physical attributes of such events that make reliable effects on their sounds. Some of these involve the timing of successive events so that, for instance, successive footstep sounds must probably occur within a range of rates and regularities to be heard as walking. Others are likely to involve mutual constraints on the objects that participate in related events. For instance, concatenating the squeak of a heavy door slowly closing with the bang of a light door slammed shut would probably sound quite unnatural. These sorts of higher-level attributes of the events are not the sorts of variables that physicists typically study, but they are likely to be quite important for everyday listening. We will consider more complex sound-producing events at some length later in this chapter.

5.8   Asking people what they hear

Considering the physical attributes of sound-producing events is useful in driving intuitions about the sorts of perceptual dimensions and features that might characterize everyday listening. But knowing how the physics of an event determines the sound it makes is not the same as knowing how a sound specifies an event. For instance, several attributes of a vibrating object, including its size, shape, and density, determine the frequencies of sound it produces. When hearing two sounds composed of different frequencies, then, how are we to know which parameters of the source have changed?

There are several possible answers to this problem. First, when several basic physical properties of an event have the same effect on the sound it produces, it is possible that a single perceptual dimension is heard, one that incorporates all of them. In other words, we may not hear size, shape, or density separately but rather a new dimension that combines all of them. On the other hand, it may be that the effects of changing some of the basic variables are much smaller than changing the others – for instance, changing the density of an object is likely to make a much smaller change in frequency than changing either its size or shape. In this case, the more effective parameters may also be more salient. That is, we may be inclined to hear a change in frequency as a change in size rather than density, just because size changes are the more significant source of frequency changes. Finally, it is quite likely that many parameters that change frequency also change other attributes of a sound. For example, changing the size of an object will change the frequencies of the sound it produces but not their pattern. Changing the shape, on the other hand, changes both the frequencies and their relationships. These complex patterns of change may serve as information distinguishing the physical parameters responsible.

In any case, we cannot base an account of everyday listening on the physics of sound-producing events alone. As Gibson (1979) pointed out, what is simple for physics may not be simple for perception, and vice versa. Instead, it is necessary to build an ecological physics, one founded on attributes relevant to listeners. For this reason, several studies have aimed at exploring the kinds of information sound conveys. Experiments of this sort complement analyses of physics: the data from such experiments constrains the sorts of physical attributes we might think we hear, while physical analyses can help in interpreting and organizing experimental data.

One approach to understanding the information people hear is basically experiential, involving introspection and self-observation. For instance,

Jenkins (1985) reported that blindfolded students were able to orient themselves within their environment on the basis of auditory information, such as "acoustic landmarks," resonances and echoes, and mixtures of near and far sounds. Note that they were not only using their ability to localize and to use reverberation as information about the environment (as discussed in Chapter 3 or so) but that the sounds themselves – people talking, relatively continuous machine noises, and the like – served as meaningful and relatively stable landmarks (see Chapter 3 for an example of an application of this observation).

Another approach to understanding what people hear is simply to ask them. For instance, in the work of Vanderveer (1980), subjects were presented with recorded tokens of 30 everyday sounds, such as clapping and tearing paper in a free identification task. Subjects were run in groups and asked to write a short phrase describing each sound. She found that subjects tended to identify the sounds in terms of the objects and events which caused them, describing their sensory qualities only when they could not identify the source events. In addition, subjects' mistakes tended to be based on the temporal qualities of sounds so that clapping might be confused with dropping a book, but seldom with tearing paper.

In the work of Gaver and Norman (1988), a similar study was run in which 17 sounds were played to subjects, who were then asked to describe what they heard. In contrast to Van Derveer's study, subjects were run individually and prompted by the experimenter to go into as much detail as they could about what they heard. Like Van Derveer, it was found that subjects nearly always described the sounds in terms of their sources. Their accuracy was often impressive. For instance, several subjects could readily distinguish the sounds made by running upstairs from those made by running downstairs, others were substantially correct about the size of objects dropped into water, and most could tell from the sound of pouring liquid that a cup was being filled. Subjects did find that some sounds were extremely difficult to identify (e.g., the sound of a file drawer being opened and closed), but they were almost always correct about some others (e.g., the sound of writing with chalk on a chalkboard). Often mistakes revealed interesting attributes that were heard. For instance, several people said the file drawer sounded like a bowling alley, both of which share rolling as an important component. In addition, attempts to identify unusual or implausible sounds were equally interesting. For example, the sound of somebody walking across a floor covered with newspaper was described variously as a person walking on snow or gravel or as somebody rhythmically crumpling paper; only one subject guessed correctly and immediately rejected the correct perception as being too implausible. Finally, their judgments followed the account of physics described previously to an impressive degree. For instance, they never confused the sounds made by vibrating objects, liquid, or aerodynamic sources.

Ballas and his colleagues (Ballas and Howard Jr 1987; Ballas et al. 1986) have used free identification tasks to study everyday sounds that are ambiguous as to their sources. They have shown that a measure of the information inherent in a given sound, based on the number of possible sources that subjects propose, can be used to predict reaction times for its identification.

Studies such as these are informative but sometimes frustrating. The result of asking people what they hear is often a list of events or attributes more akin to the list of sound effects discussed earlier than to the set of dimensions and features we want. Nonetheless, there are inherent categories in many of these studies that reveal themselves both in correct answers and (perhaps even more often) in confusion. So for instance, the fact that the file drawer sound in the work by Gaver and Norman (1988) was confused with that of bowling suggests that rolling may be a particularly salient event warranting further study (Fernström et al. 2005).

5.9 Attributes of everyday listening

Understanding the physics of sound-producing events is useful in suggesting physical attributes that might be heard, while the sorts of studies described previously help to constrain hypotheses about the attributes that actually are heard. Using our knowledge of physics and the results of these studies together, then we may begin to build up a framework for understanding some of the basic source parameters conveyed by sound. Such a framework may be tentative and speculative, but it is useful both in providing a guide to future research and in suggesting the attributes of sounds available for manipulation in the sorts of applications we describe in the next chapter.

The first part of this framework, shown in Figure 5.4, divides groups first by broad classes of materials and then by the interactions that can cause them to sound. Most generally, sounds indicate that something has happened, that an event has occurred, that there has been an interaction of materials. All sounds, then, convey this information.

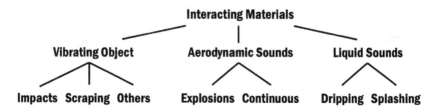

Figure 5.4 A framework for everyday sounds. Three fundamental sources (vibrating objects, liquids, and aerodynamic sounds) are shown in the three overlapping sections of the figure. Within each section, basic sound-producing events are shown in bold, and their relevant attributes next to them are in italics. Complexity grows toward the center of the figure, with temporally patterned, compound, and hybrid sounds shown.

At the next level, primitive sounds may be broken into three general categories: those made by vibrating objects, aerodynamics, and liquids. This categorization is supported both by the account of physics outlined at the beginning of this chapter and by the results of the protocol study described by Gaver and Norman (1988). Although subjects often misinterpreted the sources of sounds they heard, no misidentifications crossed these categories: none of the subjects confused the sounds made by vibrating objects, for instance, with those made by water.

Finally, various distinct sorts of sound-producing events are shown at the third level of this hierarchy, defined by sound-producing interactions involving objects, aerodynamics, and liquids. The sounds made by vibrating objects may be caused by impacts, scraping, or other interactions (such as deformation and rolling). Aerodynamic sounds may be made by discrete, sudden changes of pressure (explosions) or more continuous introductions of pressure variations (e.g., fans, leaking pipes). Similarly, liquid sounds may involve discrete drips or more continuous splashing.

This simple classification is useful in building up a more comprehensive framework of everyday sounds, as shown in Figure 5.4. This figure is broken into three main overlapping regions, corresponding to vibrating objects, liquid, and aerodynamic sounds, respectively. Within each region, several levels of sound-producing events are suggested. Finally, the overlapping regions show examples of sound events that involve hybrids of different sources.

5.10   Patterned, compound, and hybrid complex sounds

Above these basic level events are shown three sorts of complex events. The first is defined in terms of the temporal patterning of basic events. For instance, breaking, spilling, walking, and hammering are all complex events involving patterns of simpler impacts. Similarly, crumpling or crushing are examples of patterned deformation sounds. We would expect these sorts of events to convey the attributes made by their basic level constituents; in addition, other sorts of information are made available by their temporal complexity. For example, the regularity of a bouncing sound provides information about the symmetry of the bouncing object; variations in the scraping sounds produced by filing might indicate the general configuration of the object being filed.

The next level of complexity is produced by compound events that involve more than one sort of basic level event. For instance, the sounds made by handwriting involve a complex series of impacts and scrapes over time, while those made by bowling involve rolling followed by impact sounds. Again, these sounds are likely to convey information inherited from their basic level components and new information made available by their complexity. It is also worth noting that while some of these events involve more than one sort of source simultaneously (e.g., writing), others involve a series of basic events (e.g., opening a file drawer until the impacts against it stop).

Finally, hybrid events involve yet another level of complexity in which more than one basic sort of sound is involved. For instance, when water drips on a reverberant surface, the resulting sounds are caused both by the surface's vibrations and the quickly changing reverberant cavities and thus involve attributes both of liquid and vibrating object sounds. Some hybrid events involve attributes of all three basic sources: for instance, the sounds made by a speeding motorboat involve the splashing of the water, the vibrating engine sounds, and the rush of air past the body of the boat. As with other complex events, hybrid events provide information about their basic source categories and the basic events involved in their production, as well as more idiosyncratic information specific to their sources.

5.10.1 Problems and potentials of the framework

Clearly, the framework shown in Figure 5.5 is far from complete. For one thing, we know much more about how to characterize the sounds produced by vibrating objects than we do about either liquid or aerodynamic sounds. In addition, we don't yet know how to characterize the attributes of many complex events (though see the discussion of breaking, bouncing, and spilling in the next sections). Finally, the three basic categories of sounds we propose may not be enough. What of electronic sounds, such as those made by sparks or humming? Should fire be a basic sound-producing category (as suggested by our earth-air-water trichotomy)? What of vocal sounds? Though the inheritance strategy we propose here seems powerful and correct, there is much more to be discovered about how people hear events.

There are several more fundamental problems with this system. Two have to do with the sources of information used in its creation. Insofar as it relies on verbal evidence from subjects, it is liable to confuse the effects of language use for the attributes of perceptual experience. Insofar as it is based on an analysis of physics, it is liable to confuse source attributes that affect sounds with those that are actually heard. For example, the texture of an impacting object certainly affects the physics of dripping, but it is by no means obvious that this property is perceptible. Clearly, other sorts of research will be necessary to test whether these sources of information are informative.

In addition, the idea that the attributes of different sorts of events may be cataloged unequivocally is somewhat questionable. The information people obtained from the various sounds used in protocol studies often seem to be somewhat peculiar to the sounds themselves. Not all impact sounds, for instance, provide equal information about material, while some sounds convey more information about materials than interactions (for instance, many subjects heard metal but not deformation when listening to a crumpling can).

Nonetheless, this framework does seem to describe satisfactorily a great deal of the information inherent in everyday sounds. It captures our intuitions about basic sorts of sound-producing events and the information they make available for listening. It does so in a way that recognizes the mutual constraints

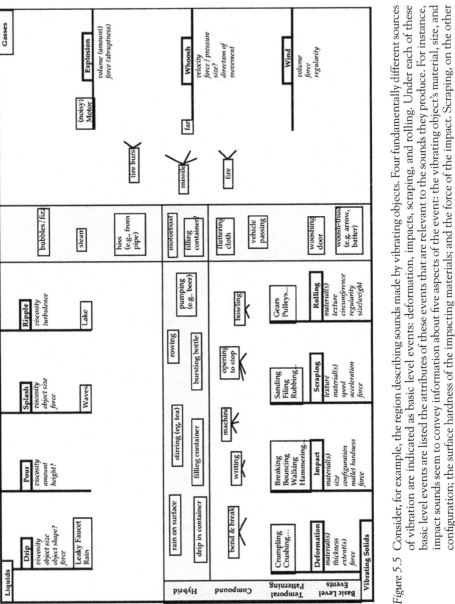

Figure 5.5 Consider, for example, the region describing sounds made by vibrating objects. Four fundamentally different sources of vibration are indicated as basic level events: deformation, impacts, scraping, and rolling. Under each of these basic level events are listed the attributes of these events that are relevant to the sounds they produce. For instance, impact sounds seem to convey information about five aspects of the event: the vibrating object's material, size, and configuration; the surface hardness of the impacting materials; and the force of the impact. Scraping, on the other hand, conveys information about the texture of the surfaces, one or more of the materials involved, the speed and acceleration of scraping, and the force or weight with which one object is scraped over another.

of materials and interactions in producing sounds. In addition, it provides a mechanism by which to understand the myriad of complex events we typically hear. Finally, and perhaps most importantly, it seems useful in suggesting the kinds of source attributes that may be manipulated when creating or shaping everyday sounds that are to be used to convey information.

5.11   How do we hear it?

Asking what people hear is useful in understanding attributes of the experience of everyday listening. As we have seen, these attributes can be expressed in terms of the physical parameters of sound-producing events – the kind of inter-action that starts an object vibrating, for example, or its force; the viscosity of a liquid, or the size of something dropped into it, and so on. Such an account is useful in knowing the sorts of dimensions we can manipulate in applications that involve everyday sounds.

Asking how we hear it, on the other hand, is meant to get at the attributes of sounds than convey information about the events that caused them. It is one thing to suggest, for instance, that people hear the material of a vibrating object and another to understand how a sound may be changed so that the perceived material changes. If the account prompted by asking what we hear expands traditional descriptions of elemental sensations, then the account of how we hear it is meant to expand traditional descriptions of the primitive physical dimensions of sounds. Even less is known about how to characterize the perceptual information that allows us to hear events in the world than is known about how to characterize what we hear of them. This is not surprising, as it is the more difficult of the two tasks. The sort of framework introduced in the last section is not definitive but suggestive. It organizes a set of semiformal hypotheses based on intuition, physics, and experimentation. Understanding how we hear these attributes requires that we test these hypotheses and that we formalize the information that leads to these supposed experiential dimen-sions. Asking what we hear is useful in orienting toward the immense range of everyday sounds, but asking how we hear is necessary if we are actually to create them.

5.12   Analysis and synthesis of sounds and events

Computer musicians have addressed a problem similar to the one we are ask-ing about here. One of the goals for some computer musicians has been for decades to find efficient means to capture and reproduce the sounds of acoustic instruments. As we have described previously, such sounds can be completely described in digital form by the output of a time-varying sum of sinusoids, but this description is likely to be huge. A method known as analysis and synthesis (Risset and Wessel 1982) has been developed, which aims at understanding how to reduce the data from such analyses so that only that necessary for recreating a perceptually identical sound is retained.

Analysis and synthesis, as the name implies, involves analyzing a real instrument sound and then synthesizing a duplicate on the basis of the analysis. The analysis data can be systematically reduced, and synthesis is driven by the results. For instance, straight line segments can be used to approximate complex time-varying attributes of the sound, and the resulting synthesized sound can be compared to the original. In this way, an understanding of which aspects of the sounds are crucial for perception may be obtained.

Understanding the effective perceptual information can be studied in similar ways. The sounds made by actual events can be analyzed, the data reduced, and then synthesized sounds can be compared to the originals. The purpose of this comparison, however, is not to produce an identical sound (one which produces the same sensations) but to produce a sound that retains information for relevant source properties. For instance, if we were interested in understanding how we hear the texture of a scraped surface, we might record and analyze a number of surfaces being scraped by various objects. In resynthesis, we would be concerned only with maintaining the information relevant to texture, not the size or material of the surface or the scraping object. In this way, we reduce the data from the analysis until only that which conveys the relevant information remains. The result is a description of the information relevant for scraping, independent from that relevant for other source attributes.

We can go a step further and explicitly consider the source in our account. Now we don't only analyze the acoustics of the source but the physics of the event. And similarly, we can reduce our description of the source until only those attributes relevant to a particular source attribute are described. Resynthesis, then, can be driven not only by a reduced description of natural sounds but reduced descriptions of sound-producing events. Basing synthesis on the analyses of events and sounds is valuable in helping to suggest what acoustic attributes will indeed be relevant and what will not. As will become evident in the following examples, many of the acoustic attributes which provide information for events are subtle and unlikely to be made evident by inspection of acoustic analyses alone. Using analysis and synthesis of events and sounds, then, is a powerful method for understanding the effective information for everyday listening.

5.12.1   *Breaking and bouncing bottles*

An early example of analysis and synthesis of everyday sounds is the study of Warren and Verbrugge (1984) about breaking and bouncing sounds. In this study, they used physical and acoustic analyses to examine the auditory patterns which characterize breaking and bouncing and verified their results by testing subjects on synthetic sounds.

Consider the mechanics of a bottle bouncing on a surface (see Figure 10.3 A). Each time the bottle hits the surface, the impact causes the bottle to vibrate in a characteristic way depending on its shape, size, and material (as discussed in the earlier section on physics). Energy is dissipated with each bounce so that, in general, the time between bounces and the force of each impact becomes less (some irregularities in the pattern are likely to occur due to the bottle's asymmetry). Thus, bouncing sounds may be expected to be characterized by a repetitive series of impact sounds with decreasing period and amplitude. When a bottle breaks, on the other hand, it divides into many separate pieces of various sizes and shapes (see Figure 10.3 B). Thus, a breaking sound should be characterized by an initial impact sound followed by several different, overlapping bouncing sounds, each with its own frequency makeup and period. The differences between breaking and bouncing, then, should be conveyed largely by the temporal patterning of the sounds.

Sound Examples: Breaking and bouncing bottles.

This informal physical analysis is born out of acoustic analyses of natural tokens of breaking and bouncing sounds (see Figure 10.3). Spectrograms of recorded bouncing sounds clearly show a series of impacts, each with identical frequency components, which repeat at a decaying rate. Spectrograms of breaking sounds, on the other hand, show a more complex pattern; individual bouncing patterns of the pieces are overlapped but still may be distinguished. Individual spectral components may play a role in distinguishing different bouncing patterns, but temporal patterning seems the most salient distinguishing feature between the sounds.

Warren and Verbrugge (1984) created artificial tokens of breaking and bouncing sounds by combining natural tokens of single impacts in various temporal patterns (see Figure 10.5). The sounds made by four individual pieces of a broken bottle were recorded separately. In order to create an artificial bouncing sound, the individual sound tokens were synchronized to the timing of a real bouncing bottle so that all four played simultaneously. To create an artificial breaking sound, each of the four component sounds was synchronized to a different bouncing pattern (taken from a natural bouncing bottle sound) so that they were not in phase. Thus, the spectral components of the artificial breaking and bouncing sounds were identical, and they could only be distinguished by their temporal patterning.

Subjects were asked to rate natural and artificial bouncing and breaking sounds in order to verify these analyses. When presented with natural tokens and asked to rate them as "bouncing," "breaking," or "don't know," subjects were 99.3% correct for "bouncing" and 98.5% for "breaking." Clearly, subjects were able to obtain and use the information for the events. When asked to rate artificial tokens, subjects were 93% correct for bouncing patterns and 86.7 % correct for breaking. Despite some performance degradation, the characterization of Warren and Verbrugge (1984) of the information for breaking and bouncing appears to have been substantially correct.

Two things should be noted about these results. First, the breaking sounds they constructed were quite simple. Natural breaking sounds are likely to have an initial impact and rupturing sound different from those following, but the constructed tokens of Warren and Verbrugge (1984) did not. In addition, natural breaking sounds are probably characterized by many more than four overlapping bouncing sounds. Second, note that the rating task they used is a fairly coarse test. Asking subjects to rate breaking versus bouncing places constrains the events that subjects might think they heard. Subjects were offered a third category, "don't know," to try to reduce this constraint. Nonetheless, we might suspect that their judgments indicate that a particular sound is more representative of breaking than bouncing, for instance, without necessarily sounding like breaking. The coarse grain of the empirical methodology of Warren and Verbrugge (1984), then, seems likely to have balanced the simplicity of their sounds.

Nonetheless, this work is a good representative of analysis and synthesis studies. The combination of an intuitive physical analysis with acoustic analyses seems quite useful in discovering the informative properties of everyday sounds. These analyses can be tested by constructing versions of the sounds. In this case, the result is a simple description of the features distinguishing two sound-producing events, a description that can be used in synthesizing representative sounds.

5.12.2   Impact sounds

In our discussion of the physics of vibrating objects earlier in this chapter, we suggested several properties of objects that might be conveyed by impact sounds, including those of the vibrating object's material and configuration and those of the type and force of impact. A number of studies have been concerned with understanding the information for these properties conveyed by sounds and the accuracy with which people hear them.

Freed (1990) studied people's perception of the hardness of mallets used to strike objects. He recorded the sounds made by hitting cooking pans with mallets of various hardnesses. Four different-sized pans were used: one each of 1-, 2-, 3-, and 6-quart saucepans. Six mallets with heads of different hardnesses were used: metal, wood, rubber, cloth-covered wood, felt, and felt-covered rubber. The sounds were analyzed using a model of the peripheral auditory system. The model first passed the signal through a bank of critical-band filters, squared the magnitude of the output signals, converted the results to decibels, and transformed them by an A-weighting function to approximate loudness (rather than amplitude). The resulting description of the sounds is similar to that provided by a Fourier analysis but is held to be more similar to the output of peripheral auditory processing.

Freed described the results of this analysis in the form of four summarizing parameters that were meant to capture the information for mallet hardness in these sounds. The first two, spectral level and spectral level slope, are measures of overall loudness and change of loudness with time, respectively; the second two, spectral centroid and spectral centroid TWA (time-weighted average), are measures of the ratio of high- to low-frequency energy in the sounds and their change, respectively. Finally, multiple regression was used to assess the usefulness of these parameters in predicting hardness judgments made by nine skilled listeners. The parameters seemed to perform as accurate predictors, with an overall multiple R-squared of .725. However, individual parameters varied widely in their predictive power. Most useful were measures of the spectral centroid and the spectral centroid TWA. To a first approximation, then, mallet hardness is conveyed by the relative presence of high- and low-frequency energy.

5.12.3 *Material and length*

Gaver and Norman (1988) studied people's abilities to judge the length and material of struck wooden and metal bars based on the sounds they made when struck. He recorded the sounds made by striking ten wooden and metal bars of five different lengths (10, 20, 30, 40, 50, and 60 cm) three times each, for a total of 30 sounds. A model of the physics of the events was developed, which combined analytical solutions to the wave equation for transverse vibrations in a bar (see, e.g., Lamb [2004]) with empirical measurements of damping and resonance amplitudes. This model was used both to aid the interpretation of acoustic analyses of the sounds and to synthesize new tokens.

According to this model, the material of the bars had several effects on the sounds. Perhaps most importantly, materials have different characteristic frequency-dependent damping functions: the sounds made by vibrating wood decay quickly, with low frequencies lasting longer than high ones, while the sounds made by vibrating metal decay slowly, with high-frequency components lasting longer than low ones. In addition, metal sounds had partials with well-defined frequency peaks, while wooden sound partials were smeared over frequency space. The sounds made by wooden bars tended to have fewer high-frequency components than those made by metal bars, and each material seemed to support a band of frequencies better than those higher or lower; for wood, this reverberant range was lower than for wood. Finally, the sounds made by a given length of metal tend to be higher than those made by a given length of wood because of metal's greater density. The many and complex effects of material-on-impact sounds contrast with the simple effect of length. Changing the length of a bar simply changes the frequencies of the sound it produces when struck so that short bars make high sounds and long bars make low ones. However, the effects of length interact with the effects of the material. For instance, frequencies change monotonically with length, but the frequency of the partial with the highest amplitude changes nonlinearly with length (see Gaver and Norman [1988]). Thus, according to this model, information for the material of the bars is more salient than that for length.

In the work of Gaver and Norman (1988), subjects were asked to judge the material and rate the length of struck bars based both on recorded sounds and sounds synthesized on the basis of his model. Subjects were excellent at judging material – 96% and 99% correct for natural wood and metal sounds and 91% and 97% for synthesized ones. They were much less accurate at judging length: their judgments showed large interactions with the material. However, with a brief training session in which they received feedback about their judgments, their accuracy improved dramatically. In addition, almost all subjects' ratings correlated with frequency so that low sounds were judged as indicating long bars and high sounds as indicating short bars. In sum, the studies by Gaver and Norman (1988) supported his analysis of the information for material and length but suggested that judgments of length were disrupted by interactions between the effects on sounds of length and material.

5.12.4   *Internal friction and material*

Wildes and Richards (1988) also studied material identification based on impact sounds. Their approach differed from Gaver's in two ways. First, they rely entirely on analytical physics in their approach and present no empirical data or any acoustic analyses. Second, they focused on identifying a property of the sound that is identified with material, where Gaver focused on finding all effects of material on sounds.

Wildes and Richards (1988) noted that for many materials, the amount of deformation produced by an impact, as well as the material's return to equilibrium after the removal of the impact force, lags compared to the impact. This characteristic is embodied in their model of a standard anelastic linear solid. The dynamic behavior described by this model depends on an intrinsic parameter of material called internal friction. Internal friction determines both the sharpness of the peaks around a vibrating object's partials and the rate of its decay. Thus, Wildes and Richards (1988) concluded hearing material depends on assessing internal friction on the basis of peak bandwidth and decay rate. Note that this conclusion corresponds with the observations of Gaver and Norman (1988) that wood and metal are differentiated both by their decay rates and by the fact that partials of metal sounds are more sharply defined than those made by wood.

5.13   Sound synthesis by physical modeling

An ecological approach to sound synthesis may look at the sources and try to mimic the physical behavior of sounding objects. Physics-based modeling of everyday sounds relies on detailed simulation of basic physical phenomena and introduces simplifications and abstractions for complex physical phenomena. Much of the physical-modeling literature focused its attention on the properties of resonating objects (Van Den Doel et al. 2001; Cook 2002a; Aramaki and Kronland-Martinet 2006). The idea of linking sound and event perception to action possibilities has been used to design different synthesis algorithms to produce and manipulate sounds according to the physical attributes of the sources. For example, a physical modeling synthesizer, designed to simulate how different materials (e.g., wood, metal), resonates when they are struck. This framework has guided recent designs of technologies for sound and interaction design, focusing on the model of interaction itself rather than sound engines based on conventional sound synthesis techniques (Monache et al. 2010). This has given the Sound Design Toolkit (Baldan et al. 2017), a software that focuses on dynamic nonlinear interactions. A bottom-up hierarchy represents the dependencies between low-level models and temporally patterned textures and processes, organized into four classes: solids, liquids, gases, and machines. These classes are grounded on different physical mechanisms, and they mirror the perceived categories of everyday sounds.

5.14 Conclusions

In this chapter, we have introduced the concept of everyday listening, together with different experiments showing how humans are able to judge the physical properties of objects merely based on their sounds. Few studies have focused on everyday sound perception engaged in active processes, perhaps because they were judged not technologically feasible in terms of real-time sound control, motion capture, and experimental setup. However, such sonic interaction systems are increasingly common in a variety of fields of applications, such as industrial products (to promote manipulations with an object), sports (to improve an athlete's performance), health (to assist in the rehabilitation of a patient), robotics (to control the movement of an operator), games (to strengthen a multisensory immersion of a player), and virtual and augmented reality applications. Everyday listening represents the foundation of auditory icons, which will be described in the following chapter.

6 Auditory icons

6.1 Introduction

An account of everyday listening, as described in the last chapter, gives us a new foundation for creating auditory interfaces. Instead of mapping information to sounds and their dimensions, as the interfaces we described in Chapters 3 and 4 do, we can encode information using audible events and their dimensions. The results are auditory icons, everyday sounds designed to convey information about events by analogy to everyday sound-producing events.

For instance, when we mark a computer file for deletion, we might hear the sound of an object crashing into a wastebasket. The type of object we hear might indicate the type of object we've discarded, whether it is a document, a program, or some other file, while its size might be indicated by the size of the object we hear. The number of other objects awaiting deletion might affect the sound of the crash, and their types and sizes could also be indicated. Finally, when the files are eventually deleted, we might hear an appropriate sound (for instance, a trash compactor) as the deletion occurs or, better, enough in advance that we can abort the deletion.

Auditory icons such as these are like sound effects for computers, complementing visual events with appropriate sounds. But they are not designed merely to provide entertainment; rather, they convey rich information about events in computer systems, allowing us to listen to computers as we do to the everyday world. They use a strategy similar to that used in creating visual icons, mapping events in computer systems to related everyday events in order to aid learning and comprehension. This strategy contrasts with those based on musical listening. For instance, compare the wastebasket sound of our example with the simple two-note earcon for indicating file deletion proposed by Blattner et al. (1989), as described in Chapter 4. Not only does the wastebasket sound convey more information about the event and objects involved in it, but it does so in a more intuitive way and one that fits better with the graphical components of the interface.

The richness of everyday sounds, their ease of comprehension, and their ability to help create a virtual world lead to a number of powerful advantages for auditory icons. In this chapter, we review work on auditory icons, describing

DOI: 10.4324/9781003260202-6

how they may be created and some of the issues to keep in mind when doing so. A number of systems that use auditory icons are described, both to give an idea of the kinds of auditory icons that might be created and to illustrate the range of functions they can perform. A number of issues that are raised by this work are discussed, and their importance for all auditory interfaces is considered. Finally, we discuss the design and implementation of systems that use auditory icons.

6.2   Advantages of auditory icons

As the previous example suggests, auditory icons are simply everyday sounds mapped to events in the computer. So marking something as deleted is expressed by the sound of throwing it into a trashcan. Selecting an object might sound like touching it. Moving an object might make a scraping sound.

But auditory icons don't serve merely as labels for categories of events and objects, as most visual icons do. They can be parameterized to reflect their relevant dimensions as well (see Figure 6.1). To return to the example of deleting a file, the computer event (deletion) is mapped to an everyday event (throwing an object into a trashcan). Then parameters of the everyday event can be used to indicate parameters of the computer event: the size of the object represents the size of the computer file, its material reflects the file type, and so on.

Thus, auditory icons convey multidimensional information by mapping the dimensions of the information to be displayed to dimensions of everyday events. In this way, any sound can convey a great deal of information. Moreover,

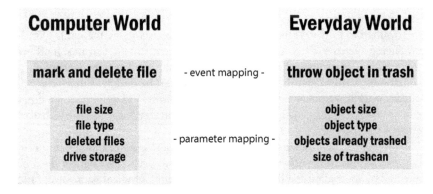

Figure 6.1 Auditory icons are created by mapping events in the computer world to sound-producing events in the everyday world. They may be parameterized by mapping parameters of the computer events to dimensions of the everyday event that affect the sound it makes.

"families" of auditory icons can be created by exploiting the organization inherent in everyday events. For instance, if the material of a sound-producing event is used to represent the type of object, all auditory icons concerning that type of object would use sounds made by that kind of material. So text files might always sound wooden, whether they are selected, moved, copied, or deleted. In this way, a rich system of auditory icons may be created that relies on relatively few underlying metaphors.

Because auditory icons rely on everyday sounds, it is relatively easy to make them compatible with existing graphic interfaces. Objects can sound like what they look like: files can sound like solid objects being tapped or scraped, windows can sound like glass surfaces, objects clatter when they are thrown away.

Achieving this correspondence between sound and graphics is more difficult using the strategies described in Chapter 4 because they rely on the musical parameters of sound. The earcon for deleting a file described in Chapter 4, as an example, bears little relation to the graphic counterpart of dropping a file icon over a trashcan icon. A different set of rules must be learned for the auditory and graphic components of such systems. Using auditory icons, in contrast, a single set of metaphors can guide both aspects of the interface.

When the same analogy underlies both auditory and visual icons, the increased redundancy of the interface can help users learn and remember the system. In addition, making the model world of the computer consistent in its visual and auditory aspects increases users' feelings of direct engagement (Hutchins et al. 1986) or direct mimesis (Laurel 1986) with that world. The concepts of direct engagement and mimesis refer to the feeling of working in the world of the task, not the computer. By making the model world of the computer more real, one makes the existence of an interface to that world less noticeable. Providing auditory information that is consistent with visual feedback is one way of making the model world more vivid. In addition, using auditory icons may allow more consistent model worlds to be developed because some computer events may map more readily to sound-producing events than to visual ones.

To summarize, the strategy of creating auditory icons by mapping sound-producing events to events in the computer has many useful features. It allows the creation of parameterized auditory icons that convey rich, multidimensional information. Families of auditory icons can be designed that relate to one another in systematic ways. Consistent auditory and graphical mappings can be created, producing a coherent model world that increases the transparency of the interface.

However, as pointed out by Mynatt (1994), there is a need for a methodology to design auditory icons. The usability of auditory icons might indeed be affected by their identifiability, conceptual mapping, physical parameters, and user preference. In the same paper, a methodology is proposed to design auditory icons, which consist of choosing sounds with large bandwidth and where length, intensity, and sound quality are roughly equal; the identifiability of auditory icons needs to be evaluated; learnability, conceptual mapping, and possible perceptual situations, such as masking, also need to be evaluated.

In the next sections, we describe a variety of interfaces that have used auditory icons as a way of illustrating these points. In addition, these examples stress the variety of functions that auditory icons and sounds, in general, may perform in the interface. Examples such as these are the best way to communicate the concept of auditory icons and to explore their creation and functionality.

6.3   Systems that use auditory icons

The benefits of auditory icons can be more fully illustrated by examples of systems that have used them. A number of systems have been created that illustrate the potential for auditory icons to convey useful information about computer events. In particular, these systems suggest that sound is well suited for providing information, among others, about previous and possible interactions, indicating ongoing processes and modes can be useful for navigation and support collaboration.

In the following sections, a variety of systems that have used auditory icons are briefly described. Their order is roughly chronological and, not surprisingly, also reveals the increasing functionality that auditory icons can provide.

6.3.1   Case study 1: SonicFinder: creating an auditory desktop

The SonicFinder (Gaver 1989a) is the first interface to incorporate auditory icons. Developed for Apple Computer Company, it was an extension to the Finder, the application still used to organize, manipulate, create, and delete files on the Macintosh. The Finder is automatically run when the machine is booted, and thus, it is probably the program most frequently encountered by Macintosh users. Because of this, and because the SonicFinder was easily portable (requiring no special hardware, it could be distributed on a single 800 KB floppy disk), many people have encountered the SonicFinder and have provided useful feedback about its utility.

Creating the SonicFinder required extending the Finder code at appropriate points to play sampled sounds modified according to attributes of the relevant events. Thus, a variety of actions make sounds in the SonicFinder: selecting, dragging, and copying files; opening and closing folders; selecting, scrolling, and resizing windows; and dropping files into and emptying the trashcan. Most of these sounds are parameterized, although the ability to modify sounds is limited. So for instance, sounds that involve objects such as files or folders indicate not only basic events such as selection or copying but also the objects' types and sizes via the material and size of the virtual sound-producing objects. In addition, the SonicFinder incorporates an early example of an auditory process monitor in the form of a pouring sound that accompanied copying, and that indicates, via changes of pitch, the percentage of copying that had been completed (cf. Cohen and Ludwig 1991).

Because the first-generation Macintosh was a single-processing machine with a fairly simple interface, the sounds used in the SonicFinder basically provide feedback and information about possible interactions (as well as more general information about file size and type, dragging location, and the like). Nonetheless, it provided a valuable example of the potential of auditory icons, showing that sounds such as these can be incorporated in an intuitive and informative way.

Apple has never released the SonicFinder (although it did appear on a developer's CD-ROM). There are several reasons for this. Most fundamentally, the perceived benefit to disk-space ratio was not high enough: because it uses sampled sounds, the SonicFinder could never be reduced below about 100 KB in size; it was prohibitively large to release back in the days before high-density floppy disks and CD-ROMs. Although many people found the auditory cues useful, others found them irritating or thought of them as merely entertaining. This provides a valuable example of the real-world challenges that designers of auditory interfaces must face. Nonetheless, the interface has spread around the world in what Buxton has termed the "research underground" and has hopefully helped to demonstrate the potential and appeal of auditory interfaces in general.

6.3.2   Case study 2: SoundShark: sounds in a large collaborative environment

Although the SonicFinder was useful in incorporating auditory icons into a well-known and often-used interface, its simplicity led people to underestimate the functions that auditory icons could serve. For this reason, Gaver et al. (1991) demonstrated auditory icons used in a large-scale, multiprocessing, collaborative system called SharedARK and dubbed the resulting auditory interface SoundShark.

SharedARK was a collaborative version of ARK, the Alternate Reality Kit. Developed by Gaver et al. (1991), ARK was designed as a virtual physics laboratory for distance education. The "world" appeared on the screen as a flat surface on which a number of 2.5D objects could be found. These objects could be picked up, carried, and even thrown using a mouse-controlled "hand." They could be linked to one another, and messages could be passed to them using "buttons." In using this system, a number of simple physical experiments were performed. In addition, SharedARK allowed the same world to be seen by a number of different people on their own computer screens (and was usually used in conjunction with audio and video links that allow them to see and talk to one another). They could see each other's hands, manipulate objects together, and thus collaborate within this virtual world.

SharedARK was a multiprocessing system with the potential for several "machines" or self-sustaining processes to run simultaneously. In addition, it provides a very large world to users in that the space for interaction is many times larger than the screen (depending on available memory, it may cover literally acres of virtual space). Users move around this space by moving their hand near the edge of the window, causing it to scroll over adjacent territory.

To help with navigation, a "radar view" is presented, which shows a much-reduced representation of the world and objects within it.

This interface was extended by adding auditory icons to indicate user interactions, ongoing processes, and modes, to help with navigation, and to provide information about other users. Sounds were used to provide feedback as they were in the SonicFinder: many user actions were accompanied by auditory icons, which were parametrized to indicate attributes such as the size of relevant objects. In addition, ongoing processes made sounds that indicated their nature and continuing activity even if they were not visible on the screen. Modes of the system, such as the activation of "motion," which allows objects to move if they have a velocity, were indicated by low-volume, smooth background sounds. Collaborators could hear each other even if they couldn't see each other, which seemed to aid in coordination. Finally, the distance between a given user's hand and the source of the sound was indicated by the sounds' amplitude and by low-pass filtering, aiding with navigation. The apparent success of this manipulation led us to develop auditory landmarks, objects whose sole function was to play a repetitive sound that could aid orientation.

SoundShark was implemented using an external sampler that was triggered and controlled via MIDI. This allowed a number of features that would have been more difficult to achieve had the sound playback been handled by the workstation. Multiple sounds could be played simultaneously, and manipulations, such as varied attack times and low-pass filtering, could be used. Nonetheless, the use of external hardware meant that the system was not as portable as the SonicFinder.

6.3.3 Case study 3: ARKola: studying the use of sound in a complex system

Our experiences with SoundShark suggested that auditory icons could provide useful information about user-initiated events, processes, and modes and about location within a complex environment. To test this, we developed a special application within SoundShark, which we used as a basis for observing people's use of the system. This application, developed in collaboration with Tim O'Shea, was a model of a soft drink plant called the ARKola bottling factory (Gaver et al. 1991). It consisted of an assembly line of nine machines that cooked, bottled, and capped cola, provided supplies, and kept track of financing. The plant was deliberately designed to be too large to fit on the computer screen, so participants could only see about half the machines at any given time. In addition, we designed the plant to be fairly difficult to run, with the rates of the machines requiring fine-tuning and with machines occasionally breaking down, necessitating the use of a repair button.

Each of the machines made sounds to indicate its function. For instance, the nut dispenser made wooden-impact sounds each time a nut was delivered to the cooker, the heater made a whooshing flame-like sound, the bottler clanged, and the capper clanked. In addition, the rate of each machine was indicated by the rate of repetition of the sounds it made, and problems with the machines were indicated by a variety of alerting sounds such as breaking glass, overflowing liquid, and so forth.

With as many as 12 sounds playing simultaneously, designing the sounds so that all could be heard and identified was a serious challenge. In general, we used temporally complex sounds to maximize discriminability and designed the sounds to be semantically related to the events they represented. Two strategies were found to be useful in avoiding masking. First, sounds were spread fairly evenly in frequency so that some were high-pitched and others lower. Second, we avoided playing sounds continuously and instead played repetitive streams of sounds, thus maximizing the chance for other sounds to be heard in the gaps between repetitions.

Six pairs of participants were asked to run the plant with the aim of making as much "money" as they could during an hour-long session. Each pair ran the plant for two hours, one with and one without auditory feedback (with the order, of course, being counterbalanced). We observed their performance from a "control room" via video links as they ran the plant and videoed their activities for later analysis.

Our observations indicated that sounds were effective in two broad areas. First, they seemed to help people keep track of the many ongoing processes. The sounds allowed people to track the activity, rate, and functioning of normally running machines. Without sound, people often overlooked machines that were broken or that were not receiving enough supplies; with sound, these problems were indicated either by the machine's sound ceasing (which was often ineffective) or by the various alert sounds. Perhaps most interestingly, the auditory icons allowed people to hear the plant as an integrated complex process. The sounds merged together to produce an auditory texture, much as the many sounds that make up the sound of an automobile do. Participants seemed to be sensitive to the overall texture of the factory sound, referring to "the factory" more often than they did without sound.

The second set of observations is related to the role of sound in collaboration. In both the sound and no-sound conditions, participants tended to divide responsibility for the plant so that each could keep one area on the screen at all times. Without sound, this meant that each had to rely on their partner's reports to tell what was happening in the invisible part. With sound, each could hear directly the status of the remote half of the plant. This seemed to lead to greater collaboration between partners, with each pointing out problems to the other, discussing problems, and so forth. The ability to provide foreground information visually and background information using sound seemed to allow people to concentrate on their own tasks while coordinating with their partners about theirs.

Sound also seemed to add to the tangibility of the plant and increased participants' engagement with the task. This became most evident when one of a pair of participants who had completed an hour with sound and were working an hour without remarked, "We could always make the noises ourselves."

In sum, the ARKola study indicated that auditory icons could be useful in helping people collaborate on a difficult task involving a large-scale complex system and that the addition of sounds increased their enjoyment as well.

6.3.4 Case study 4: ShareMon: background sounds for awareness

As we have pointed out earlier, continuous or repetitive sounds have the interesting property that they fade to the background of attention over time. They become part of the peripheral information that people have access to but don't consciously attend to at a given time. People can bring them into the focus of attention, and when the sounds change in some way, they are likely to force a switch of attention, but when they remain relatively unchanging, they are relatively unnoticeable.

Continuous and repetitive sounds thus have great potential for use as background status indicators. Both SoundShark and the ARKola factory used continuous sounds to help people keep track of ongoing processes and modes. Some attempt was made to keep these sounds unobtrusive, but for the most part, they were about as noticeable as any of the other sounds used in this system. Though these systems began to explore the potential of sounds used as unobtrusive status indicators, much of the potential for using sound in this way remained unexplored.

6.3.5 Case study 5: EAR: environmental audio reminders

Where SoundShark and ARKola explored the use of auditory icons to support collaboration in software systems, another system, called EAR (Environmental Audio Reminders), demonstrates that auditory icons are also helpful for supporting collaboration in the office environment itself (Gaver et al. 1991). This system plays a variety of nonspeech audio cues to offices and common areas inside EuroPARC to keep us informed about a variety of events around the building. It is one element of ongoing research at EuroPARC on environmental interfaces, which are aimed at merging the power of the computational and everyday environments. EAR works in conjunction with the RAVE audio-video network (Gaver et al. 1992; Buxton and Moran 1990), which connects all the offices at EuroPARC with audio and video technologies using a computer-controlled switch, and Khronika (Lövstrand 1991), an event server that uses a database of events in conjunction with software daemons to inform us of a wide range of planned and spontaneous electronic and professional events. EAR, then, consists of sounds triggered by Khronika when relevant events occur, which are routed using the RAVE system from a central server (in this case, a Sparcstation) to any office in the building.

A wide variety of sounds were used to remind about a range of events. For instance, when a new email arrived, the sound of a stack of papers falling on the floor was heard. When somebody connected to a video camera, the sound of an opening door was heard just before the connection was made, and the sound of a closing door just after the connection was broken. Ten minutes before a meeting, the sound of murmuring voices slowly increasing in number and volume was played in the office, then the sound of a gavel. And finally, when one of the colleagues decided to call it a day, they often played the "pub call" to the office, the sound of laughing and chatting voices in the background with the sound of a pint glass being filled with real ale in the foreground.

Many of the sounds used in EAR may seem frivolous because they are cartoon-like stereotypes of naturally occurring sounds. But it is precisely because they are stereotyped sounds that they are effective. More "serious" sounds, such as electronic beeps or sequences of tones, would be likely to be less easily remembered than these. In addition, some care was taken in shaping the sounds to be unobtrusive. For instance, many of the sounds are very short; those that are longer have a relatively slow attack so that they enter the auditory ambiance of the office subtly. Most of the sounds have relatively little high-frequency energy, and we try to avoid extremely noisy or abrupt sounds. So though the sounds we use are stereotypes, they are designed to fit into the existing office ambiance rather than intruding upon it.

In sum, the auditory cues used in the EAR system can be unobtrusive, informative, and valuable. They serve to indicate events in the same way that they might be heard in everyday life, with the added advantage that the events cued are chosen by users. They allow us to hear distant events or events that don't naturally produce informative noises, helping to blur the distinction between the electronic and physical environments. By informing us about ongoing events in the building, they help to ease the transition between working alone and working together.

6.3.6   Case study 6: Shoogle: excitatory multimodal interaction on mobile devices

A relatively more recent example is Shoogle, presented by Williamson et al. (2007). Shoogle is a novel interface to sense information on mobile devices. It is possible to interact with the device, for example, by shaking it, which results in vibrotactile and auditory feedback. In Shoogle, the user excites information from the mobile device and then negotiates with the system in a continuous, closed-loop interaction. Shoogle uses sonic and haptic rendering of the contents of inboxes, the state of battery life, or remaining memory. The feedback is tightly coupled to the input. In contrast to static display approaches, this active perception approach takes advantage of people's expectations about the evolution of physical systems. This avoids disturbing the user unnecessarily and potentiates richer, more informative feedback. Users know what motions they have applied and interpret the display in that specific context. The Shoogle interface uses inertial sensing for natural motion-sensing without external moving parts; the user just shakes, tilts, or wobbles the device to stimulate the auditory and vibrotactile feedback. This can either be explicit or occur as part of a user's background motion – walking, running, standing up, or other everyday motions.

Shoogle, for example, simulates a certain number of balls, each representing a message on a mobile device. The user, while shaking the mobile, excites the balls in motion, which bounce around the virtual container. When an impact is produced, it generates sound and vibration. This natural interaction is interpreted as the number of messages in the device. Another interesting interaction is the checking of the battery life: the user shakes the device to gain a sense of its fullness. When the battery is full, the sensation is like that of a full bucket of water sloshing around. As the battery drains, shaking the device sounds like a few droplets splashing until finally all power evaporates. This is similar to the virtual maracas approach for resource sensing suggested by Fernström et al. (2003).

The audio is transformed based on the properties of each particular collision. The intensity of the impact sound is proportional to the kinetic energy of the impact, while the pitch of the sample is related to the size of the impacting object.

The Shoogle prototypes illustrate how model-based interaction can be brought into practical mobile interfaces. The resulting interface is based on active sensing and ecological auditory cues, letting the user drive the interaction and interpret the natural feedback received.

6.3.7   Summary

These systems demonstrate the wide range of functions that auditory icons can perform. They can provide information about user actions, about possibilities for new actions, and about nonvisible attributes of objects in the system. They can provide background information about processes and modes in a more complex system. Continuous or repetitive sounds, which are varied according to distance, may serve as auditory landmarks, supporting navigation in complex systems. Finally, auditory icons can work with graphic displays, supporting a smooth flow between individual and cooperative work.

These examples also demonstrate the range of systems that may benefit from auditory icons, from traditional desktop graphical interfaces to more complex virtual realities and process simulations and to systems that introduce computational power into the everyday environment itself. By building these systems, using them ourselves, and observing others use them, we have gained a great deal of valuable information about their utility, their problems, and issues for their design.

Finally, these systems illustrate the broad range of sounds that may be used as auditory icons, from the simple impact and scraping sounds that are designed for graphical user interfaces, such as the SonicFinder, to the more complex and continuous process sounds used in SoundShark, ARKola, and ShareMon, to the very complex and stereotypical sounds used in EAR. They also illustrate some of the issues that must be tackled when designing sounds for interfaces, particularly the tension inherent in designing sounds that are simultaneously identifiable and subtle, memorable but not annoying. The rest of this chapter focuses on the creation of such auditory icons, discussing some of the issues that are important for the creation of auditory icons and, more generally, for the creation of any auditory interface.

6.4   Issues with auditory icons

A number of issues become clear in considering the interfaces described previously. These include questions regarding auditory icon's functions, mapping, vocabulary, and annoyance:

- Functions: What are auditory icons good for? We have addressed this already through the examples we have described.
- Mapping: How should sounds be mapped to events? The different sorts of mapping from perceptible representations to underlying events.
- Vocabulary: What sounds should be used? Is hearing a telephone an example of everyday listening? How can sounds be both recognizable and discriminable?
- Annoyance: How can we use sounds without driving users crazy?

In the rest of this chapter, we consider each of these issues in turn with the exception of functions, which we have discussed in the previous sections on examples of systems that use auditory icons. In addition, we discuss practical issues concerning the implementation of auditory icons in the next chapter of this book.

6.4.1   *Mapping sounds to events*

The two defining features of auditory icons are (1) the use of environmental sounds controlled along with parameters of the events that cause them and (2) the use of intuitive mappings between the sounds and the computer events they indicate. In fact, the type of mapping has priority over the sounds used. It is entirely possible to use environmental sounds in a way that is incompatible with the concept of auditory icons. For instance, Brown et al. (1989) reported an experiment in which they showed that everyday sounds were as effective at facilitating a spatial search task as graphical cues were. In order to indicate the six columns of their visual display, they used applause sounds differentiated by the number of people clapping (one or three) and the repetition rate (from 50 to 208 bpm). This mapping between applause and spatial location is extremely arbitrary, a fact that the authors recognized, pointing out that any mapping between everyday sounds and spatial location is liable to be arbitrary. So while this is an impressive demonstration of the utility of nonspeech audio, it is a poor example of the use of auditory icons. It is easy to say that the mapping between an auditory icon and the event it represents should be intuitive, but it is more difficult to know what makes a particular mapping intuitive. In order to understand this, it is necessary to discuss what is being mapped to what and the variety of mappings that might occur.

6.4.2   What is being mapped to what?

Consider what happens when we delete a computer file. There are several ways to consider what is going on. At the level of the display, we are simply dragging the file icon into that of the trashcan, knowing the file icon will disappear when the trash is emptied. There are two sorts of mappings, conceptual and perceptual, between the display the user sees and the reality of the computer. Conceptual mappings are always metaphorical abstractions, but a variety of perceptual mappings may be used.

But of course, the purpose is to get rid of not just the icon but also the file itself. We are happy with throwing the icon away because it stands for the real file; it is the perceptual reality of the file. Throwing its icon becomes equivalent to throwing a real file into the trash; not only does its apparition go away, but the file itself goes away with all the attendant consequences (e.g., it is no longer accessible for reading, copying, etc.). The display is the outward appearance of the model world of files and wastebaskets set up by the computer, a model world that determines not only the current display but also future possibilities for action.

Still, in reality, we aren't throwing away a file at all. Instead, we are manipulating a graphical output, which is linked to data structures in the computer. What we are really doing is something like switching an address bit from one to zero, or . . . The point is that we don't need to know. The reality of the computer is simultaneously hidden and made accessible to us by the conceptual mapping that allows electronics to be thought of as information, information to be thought of as variables, variables to be grouped into structures, and structures to be called files.

6.4.3   Types of mapping

Conceptual mappings between the reality of silicon gates and the like and the model world of files, trashcans, and so on are always metaphorical (Hutchins 1987). But there are three different kinds of mappings that may allow the model world to be expressed as a display: symbolic, metaphorical, and iconic. Symbolic, metaphorical, and iconic mappings are distinguished by the degree to which they are arbitrary or lawful; this also has profound effects on the ease with which they are learned and remembered. Symbolic mappings are difficult to learn because they are entirely arbitrary and rely on social convention for their establishment. Metaphorical mappings are easier to learn because they rely on similarities between the representation and the thing to be represented. Iconic mappings are easiest to learn because they rely on the similarity between a representation and the thing it represents: in the case of perceptual mappings, this means that the representation must look like (or sound like) the event

Perceptual and Conceptual Mapping

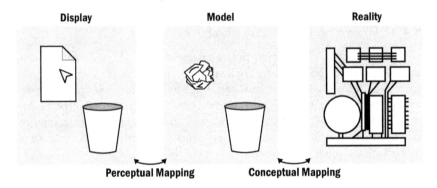

Display   **Model**   **Reality**

Perceptual Mapping   **Conceptual Mapping**

Figure 6.2 In light of this example, it is clear that there are two sorts of mappings that mediate between throwing a file icon away and the actual physical events that occur in the computer. The first is conceptual mapping, which allows the electronic events to be thought of in terms of everyday analogies. The second is perceptual mapping, which allows the model world set up by these analogies to be expressed in terms of perceptible entities such as icons (or sounds).

it represents. Note that this similarity is not a subjective quantity, but rather it depends on the lawful, physical mapping between physical structure and perceptible appearance in the everyday world. Iconic mappings allow learners to apply the skills they already possess in the everyday world to the new model worlds created by computer technology.

Figure 6.3 shows examples of the three for both visual and auditory displays showing that a file has been marked for deletion. The first kind of mapping is symbolic: an arbitrary sign is used to mark the file: an X for the visual display and a simple beep for the auditory one. The second kind of mapping is metaphorical: the displays form an analogy to the real-world metaphor of deletion. For the visual display, this is accomplished by fading the icon as if it were in the process of disappearing. For the auditory display, an earcon is used in which a motive standing for a file is diminished in amplitude. Finally, the third kind of mapping is iconic: the display resembles the real-world event in a lawful way. In the graphical version, an icon of the file is dropped over the icon of the trashcan. For the auditory display, the sound of an object dropping into a (full) trashcan is played.

From this point of view, designers of auditory interfaces should be concerned with using mappings between sounds and events that are as physically plausible as possible. In other words, they should avoid creating new symbolic languages for sounds and instead seek iconic or metaphorical mappings. This is one of the key concerns behind the concept of auditory icons.

PERCEPTUAL MAPPING

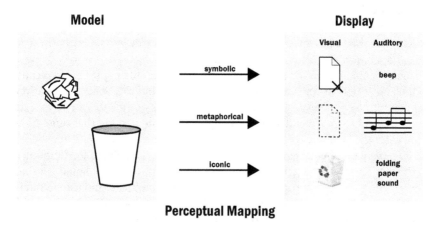

Perceptual Mapping

Figure 6.3 Three types of mappings used between the model world of the computer and the display: symbolic, metaphorical, and iconic.

6.5   The vocabulary of auditory icons

At the beginning of this chapter, we defined auditory icons as everyday sounds that convey information about computer events by analogy with everyday events. As the previous discussion emphasizes, it is the mapping between sound and event that is crucial for auditory icons; auditory icons could be constructed from musical tones or motives if they are mapped in an iconic or strongly metaphorical way to their intended message. From this point of view, the use of everyday sounds for auditory icons may seem accidental and unnecessary.

But the fact that most auditory icons use everyday sounds is no accident. Instead, it is precisely because everyday sounds are defined in terms of events that lawful mappings can be created between auditory icons and the events they convey. The new framework for sound offered by a study of everyday listening, as outlined in Chapter 5, serves as a new palette for designers of auditory interfaces. Instead of trying to map the dimensions of a computer event to dimensions of sound, one can now map events to events. This offers the possibility of the sort of lawful, iconic, and metaphorical mappings illustrated by the systems described in this chapter.

Thus most auditory icons should use everyday sounds. If a file is selected by clicking the mouse over it, then a tapping sound should be produced. If it is moved by dragging it over a background, then a scraping sound provides appropriate feedback. Whenever possible, an iconic mapping between the event in the model world and the sound that is heard should be used.

6.5.1   *Beyond literal mappings: metaphors, sound effects, cliches, and genre sounds*

In some cases, however, iconic mappings between sounds and computer events are impossible to achieve. For instance, what sound should copying a file make? It might be tempting to use the real-world analogy of photocopying a document. But this seems misleading in using the sound made by a repetitive, piece-meal operation to indicate a more continuous one (i.e., I can stop copying a paper document after one page, whereas electronic file copies are typically all-or-nothing). In addition, such a sound doesn't indicate some information that might be of value to users, such as the progress of the job. In this case, it seems useful to go beyond a literal mapping to create a sound that more fully indicates the attributes of copying in the model world of the computer.

One way to go beyond literal mappings is to use metaphors. In the Sonic-Finder, for instance, copying a file was indicated by the sound of liquid pouring into a container. As the operation neared completion, the sound rose in pitch to indicate that the container was getting full. Thus, the sound conveyed useful attributes of the copy operation: that it involves transferring "stuff" (in this case, data bits) into a new container, that the operation is relatively continu-ous, and that it is possible to predict how close it is to completion. However, metaphors such as these may also have unwanted implications: for instance, since the liquid must come from somewhere, the sound might be taken as indicating a move rather than a copy. The sound also does not differentiate the reading and writing stages of a copy operation, which might be useful informa-tion in some circumstances. Finally, using the sound of a container being filled implies a constrained space waiting for the new information. In the case of the copy operation, this space is determined by the size of the information to be transferred, as if bottles changed size to automatically hold just the amount of liquid to be poured. As this example indicates, there is a trade-off in designing and using metaphors such as this: they provide a lawful structure that can guide users' expectations but may sometimes be misleading.

Another approach to going beyond literal mappings is to use exagger-ated sound effects. Although such effects are not naturally occurring every-day sounds, they seem to be heard in many of the same ways if they are well designed. Think of the sound made by a ray gun in a science fiction movie, for example. If well designed, it will indicate many of the properties of the event: that it is electronically produced, quick, powerful, and hot enough to sear the air. Such sounds have never existed, but they are not arbitrary: they seem to extend the laws relating events to sounds.

Exaggerated sound effects can be very useful in creating auditory icons. For example, in designing the SonicFinder, it became clear that sounds should accompany opening and closing windows. Many attempts were made to use, literally, the sounds made by opening and closing (glass) windows, but none sounded appropriate. Finally, it became clear that opening and closing windows in a computer is only metaphorically related to the real-world event. In the graphic interface, windows do not slide open but instead expand into existence from their associated icon. They appear from nowhere in a way that has no literal analog in the real world, though such appearances are common in science fiction movies. Thus, it was more appropriate to use a kind of whooshing noise to indicate this event, as if air rushed around the window as it expanded into existence.

Sound effects such as these are closely related to the genre sounds used by Cohen (Cohen 1993). As he points out, sounds from popular TV shows, movies, and the like can be incorporated successfully into auditory interfaces. In some cases, they may provide information that is difficult to convey using more literal sounds. For instance, designing a sound for the teleporter in SoundShark might have a challenge because, clearly, no analogous mechanism exists in the everyday world, but it does in science fiction. Thus, the sound used to convey this event, basically a slowly growing, inharmonic sound, was based on the sounds used to indicate teleportation in popular TV shows.

One of the drawbacks of genre sounds, as Cohen (1993) notes, is that they may not be interpretable by people who are not familiar with their sources. This problem may be overcome to some degree by creating sound effects that are custom-made for particular applications. Insofar as they rely on extensions of physics rather than familiarity with particular movies or television shows, such sounds can be expected to be more readily recognized even by users unfamiliar with the specific reference.

Finally, both sound effects and genre sounds are closely related to another class of sounds that can be used to extend auditory icons. These are auditory cliches: sounds that are arbitrarily related to their meaning, even in the everyday world, but that are so firmly embedded in the culture that they can be used as everyday sounds are. For instance, from the point of view of everyday listening, the sound of a ringtone simply conveys information about a hard mallet repetitively striking a small metal one. But because in many cultures, this sound is strongly linked with the request to make an electronic connection to a remote colleague for the purposes of communication, it can be used to indicate analogous computer connections (as it is, for instance, in EAR). Similarly, from the point of view of everyday listening, the sound of somebody knocking on a door simply indicates a somewhat softer mallet striking a large wooden surface, for instance. Again, because the symbolic message it conveys is so widely recognized, auditory icons can be created that map to this message rather than the more literal meaning of the sound.

In sum, the vocabulary for auditory icons is driven more by the efficacy of the mappings allowed than by the sounds themselves. In general, this means using everyday sounds that indicate their real-world meaning due to the laws of physics. But it is also possible and useful to expand the vocabulary for auditory icons to include metaphors, sound effects, genre sounds, and cliches. Such sounds can vastly expand the repertoire of auditory icons and the information they convey. Nonetheless, it must be recognized that the mapping from sound to meaning becomes more arbitrary the greater the move from everyday sounds and iconic mappings. In general, mapping a file selection to a tapping sound can be expected to be more readily guessed, learned, and remembered than mapping, for instance, an instantaneous move to the sound of a television transporter.

6.6   Annoyance

A final issue for auditory icons and for auditory interfaces in general is how to design sounds that will not prove annoying to users. As we pointed out in the introduction, one of the first responses most people have to the idea of auditory interfaces is to say, "I like to work in peace and quiet. Why would I possibly want a computer that makes noise?"

One response to this is a variation of the story about John Cage that we told in the introduction; his experience in an anechoic chamber illustrated the fact that there's no such thing as silence. As a less extreme but perhaps more telling model, listen carefully to the sounds around you right now. Even in a quiet office, you are likely to hear many subtle sounds: the whoosh of a ventilator, the hum of a computer, the shuffle of papers on nearby desks, footsteps as somebody walks by. Most of these sounds are hardly noticed, most of them are not annoying, and many of them are useful in maintaining a background awareness of ongoing events.

The point is not to say that concerns about auditory interfaces being annoying are misplaced. Rather it is to provide a model of how sounds can be used without being obtrusive: in general, the goal is to create sounds that are as subtle, unobtrusive, and informative as the sounds we already hear in the office. How can we do this? One answer is simply to use common sense in designing sounds: don't make them too loud, too cute, too complex. Beyond this, however, we can turn to relevant basic research in understanding what makes sounds annoying.

Experimental studies of aesthetics, emotion, and psychoacoustics can provide a useful guide to the design of unobtrusive sounds (see Patterson [1990] and Gaver and Mandler [1987]). Such studies break into two groups. The first concern is the acoustic properties of sounds that seem to make them more or less annoying: this is the psychoacoustics of annoyance. The second group studies the interplay between acoustic variables of sounds, or patterns of sounds, and the experience of listeners in determining what will be annoying. This second group comes largely from those attempting experimental studies of aesthetics and emotion, though many psychoacousticians also recognize the relevance of such factors.

6.7   The psychoacoustics of annoying sounds

Edworthy et al. (1991) provided an excellent example of psychoacoustic studies relevant to annoyance. They were concerned with determining the acoustic correlates of urgency, the converse of annoyance to guide the development

Table 6.1 Acoustic parameters affecting urgency

Parameter	Most urgent		Least urgent
Individual tones			
Fundamental freq.	530Hz	-	150 Hz
Amp. envelope	rectangular	slow onset	slow offset
Harmonic series	random	10% irregular > %50 irregular	harmonic
Delayed harmonics	no delay	-	delayed harmonics
Sequences			
Speed	fast	moderate	slow
Rhythm	regular		syncopated
Number of units	4	2	1
Speed change	speeding	regular	slowing
Pitch range	large	small	moderate
Pitch contour	random		down/up
Musical structure	atonal	unresolved	resolved

Source: From Edworthy et al. (1991).

of auditory warning systems such as those developed by Patterson (1990; see Chapter 4). For each of their experiments, several acoustic factors were varied, and the subjects were asked to rate the urgency of the resulting sounds. The factors they varied were divided into two groups: the first affected individual sounds, or pulses, while the second applied to melodies, or bursts (see Table 6.1). Their findings showed that subjects were very consistent in judging urgency, which implies both that it is a psychologically real construct and that acoustic factors have consistent effects on it.

The effects of acoustic parameters affecting urgency are summarized in Table 6.1. Each of these factors was found to be significant and consistent in the studies that Edworthy et al. (1991) ran. It should be noted, however, that the relative effects of the factors were not tested. Thus, it is not clear, for instance, whether changes in pitch make larger differences in urgency than the inharmonicity of sounds. Nonetheless, these results provide extremely useful information for creating sounds and sequences that are more or less urgent (and thus annoying).

6.7.1 The principle of optimal complexity

Results of psychoacoustic studies of urgency and annoyance can be extremely helpful in developing guidelines for the creation of auditory interfaces. However, experiential factors also affect the annoyance of sounds and thus must also be taken into account. The old saying that "familiarity breeds contempt" has a lot of truth to it: we often find that the melody that was so instantly hummable becomes sickening after repeatedly hearing it. Clearly, experiential effects play a large role in determining what we will find annoying.

Experimental and theoretical studies of emotion and aesthetics are useful in understanding the role of experience. Two simple factors have emerged as most relevant: familiarity and complexity. In general, both are related to liking by an inverse-U curve: both highly familiar and unfamiliar things are liked less than some moderately familiar items; both highly complex and simple things are less preferable than intermediate values. These findings can be summarized succinctly in the principle of optimal psychological complexity: moderately complex sounds are less annoying than very simple or very complicated ones; however, perceived complexity decreases with familiarity.

This principle implies a variety of possibilities for the design of informative sounds. Complicated sounds may be used if they are heard relatively frequently: although initially likely to be annoying, they will usually become acceptable over time. Conversely, very simple sounds should not be repeated too often: though initially acceptable, they become irritating if heard too often.

Perhaps the middle route is best: use moderately complex sounds, but make subtle variations fairly often. This approach works well with the strategy behind parameterized auditory icons in that it encourages more information to be conveyed by sounds, thus producing richer auditory icons. For example, in the SonicFinder, the size of objects usually affected the sounds they made, with large objects making lower sounds than small ones. This had the effect not only of conveying potentially valuable information but also of preventing the (often simple) impact and scraping sounds from becoming too annoying. It is fortunate that the least annoying auditory interfaces may also be the most informative.

6.7.2   *Semantic effects*

To acoustic and experiential factors that influence annoyance must be added semantic factors. For instance, people regularly find highway sounds more annoying than birdsong, despite the fact that birdsongs have more of the acoustic parameters corresponding to annoyance (e.g., high pitch, abrupt envelopes, fast changes). It appears that the semantic connotations of the sounds can override acoustic and even experiential considerations in determining annoyance.

Note that semantic effects like these cannot be addressed from traditional views of sound and hearing because the meaning of sounds is outside the scope of such inquiries. Accounts of everyday listening (Chapter 5) can provide a somewhat better basis for understanding semantic effects on annoyance since they focus on the sources of sounds. But even everyday listening does not directly address higher-level semantics of many sounds as can be seen, for instance, by the fact that a literal account of everyday listening would describe a telephone bell in terms of a piece of metal being struck repeatedly by a hard clapper. Still less can the emotional reactions to the semantics of sounds be predicted from theory. Nonetheless, designers can and must be sensitive to issues surrounding the semantics of sound in developing auditory interfaces.

6.7.3   *The tension between clarity and obtrusiveness*

The principles guiding the design of intuitively obvious and unobtrusive auditory icons may often be at odds with one another. Everyday sounds tend to have many acoustic features that characterize annoying sounds. For instance, consider a metallic impact sound often used in the auditory interfaces described previously. For many object mappings, the sound will be high-pitched, inharmonic, abrupt, and atonal. This is the recipe for an urgent sound, according to our previous discussion. On the other hand, consider trying to create unobtrusive sounds based on the acoustic guidelines we have described. According to these principles, the sounds should be low-pitched and harmonic, have smooth envelopes, and have tonal relations with one another. This implies severe constraints for the creation of auditory icons based on auditory icons.

There are several heuristics for reducing this tension between identifiability and obtrusiveness. First, everyday sounds may be shaped acoustically to reduce their annoyance. For instance, the attack of percussive sounds can be slowed slightly to reduce the tendency for abrupt sounds to demand attention. Most sounds can be low-pass filtered, reducing the amplitude of annoying high-frequency partials. Many long sounds can be shortened considerably and thus made to convey information concisely. In all these cases, effective variations can be made without reducing sounds' identification if the changes are kept small. In addition, the tension between the acoustic factors leading to identifiability and those that produce annoying sounds can be mitigated by taking advantage of experiential and semantic factors. This is, in fact, one of the major advantages of auditory icons: they are designed to be similar to the sorts of sounds one hears in the everyday world and thus less distracting than introducing a new vocabulary (e.g., music). Because they fit with the existing auditory ambiance, they benefit from familiarity and semantic congruity. Moreover, they can be designed to reach an optimal level of familiarity, as described previously, and with the aim of using semantically pleasing or better, neutral sounds.

6.8   Conclusions

Auditory icons have great potential as a strategy for creating informative, intuitively accessible, unobtrusive auditory interfaces. Already they have been shown to increase the tangibility of and promote direct engagement with the model world evoked by most graphical interfaces. They can provide feedback about users' actions and feedforward about what might be done next. They serve as useful status monitors, helping people maintain a background awareness of ongoing processes and modes. They have been found to support a sense of the coherence of related processes. Finally, they are useful in providing a new medium for supporting collaboration, allowing colleagues to maintain awareness of one another while working independently. The strategy behind auditory icons highlights a number of issues that have largely been left implicit by other auditory interfaces. In particular, the mapping between sounds and the information they convey is a crucial issue, with auditory icons suggesting the possibility and desirability of using iconic and metaphorical mappings rather than the symbolic mappings typically employed by the interfaces discussed in Chapters 3 and 4. In addition, they serve to indicate the range of auditory vocabularies that might be used, with abstract musical tones and literal recordings of everyday sounds being extremes in a continuum that also includes genre sounds, sound metaphors, and sound effects. Finally, they serve to emphasize the acoustic, experiential, and semantic factors that help determine the obtrusiveness and, ultimately, the acceptability of auditory interfaces.

6.9   What's next?

Despite the promise of the systems we have described in this chapter, there is much potential for the development of systems that use auditory icons. The development of auditory icons as a widespread interface technique, though, depends on making their creation more readily available to nonspecialized designers. There have been several developments to this end. First, creating and manipulating sounds on any computer or mobile device has been greatly facilitated by rapid developments in hardware and software technologies. Second, the increasing power of today's computers is enabling the creation of synthesis algorithms specialized for generating parameterized everyday sounds for use as auditory icons, as first suggested by Gaver (1993) and more recently explored by other research groups, such as in the context of the Sounding Object research project (Rocchesso and Fontana 2003) that facilitated the development of physics-based toolkit for the design of auditory icons (Monache et al. 2010).

In the end, though, it is not just technical issues that will determine the success of auditory icons. While many researchers working with musical sounds call for research teams to include musicians in the design of auditory cues, we might be better off with good sound-effect designers. The creation of systems that use auditory icons will depend on designers who have a good feel for how people hear sounds in the everyday world, the kinds of information that sounds can convey, the uses to which we put them, and the aesthetic possibilities of everyday sounds. With the help of such designers, we may expect to see more and more powerful systems that do not blare out incongruous, annoying sounds but instead sounds with the subtlety and communicative power of those we hear in the everyday world.

7 Sonic interaction design

7.1 Introduction

Sonic interaction design (SID) is a novel interdisciplinary field that has recently appeared as a combined effort of researchers and practitioners working at the intersection of sound and music computing, interaction design, human-computer interaction (HCI), novel interfaces for musical expression, product design, music psychology and cognition, music composition, performance, and interactive arts. Compared to the field of auditory display, which is more broadly concerned with the use of nonspeech sound to present information, SID shifted the focus on the role of sound under the perspective of interaction, especially continuous and multisensory. SID can, therefore, be considered as the sonic effort into the third-wave HCI that describes how the scope of HCI design moved from work and task orientation toward everyday lives and meaning-making (Bødker 2006). Within the field of human-computer studies, the subtopics of auditory display and sonification have been of interest for a couple of decades, as extensively described in this book. In sound and music computing, researchers have moved away from the mere engineering reproduction of existing musical instruments and everyday sounds in a passive context toward investigating principles and methods to aid in the design and evaluation of sonic interactive systems. This is considered to be one of the most promising areas for research and experimentation (Serra et al. 2007). Moreover, the design and implementation of novel interfaces to control such sounds, together with the ability to augment existing musical instruments and everyday objects with sensors, actuators, and auditory feedback, is currently an active area of exploration in the New Interfaces for Musical Expression (NIME) community (Jensenius and Lyons 2017).

Among scholars in perception and cognition, there has been a shift in attention from the human as a receiver of auditory stimuli to the perception-action loops that are mediated by acoustic signals (Leman et al. 2008). Such loops have become an important topic of research also in the sonification domain, where the topic of interactive sonification has emerged. Interactive sonification can be defined as the use of sound within a tightly closed HCI where the auditory signal provides information about data under analysis, or about the

DOI: 10.4324/9781003260202-7

interaction itself, which is useful for refining a specific activity (Hermann and Hunt 2005; Dubus 2013; Rocchesso et al. 2019).

SID explores ways in which sound can be used to convey information, meaning, and aesthetic and emotional qualities in interactive contexts. One of the ultimate goals of SID is the ability to provide design and evaluation guidelines for interactive products with a salient sonic behavior. SID addresses the challenges of creating interactive, adaptive sonic interactions, which continuously respond to the gestures of one or more users. At the same time, SID investigates how the designed gestures and sonic feedback are able to convey emotions and engage expressive and creative experiences.

SID also aims at identifying new roles that sound may play in the interaction between users and artifacts, services, or environments. By exploring topics such as multisensory experience with sounding artifacts, perceptual illusions, sound as a means for communication in an action-perception loop, and sensorimotor learning through sound, SID researchers are opening up new domains of research and practice for sound designers and engineers, interaction and interface designers, media artists, and product designers, among others.

A long-lasting problem in the design of auditory displays is how to design audio feedback that is aesthetically appealing and comfortable to listen to. Many systems focus solely on function and do not consider these other factors. Several efforts in these research areas were unified under the SID umbrella thanks to a European COST (Cooperation in Science and Technology) action, which started in 2006. Many of the results from this cooperation are presented by Rocchesso (2011).

7.2   Psychology of sonic interactions

The next paragraphs will consider some basic psychological phenomena involved in sonic interactions. To do so, we will examine a specific type of sonic interactions: closed-loop interactions. During such interactions, the users manipulate an interface that produces sound, and the sonic feedback affects in turn the users' manipulation. Such interactions have been used in applied (Schaffert et al. 2010; Eriksson and Bresin 2010) and experimental settings (Lemaitre et al. 2009; Rath and Rocchesso 2005). In fact, the design of these interactions brings under a magnifying glass a phenomenon that has recently received a great deal of attention on the part of psychologists interested in perception: the tight coupling between auditory perception and action (Aglioti and Pazzaglia 2010).

A useful example of such an interaction is the real-time sonification of a person rowing, aiming to improve the athletes' performance (Schaffert et al. 2010). In this design, the athletes' movements modulate the auditory feedback in real time. In turn, the sound helps the athletes to adapt their movements. Sounds have a great advantage in this case because auditory perception and action are naturally and tightly coupled. Therefore, the intention is that the rowers would not be expected to consciously decode the information conveyed by the sounds nor to think about how modifying their actions would modify the sound.

Other useful examples can be found in the dissertation of Boyer (2015), which examines the contribution of continuous auditory feedback to sensorimotor control and learning. The main question addressed in the dissertation is how feedback can be integrated and which gesture-sound parameters are relevant to learning. Results show the benefits of continuous movement sonification for motor learning. Other interesting examples related to the use of sonic interactions for rehabilitation are presented in (Avanzini et al. 2009). In artistic settings, the Gamelunch is an application that provides a useful scenario of SID. In the Gamelunch, the authors apply basic design methods to the new content of interactive artifacts by means of a series of prototypical interaction primitives that are summarized by multistage yet continuous coupling, divisible into clear stages: a first stage is a cyclic interaction with continuous and rhythmic feedback, giving a sense of progress to emphasize the coordination and the expressiveness of gestures; the second stage is a counter-interaction, where contradictory feedback is provided to mislead the perceptual experience. An example of contradictory feedback is hearing the sound of pouring water when the action is cutting a vegetable.

The examples just described show how the sound-action loop is supposed to be intuitive. After all, this is what happens in natural interactions through sound. A user filling a vessel with water does not need to understand the relationship between pitch and volume to fill a recipient without overflowing (Cabe and Pittenger 2000). Nor does a beginner violinist need to be aware of the physics of the bowstring interaction to avoid squeaky sounds, at least after a bit of practice. In a designed sonic interaction, the richness of the added auditory feedback has the potential to let the users explore the complex patterns and discover how their actions can modulate the sound. In turn, the auditory feedback guides the actions. As such, sonic interactions have a great potential to help a user become more proficient at the fine movements required in sports, as illustrated by the rowing example, but also in music, dance, surgery, and the complicated manipulation of tools (Barrass and Kramer 1999). As discussed later in this chapter, there are also other aspects of sounds to consider.

7.3   Sonic interactions in products

When we interact with physical objects in the world, these interactions often create sound. The nature of this sound is a combined product of our actions and the physical attributes of the objects with which we interact – their form, materials, and dynamics, as well as the surrounding environment. As we saw in Chapter 5, people possess a natural capacity for deriving information from sound: we can infer, from the sound arriving at our ears, rich information about its source.

Today, more and more sounds for products are being more carefully designed. This includes both sounds that are produced through physical phenomena and sounds that are digitally created. As an example of both types, the physical manipulation of materials and fine-tuning of internal components have been used to create the distinct sound of the Harley Davidson engine, a sound that the company tried to protect as a trademark (Bernsen 1999). With the recent advent of electric cars that create very little noise (Robart and Rosenblum 2009), digitally produced sounds have been introduced into cars both for pedestrian safety and for driver experience (Otto et al. 1999). The long-awaited Fisker Karma, the first hybrid sports car, is said to have external speakers that generate *a sound somewhere between a Formula One car and a starship* but can be configured by the owner.

Obviously, these corporations realized the impact of sound on the perception of product quality. The field of sound design for products, specifically the design of nonspeech, nonmusical sounds, is quite young. A main source of knowledge on which it builds is the domain of film, where sound has been used extensively and in complex ways to affect the viewer's experience. Michel Chion, a researcher of film sound, has referred to two types of the added value of sound in film: informative and expressive (Chion 1994). These are useful in thinking about sound for products as well: sound can add information to the use of a product and can enhance its perceived quality and character. The development of the field of sound design is such that sound designers today use their skills to create auditory logos and signals (such as the attention-getting tone, or attenson [Hellier and Edworthy 2009], that precedes an announcement in a train station), sound effects for website navigation and for computer games, and more.

Interactive physical products bring a new level of potential and challenge into this field. The lack of an inherent relation between form and functionality, as found in many consumer-electronic products, makes feedback a prominent factor. The complexity of functions makes the dialogue between user and system more critical. Fortunately, these products are embedded with technological components and can be equipped with micro-controllers and sound-producing elements. Thus, there is great potential for rich responsive sound in interactive products.

When we think of the sounds of products, we may still think about the beeps and bleeps of our household appliances or the ding of the PC error. However, things are changing. Our input methods for digital products are no longer limited to pressing or pointing, and continuous interactions such as finger gestures and body movements are those for which sonic feedback may be the most beneficial (Rocchesso et al. 2009). Knowledge from the realm of interaction design, sound design, and software development is needed to tackle continuous interactive sound projects.

When feedback provides information about data under analysis or about the interaction itself, then we talk about interactive sonification (Hermann and Hunt 2005). A successful example of interactive sonification is the one proposed in Rath and Rocchesso (2005). Here, the task of balancing a marble ball on a wooden stick is improved by providing augmented auditory feedback given by rolling sounds. This example will be described in more detail later in this chapter.

7.4 Examples of objects with interesting sounds

Not surprisingly, some of the best examples of continuous sound for interaction come from the world of mobile devices. The reasons are twofold: (1) the price and positioning of these products make the embedding of high-quality audio components most feasible and (2) the fact that these devices are used on the move motivates the provision of information in a nonvisual way. The first iPod Classic model used a mechanical scroll wheel as an input device: a wheel that turned to allow scrolling between menu items. Consequent iPod versions replaced the mechanical wheel with the click wheel: a round touch-sensitive surface on which users slide their finger clockwise and counterclockwise, as if on a moving wheel.

One element that was introduced to the click wheel is the clicker: a clicking sound that provides feedback for the movement between menu items. This feature gives a haptic feel to the click wheel (a pseudo-haptic illusion), somewhat similar to the rotary dial on old phones, making the scrolling more expressive and more informative. Since the scrolling reacts to acceleration, the more one scrolls, the faster menu items move per rotation; the clicker provides information that is not evident from the scrolling action per se. The click sound is the only sound made by the iPod outside of the headphones and is generated via a small piezoelectric speaker inside the device.

The Apple Mighty Mouse, introduced in 2005, contained an embedded speaker that gave sonic feedback to scrolling gestures. Apple seemed to abandon this line completely in 2009, when the Magic Mouse was introduced. This symmetric, uniformly smooth, and perfectly silent object supported multi-touch gestures and contained no apparent usability clues. Interestingly, despite the success of the Magic Mouse, Microsoft decided to go the other way and, in 2010, unveiled the Arc Touch Mouse, which includes both haptic and sonic feedback to scrolling gestures over a central capacitive scroll strip. The Wii Remote was the primary controller for the Nintendo Wii game console, introduced in 2006. A main feature of the Wii Remote is its motion sensing capability, which allows the user to interact with and manipulate items on-screen via gesture recognition and pointing through the use of accelerometer and optical sensor technology. The Wii Remote has basic audio functionality via its own independent speaker on the face of the unit. This audio is used in different games to enhance the experience of the gestures through tightly coupled sound. Sonic and vibro-tactile feedback can be experienced, for example, in *Wii Tennis* (a swish sound when swinging the racket) or in *The Legend of Zelda: Twilight Princess* (the sound is altered as the bow is shot to give the impression of the arrow traveling away from the player).

7.5   Methods in sonic interaction design

In the following, we examine the different elements which relate to the design of interactive products with a salient sonic behavior. One of the main challenges in creating sounds for products is finding the design language (e.g., the selection of sound type and sound character to fit the product and the interaction). Now that we are no longer limited by piezoelectric buzzers in our products, the wealth of possible sounds is great; which sounds should we choose? From which category? Musical sounds and everyday sounds all hold benefits, as we saw in previous chapters.

Creating sounds for continuous interaction, where the sonic behavior changes rapidly and dynamically, is a challenging task. To the designer, thinking and sketching in sound are not as readily accessible as using pen and paper, whiteboards, and Post-its.

A number of methods have been proposed to help designers think and sketch sound. Different ways to increase designers' sensitivity to the auditory domain include sound walks (Westerkamp 1974; Adams et al. 2008). Sound walks, as the name implies, are explorations of the surrounding sonic environment by walking. Participants in a sound walk are required to carefully listen to the everyday sounds around them. Sonic maps are an example of a technique for analyzing characteristic features of an acoustic environment based on listening (Schafer 1993; Coleman et al. 2008). These are textual or graphic descriptions of sounds collected by listening to specific places, sites, or activities. One of the possible basic classifications in sound maps consists of identifying foreground, background, and contextual sounds (Coleman et al. 2008). These can be divided into other information categories to note the users' emotions, actions, and perceived signals or signifiers (Brazil 2009). Narrative aspects of sounds could be gathered using the EarBenders technique. EarBenders was a technique used to classify narratives into task, information, and data categories as a means of providing inspiration for new designs and as an approach to help structure how and where sonic interactions might be used (Barrass 1996).

In using this technique, the sounds narrated in the stories of listening were categorized according to psychoacoustic analysis and auditory perception (such as timbre, nature of sound, perceptual grouping, patterns, and movement) and provided an array of qualities that could be used in the design of auditory interfaces (e.g., the auditory component of a system for monitoring pollution of a river over a one-year period). Architects, industrial designers, and HCI designers all use good examples as a starting point for new designs. In auditory interface design, there are not many documented and classified examples around. This led to the collection of an alternative source of examples in the form of the EarBenders database of stories about everyday listening experiences. This database supported a method for designing auditory interfaces by example, which had four steps: situation description, situation analysis, example lookup, and design synthesis. Situation description consisted of a story-like description of the situation and an identification of key features in terms of a question, answers, elements, and sounds. Situation analysis extracted the task, information, and data structure from the situation description. Example lookup used the situation analysis to search the EarBenders database for everyday examples with similar structures. Design synthesis used the sound analysis of the most similar examples as the basis for the specification of a perceptual representation that is aligned with the information requirements of the task. The everyday examples in the EarBenders database were a source of metaphorical representations, which could improve the accessibility of an auditory interface for a general audience. Unfortunately, the database is not found anymore.

Vocal sketching (Ekman and Rinott 2010) is simply the practice of describing sounds using the voice; the idea was that with the right setting, designers can easily and intuitively communicate sonic ideas through nonverbal vocal sounds. It has been shown that people spontaneously use vocal imitations in everyday conversations and that imitating a sound allows a listener to recover what has been imitated (Aura et al. 2008; Lemaitre et al. 2011). Some methods from interaction design, mostly focused on the visual domain, have been adapted to the sonic domain. Sonic overlay refers to video prototypes in which sound is designed and overlaid over the video footage at a later time to create a fake sonic interaction for the viewer. The Wizard of Oz technique (Green and Wei-Haas 1985) has been useful for sound behaviors, and methods of developing a narrative through sound, inspired by film sound, have been used to develop interactive narrative objects (Hug 2009).

Creating functional prototypes, which enable the direct experience of interaction firsthand, is of great value in iterating and improving designs. Microcontroller kits that enable the easy connection of sensors to sound-producing software together create a way to embed (at least part of) the electronics inside objects and to prototype sound behaviors. Parameter-based sound models, as the ones described in Chapter 10, help link between sensor input and dynamic output. The plethora of techniques from different fields serve the goal of sensitization to designing interactions with sound, helping to overcome a visually oriented tendency that design students may have and encouraging exploration of the audible and the sonic in their designs.

An important element of transferability of techniques and approaches between design practices and sound computing is the development of pedagogical tools and methods. Designers who are not used to working with sound in their practice may lack particular skills, languages, means, and processes to facilitate their work.

Workshops comprise an important part of research methods frequently deployed in SID. They include techniques from HCI and interaction design, such as bodystorming (Schleicher et al. 2010) and Wizard of Oz techniques (Dahlbäck et al. 1993). In addition, we can find approaches based on sound practices and inspired by theater, such as sonic narrative playing (Pauletto et al. 2009; Pauletto 2014). Pauletto examines the design of sonic interactions and how they can have many starting points. It can start with an idea, a concept, an understanding, or maybe a context, not always necessarily with a well-defined object with clear physical properties. The use of theatrical strategies for experimenting, prototyping, and sketching the design of sonic interactions was first proposed by Pauletto as a part of a workshop, SID and Its Relation to Film and Theatre Sound, which took place at the University of York in 2009. Film and theater offer settings in which one can experiment, use creativity freely, and also employ existing sound design knowledge and practices already developed in new ways. The main idea for the workshop was that sound designers would create sounds for a short theatrical scene. The text of the scene was fixed and given in the Call for Sound Designs. The proposed sound designs would then be played as part of a performance of the scene in front of the workshop participants. In the performance, the actor would respond and react to the sounds (and by inference to the objects that caused them). The audience would then be asked to observe the overall scene and discuss, with the sound designer and the actor, how well the sounds communicated the intended experience. The aim of this exploration of the theatrical representation of SIDs was to discuss the effectiveness of the SIDs in light of the original designer's intentions and the feedback produced by the actors and the audience and to evaluate the advantages and limitations of using theatrical setups as a tool for testing and evaluating SIDs. The workshop showed the power of theatrical methods to bring sonic interaction scenarios to life and to explore various possible associations of objects, sounds, and actions.

Workshops on participatory design and everyday sonic interactions can also be organized in a series of different activities. In the work of Hug et al. (2007), it is described the structure of a workshop in SID. The focus is on the exploration of physical action and sound feedback using computational artifacts for generating future scenarios and concepts of interactions, using inventive methods generated in interaction design. The four phases described for the workshops are (1) warm-up exercises, (2) creative idea generation, (3) concept exploration and bodystorming, and (4) final presentation and discussion. The warm-up phase aims to sensitize participants to the sonic domain of the workshop using techniques such as vocal sketching, sound walking, and haptic listening. These exercises explore the existing sonic experiences of the users to generate sonic interaction concepts. They use bodystorming and interaction relabelling to think about interaction scenarios using the body and novel object-action functionality that can be mediated by sound. Finally, the presentation phase shows the project ideas, which remain at a prototypical, non-technologically implemented status and set the basis for a discussion of the workshop.

Daniel Hug proposes a series of design methods and prototyping techniques for aiding the process of sound design of interactive artifacts for non-specialists or early-stage students. Mixing pedagogical approaches to sound design and interaction design, he identifies common challenges of teaching SID. Examples include the problematic dialectic of specialized tools, the aesthetic and technical complexity of interactive sound, and an obsession with functional design (Kemper and Hug 2014). Hug uses workshops in classroom settings to envision future sonic commodities and scenarios of interactions. One of the techniques developed by Kemper and Hug (2014) is the Foley mockup. This is based on Foley, a technique used in cinema to create sounds during studio production. The name Foley is derived from the person Foley, who is known as the first person who created sound effects for cinema in a studio. Hug uses participants' voices and objects available in the classroom to quickly generate sounds for the prototyping mockups. These sounds are then played back using a sampler to simulate the sounds that the prototypes would generate, in a way similar to the Wizard of Oz prototyping technique (Kelley 1984).

Tanaka et al. (2013) used user-centric workshops to investigate the design of future mobile music players. They used ethnographic interviews and the critical incident technique (Flanagan 1954) to investigate when, where, and in which circumstances users' experience of listening to music was considered problematic or inappropriate. After using brainstorming, sketches, and video prototyping, they developed interaction scenarios. In a second phase of the workshop, they injected a technology probe consisting of a novel multichannel interactive sound device. As a result, the participants produced prototypes that revealed three potential functions associated with the gestural manipulation with the interactive sound prototype: association, communication, and navigation. A participatory design approach (Muller and Kuhn 1993) reveals how users can generate ideas about sonic interaction scenarios that can be explored in further phases of design.

Despite all these possibilities, sound design and sketching still do not have the same developed tools as visual sketching or user experience sketching (Buxton 2010). However, Delle Monache et al. (2018) propose embodied sketching through vocalizations and gestures as an important tool for sound designers. They argue that sound design should address the sensorimotor nature of auditory experiences to be maximally effective. Embodied sound design is a process of sound creation that extensively involves the designer's body.

7.6 Case studies

7.6.1 Case study 1: naturalness influences perceived usability and pleasantness

An interesting question investigated by Susini et al. (2012) is how naturalness interplays with the user ratings on pleasantness and perceived usability of an interface – in this specific case, an automated teller machine (ATM) with buttons as an interaction method. In this case, the gestural interaction is quite simple: pressing a key. The researchers investigated three issues: if the different mappings between a keystroke and the resulting sound change the perceived naturalness of the sound, if the naturalness of the sonic feedback influences the perceived usability and pleasantness of the interface, and finally, if the influence of the naturalness is affected by the active manipulation of the interface. The last question is particularly interesting for SID to understand whether actions affect auditory perception. The study consisted of several experiments in which the subjects interacted with the interface, and the naturalness of the sound feedback was manipulated. The naturalness was manipulated by using three different mappings between the action of pressing a key and the resulting sounds. The highest degree of naturalness was achieved by using causal mapping: the actual sounds of a keystroke. The lowest degree of naturalness was achieved by using sounds that did not bear any semantic relationships with a keystroke (e.g., a bicycle bell): an arbitrary mapping. In between, the medium level of naturalness was created by using sounds that had the temporal envelope of keystroke sounds but a different timbre: an iconic mapping. The experimental design was inspired by Tractinsky et al. (2000). It consisted of five steps. In the first step, the participants were presented with the interface and required to rate the naturalness, usability, and pleasantness of the sounds. In the second step, the participants were required to perform a number of bank operations by manipulating the interface. In the third and fourth steps, they had to indicate how the manipulation of the interface had changed their appraisal of the sounds. The fifth step was used to validate some results observed in the previous steps. The results of the experiments clearly indicated that a causal relationship resulted in sounds perceived as natural, whereas an arbitrary relationship resulted in sounds perceived as not natural. Moreover, natural sounds were perceived as being more pleasant and more helpful than nonnatural sounds; manipulating the interface exaggerated the user's appraisal of the interface. After the manipulation, the users found the natural sounds more natural and more usable than before the manipulation. They perceived the natural sounds as more natural and usable than they had before the manipulation. These results provide sound designers with some interesting remarks. First, manipulating the mapping between the user's gesture and the sounds changes the perception of the naturalness of the sounds. It is in particular important to note that naturalness was not influenced by whether the sounds were synthetic or recorded sounds: in fact, the less-natural sounds were recordings. These results also emphasize that designers must test the quality of their sound design by having users actively manipulate the interface. Even with our simplified interface, our results make it clear that the manipulation of the interface greatly influences the appraisal of the sounds.

7.6.2   *Case study 2: the Ballancer: continuous sonic feedback from a rolling ball*

Rath and Rocchesso (2005) designed the Ballancer, a physical interface enhanced with continuous sonic interaction. Specifically, the Ballancer is implemented as a bar to be held with both hands. The task of the user is to balance a virtual simulated ball that is rolling along the longer axis of the bar. Rath and Rocchesso developed a sound model for rolling interaction that enables the continuous control and immediate acoustic expression of the involved parameters. The rolling model runs in real time in its complete control-feedback behavior and thus is well suited for interactive control tasks.

The sound engine used to implement this model (the Sound Design Toolkit) is presented in Chapter 10. In an experiment, subjects recognized the synthetic sound as being a rolling ball. When controlling (blindfolded) the tangible, audible device with the synthesized sound feedback, all ten subjects clearly described an object rolling from side to side, steered by the height of the held end. For all display sizes, the average time needed to perform the task improved significantly with the auditory feedback from the simulated rolling ball. All subjects solved the task with purely auditory feedback, without display. This aspect is interesting, for example, for applications for the visually impaired and could surely be strengthened through the inclusion of state-of-the-art algorithms of spatialization. The metaphor of the rolling ball is potentially useful for a variety of tasks (steering, aiming, avoiding obstacles) that are common in everyday life and in HCIs. Video games and virtual environments provide the most obvious application arena, but even tasks such as navigation of menu hierarchies might be recast to exploit such a metaphor.

7.7   Challenges of evaluation

The practice of understanding and designing sonic interactions requires different approaches involving constant evaluation. Qualitative approaches are used together with quantitative-analytical methods, as the sonic phenomena need to be studied as a whole rather than as an isolated event (Brazil 2009). Evaluation, within contextualization, is an important criterion in SID research, as in traditional interaction design. This is particularly important as SID research spans from the produced sonic artifact to the basis and the motivation of the design process itself, including social and cultural constructions and performative aspects. Brazil situates the techniques as serving three different design approaches in SID: (1) user-centered, which focuses on usability and gathering user perspectives; (2) product-centered, which deals with the interaction between users and interfaces; (3) interaction-centered, which involves emotional, sensory, and spatio-temporal aspects of interactions.

There is still much work to be done in assessing the value that sound brings to interactive products. Evaluation can be performed through laboratory experimentation or via analysis of products in the market. Both paths have their own challenges since products have complex behaviors and usage patterns, and discerning the role of sound is not obvious. Some initial work shows promise and can draw knowledge from existing research in interaction design (Hong et al. 2008; Sengers and Gaver 2006).

Finally, the emotional qualities of sound and sonic interactions can be analyzed using methods for data gathering of affective responses. In the sonic domain, Barrass proposes the interactive affect design diagram (IADD) as a grid for evaluating the affective qualities of designed sound, which is mapped to possible actions with interactive artifacts (Barrass 9). The process of designing an interactive affective sonic character begins by drawing a path in the IADD to specify the mapping from interaction to affect. Barrass argues that this technique creates interactive artifacts with emotional characteristics and personality traits through the use of sound design.

As an additional challenge, sound does not exist in isolation. Sound has the potential to intrude and annoy when wrongfully designed. Designers of sonic artifacts need to scrutinize closely the context in which their product will be used, considering both the direct users and the indirect, unintended users around. The existing soundscape also needs to be considered since it will determine whether the added sounds will be heard and how they will be perceived. In the work of Giordano et al. (2013), an introduction to the experimental study of sonic interactions is presented, with an overview of different methodologies for evaluating sounds.

7.8   Conclusions

Digital technologies and scale economies have enabled new possibilities in using sound in interactive products. Interaction can be coupled with feedback in the auditory domain, potentially benefiting objects and use-situations in which the auditory channel is superior to the visual one, such as with users who are mobile. The degree to which this potential will be achieved depends on the value sound will have for the users. This is, to some extent, cyclical since this value will depend on good sound quality and good interaction design, which, especially in small objects, is still a technological challenge and a costly endeavor. Good processes for working with sound and research directed at showing the value of sonic interaction will help designers to push forward sonic interactions. Most importantly, designers must create interactions that, through sound, enhance the beauty and utility of experiences.

8 Multimodal interactions

8.1 Introduction

This book examines the role of sound in designing interactions. However, most of our interactions with the physical world appear through a combination of different sensory modalities. Often auditory feedback is the consequence of an action produced by touch and is presented in the form of a combination of auditory, haptic, and visual feedback. Let us consider, for example, the simple action of pressing a button of a doorbell: the auditory feedback is given by the sound produced by the bell, the visual feedback is the motion of the bell, and the haptic feedback is the feeling of the displacement of the bell at the fingertip. It is important that these different sensory modalities are perceived in synchronization in order to experience a coherent action.

Since sound can be perceived from all directions, it is ideal for providing information when the eyes are otherwise occupied. This could be where someone's visual attention should be entirely devoted to a specific task, such as driving or a surgeon operating on a patient (Recarte and Nunes 2003). Another notable property of the human auditory system is its sensitivity to the temporal aspects of sound (Bregman 1994). In many instances, response times for auditory stimuli are faster than those for visual stimuli (Spence and Driver 1997). Furthermore, given the higher temporal resolution of the auditory system versus the visual system, people can resolve subtle temporal dynamics in sounds more readily than in visual stimuli; thus, the rendering of data into sound may manifest periodic or other temporal information that is not easily perceivable in visualizations (Flowers et al. 2005). Moreover, the ears are capable of decomposing complex auditory scenes (Bregman 1994) and selectively attending to certain sources, as seen in the cocktail party problem described in Chapter 2 (Cherry 1953). Audition, then, may be the most appropriate modality for simple and intuitive (see Connell et al. [1997] and McGuire et al. [2006]) information display when data have complex patterns, express meaningful changes in time, or require immediate action.

In this chapter, an overview is presented of how knowledge of human perception and cognition can be helpful in the design of multimodal systems where interactive sonic feedback plays an important role. Table 8.1 presents a

DOI: 10.4324/9781003260202-8

Table 8.1 Different interactions among modalities

Cross-modal interaction	Description	Example
Amodal mapping	Use of VE or another representational system to map abstract or amodal information (e.g., time, amount) to some continuous or discrete sensory cue	The use of color mapping and relative size in graphics and scientific visualization (e.g., color, size, depth)
Cross-modal mapping	Use of a VE to map one or more dimensions of a sensory stimulus to another sensory channel	An oscilloscope
Intersensory biases	Stimuli from two or more sensory channels representing discrepant/ conflicting information	Ventriloquism effect (Jack and Thurlow 1973)
Cross-modal enhancement	Stimuli from one sensory channel that enhance or alter the perceptual interpretation of stimulation from another sensory channel	Increased perceived visual fidelity of display as a result of increased auditory fidelity
Cross-modal transfers or illusions	Stimulation in one sensory channel leading to the illusion of stimulation in another sensory channel	Synesthesia

typology of different kinds of cross-modal interactions, adapted from (Biocca et al. 2001).

Sonic feedback can interact with visual or haptic feedback in different ways. As an example, cross-modal mapping represents the situation where one or more dimensions of a sound are mapped to visual or haptic feedback: a beeping sound combined with a flashing light. In cross-modal mapping, there is no specific interaction between the two modalities but simply a function that connects some parameters of one modality to the parameters of another.

Intersensory biases become important where audition and a second modality provide conflicting cues. In the following section, several instances of intersensory biases will be provided. In most of these situations, the user tries to perceptually integrate the conflicting information. This conflict might lead to a bias toward a stronger modality. One classic example is the ventriloquist effect (Jack and Thurlow 1973), which illustrates the dominance of visual over auditory information when spatially discrepant audio and visual cues are experienced as co-localized with the visual cue.

The name clearly derives from the ventriloquist, who is able to pretend that the speaking voice is originated from the dummy she is holding, as opposed to from the person herself. This effect is commonly used in cinemas and home theaters where, although the sound physically originates at the speakers, it appears as if coming from the moving image on-screen. The ventriloquist effect occurs because the visual estimates of location are typically more accurate than the auditory estimates of location, and therefore, the overall perception of location is largely determined by vision. This phenomenon is also known as visual capture (Welch and Warren 1980). Another classic example is the Colavita effect (Colavita 1974). In the original experiment, Colavita presented participants with an auditory (tone) or visual (light) stimulus, to which they were instructed to respond by pressing the tone key or light key, respectively. When presented with bimodal stimuli, the visual dominance effect refers to the phenomenon where participants respond more often to the visual component.

Vision is indeed the dominant sense in many circumstances. On the one hand, visual dominance over hearing and other sense modalities has been frequently demonstrated (e.g., Posner et al. 1976), and a neural basis has been posited for visual dominance in processing audiovisual objects (e.g., Schmid et al. 2011). Cross-modal enhancement refers to stimuli from one sensory channel enhancing or altering the perceptual interpretation of stimuli from another sensory channel. As an example, three studies presented by Storms and Zyda (2000) show how high-quality auditory displays coupled with high-quality visual displays increase the quality perception of the visual displays relative to the evaluation of the visual display alone. Moreover, the same study shows how low-quality auditory displays coupled with high-quality visual displays decrease the perception of the quality of the auditory displays relative to the evaluation of the auditory display alone. These studies were performed by manipulating the pixel resolution of the visual display and Gaussian white noise level and by manipulating the sampling frequency of the auditory display and Gaussian white noise level. These findings strongly suggest that the quality of realism in an audiovisual display must be a function of both auditory and visual display fidelities inclusive of each other. Cross-modal enhancements can occur even when extra-modal input does not provide information directly meaningful for the task.

Cross-modal transfers or illusions are situations where stimulation in one sensory channel leads to the illusion of stimulation in another sensory channel. An example of this is synesthesia, which in the audiovisual domain is expressed as the ability to see a color while hearing a sound. When considering inter-sensory discrepancies, Welch and Warren (1980) propose a modality appropriateness hypothesis that suggests that various sensory modalities are differentially well-suited to the perception of different events. Generally, it is supposed that vision is more appropriate for the perception of spatial location than is audition, with touch placed somewhere in between. Audition is most appropriate for the perception of temporally structured events. Touch is more appropriate than audition for the perception of texture, where vision and touch may be about equally appropriate for the perception of textures. The appropriateness is a consequence of the different temporal and spatial resolution of the auditory, haptic, and visual systems. Moreover, especially when it is combined with touch stimulation, sound increases the sense of immersion (Vi et al. 2017).

Apart from the way that the different senses can interact, the auditory channel also presents some advantages when compared to other modalities. For example, humans have a complete sphere of receptivity around the head, while visual feedback has a limited spatial region in terms of field of view or field of regard. Because auditory information is primarily temporal, the temporal resolution of the auditory system is more precise. We can discriminate between a single click and a pair of clicks when the gap is only a few tens of microseconds (Krumbholz et al. 2003). Perception of temporal changes in the visual modality is much poorer, and the fastest visible flicker rate in normal conditions is about 40–50 Hz (Bruce et al. 2003). In multisensory interaction, therefore, audio tends to elicit the shortest response time (Li et al. 2018).

In contrast, the maximum spatial resolution (contrast sensitivity) of the human eye is approximately 1/30 degrees, a much finer resolution than that of the auditory system, which is approximately 1 degree. Humans are sensitive to sounds arriving from anywhere within the environment, whereas the visual field is limited to the frontal hemisphere, with good resolution limited specifically to the foveal region. Therefore, while the spatial resolution of the auditory modality is cruder, it can serve as a cue to events occurring outside the visual field of view.

In this chapter, we provide an overview of the interaction between audition and vision and audition and touch, together with guidelines on how such knowledge can be used in the design of interactive sonic systems. By understanding how we naturally interact in a world where several sensorial stimuli are provided, we can apply this understanding to the design of sonic interactive systems. Research on multisensory perception and cognition can provide us with important guidelines on how to design virtual environments where interactive sound plays an important role. Through technical advancements such as mobile technologies and 3D interfaces, it has become possible to design systems that have similar natural multimodal properties to the physical world. These future interfaces understand human multimodal communication and can actively anticipate and act in line with human capabilities and limitations. A large challenge for the near future is the development of such natural multimodal interfaces, something that requires the active participation of industry, technology, and the human sciences.

8.2 Audiovisual interactions

Research into multimodal interaction between audition and other modalities has primarily focused on the interaction between audition and vision. This choice is naturally due to the fact that audition and vision are the most dominant modalities in the human perceptual system (Kohlrausch and van de Par 1999). A well-known multimodal phenomenon is the McGurk effect

(McGurk and MacDonald 1976). The McGurk effect is an example of how vision alters speech perception; for instance, the sound "ba" is perceived as "da" when viewed with the lip movements for "ga." Notice that in this case, the percept is different from both the visual and auditory stimuli, so this is an example of intersensory bias, as described in the previous section.

The different experiments described until now show a dominance of vision versus audition when conflicting cues are provided. However, this is not always the case. As an example, in the work of Shams et al. (2000, 2002), a visual illusion induced by sound is described. When a single visual flash is accompanied by multiple auditory beeps, the single flash is perceived as multiple flashes. These results were obtained by flashing a uniform white disk a variable number of times, 50 milliseconds apart, on a black background. Flashes were accompanied by a variable number of beeps, each spaced 57 milliseconds apart. Observers were asked to judge how many visual flashes were presented during each trial. The trials were randomized, and each stimulus combination was run five times on eight naive observers. Surprisingly, observers consistently and incorrectly reported seeing multiple flashes whenever a single flash was accompanied by more than one beep (Shams et al. 2000). This experiment is known as sound-induced flash illusion. A follow-up experiment investigated whether the illusory flashes could be perceived independently at different spatial locations (Kamitani and Shimojo 2001). Two bars were displayed at two locations, creating an apparent motion. All subjects reported that an illusory bar was perceived with the second beep at a location between the real bars. This is analogous to the cutaneous rabbit perceptual illusion, where trains of successive cutaneous pulses delivered at a few widely separated locations produce sensations at many in-between points (Geldard and Sherrick 1972). As a matter of fact, perception of time, wherein auditory estimates are typically more accurate, is dominated by hearing.

Another experiment in determining whether two objects bounce off each other or simply cross is influenced by hearing a beep when the objects could be in contact. In this particular case, a desktop computer displayed two identical objects moving toward each other. The display was ambiguous to provide two different interpretations after the objects met: they could either bounce off each other or cross. Since collisions usually produce a characteristic impact sound, introducing such sound when objects meet promoted the perception of bouncing versus crossing. This experiment is usually known as motion-bounce illusion (Sekuler 1997). In a subsequent study, Sekuler and Sekuler (1999) found that any transient sound temporally aligned with the would-be collision increased the likelihood of a bounce percept. This includes a pause, a flash of light on the screen, or a sudden disappearance of the discs. Auditory dominance has also been found in other examples with respect to time-based abilities such as precise temporal processing (Repp and Penel 2002), temporal localization (Burr et al. 2009), and estimation of time durations (Ortega et al. 2009). Lipscomb and Kendall (1994) provide another example of auditory dominance in a multimedia context (film). These researchers found that variation in participant semantic differential ratings was influenced more by the musical component than by the visual element. Particularly interesting in its implications for processing multisensory experiences is the work of Hecht and Reiner (2009), pointing to the disappearance of visual dominance when a visual signal is presented simultaneously with an auditory and haptic signal (i.e., as a tri-sensory combination). The authors concluded that while vision can dominate both the auditory and the haptic sensory modalities, this is limited to bi-sensory combinations in which the visual signal is combined with another single stimulus.

More recent investigations examined the role of ecological auditory feedback in affecting multimodal perception of visual content. As an example, in a study presented by Ecker and Heller (2005), the combined perceptual effect of visual and auditory information on the perception of a moving object's trajectory was investigated. Inspired by the experimental paradigm presented by Kersten et al. (1997), the visual stimuli consisted of a perspective rendering of a ball moving in a 3D box. Each video was paired with one of three sound conditions: silence, the sound of a ball rolling, or the sound of a ball hitting the ground. It was found that the sound condition influenced whether observers were more likely to perceive the ball as rolling back in depth on the floor of the box or jumping in the frontal plane.

Another interesting study related to the role of auditory cues in the perception of visual stimuli is the one presented by Thomas and Shiffrar (2010). Two psychophysical studies were conducted to test whether visual sensitivity to point-light depictions of human gait reflects the action-specific co-occurrence of visual and auditory cues typically produced by walking people. To perform the experiment, visual walking patterns were captured using a motion-capture system, and a between-subject experimental procedure was adopted. Specifically, subjects were randomly exposed to one of the three experimental conditions: no sound, footstep sounds, or a pure tone at 1,000 Hz, which represented a control case. Visual sensitivity to coherent human gait was measured by asking subjects if they could detect or not a person walking. Such sensitivity was greatest in the presence of temporally coincident and action-consistent sounds – in this case, the sound of footsteps. Visual sensitivity to human gait with coincident sounds that were not action-consistent – in this case, the pure tone – was significantly lower and did not significantly differ from visual sensitivity to gaits presented without sound.

As an additional interaction between audition and vision, sound can help the user search for an object within a cluttered, continuously changing environment. It has been shown that a simple auditory pip drastically decreases search times for a synchronized visual object that is normally very difficult to find. This is known as the pip and pop effect (Van der Burg et al. 2008). Visual feedback can also affect several aspects of a musical performance, although in this chapter, affective and emotional aspects of a musical performance are not considered. As an example, Schutz and Lipscomb (2007) report an audiovisual illusion in which an expert musician's gestures affect the perceived duration of a note without changing its acoustic length. To demonstrate this, they recorded a world-renowned marimba player performing single notes on a marimba using long and short gestures. They paired both types of sounds with both types of gestures, resulting in a combination of natural (i.e., congruent gesture-note pairs) and hybrid (i.e., incongruent gesture-note pairs) stimuli. They informed participants that some auditory and visual components had been mismatched and asked them to judge tone duration based on the auditory component alone. Despite these instructions, the participants' duration ratings were strongly influenced by visual gesture information. As a matter of fact, notes were rated as longer when paired with long gestures than when paired with short gestures. These results are somehow puzzling since they contradict the view that judgments of tone duration are relatively immune from visual influence (Welch and Warren 1980) – that is, in temporal tasks, visual influence on audition is negligible. However, the results are not based on information quality but rather on perceived causality, given that visual influence in this paradigm is dependent on the presence of an ecologically plausible audiovisual relationship.

Indeed, it is also possible to consider the characteristics of vision and audition to predict which modality will prevail when conflicting information is provided. In this direction, Kubovy and Van Valkenburg (2001) introduced the notion of auditory and visual objects. They describe the different characteristics of audition and vision, claiming that a primary source of information for vision is a surface, while a secondary source of information is the location and color of sources. On the other hand, a primary source of information for audition is a source, and a secondary source of information is a surface.

In the work of Ernst and Bülthoff (2004), a theory is suggested on how our brain merges the different sources of information coming from the different modalities, specifically audition, vision, and touch. The first is what is called sensory combination, which means the maximization of information delivered from the different sensory modalities. The second strategy is called sensory integration, which means the reduction of variance in the sensory estimate to increase its reliability. Sensory combination describes interactions between sensory signals that are not redundant. By contrast, sensory integration describes interactions between redundant signals. Ernst and Bülthoff (2004) describe the integration of sensory information as a bottom-up process.

The modality precision (also called modality appropriateness) hypothesis, by Welch and Warren (1980), is often cited when trying to explain which modality dominates under what circumstances. This hypothesis states that discrepancies are always resolved in favor of the more precise or more appropriate modality. In spatial tasks, for example, the visual modality usually dominates because it is the most precise at determining spatial information. However, according to Ernst and Bülthoff (2004), this terminology is misleading because it is not the modality itself or the stimulus that dominates. Rather, the dominance is determined by the estimate and how reliably it can be derived within a specific modality from a given stimulus.

A major design dilemma involves the extent to which audio interfaces should maintain the conventions of visual interfaces (Mynatt and Edwards 1992), and indeed most attempts at auditory display seek to emulate or translate elements of visual interfaces to the auditory modality. While retrofitting visual interfaces with sound can offer some consistencies across modalities, the constraints of this approach may hinder the design of auditory interfaces, and native auditory interfaces would likely sound much different from interfaces designed with a relative visual counterpart in mind. While visual objects exist primarily in space, auditory stimuli occur in time. A more appropriate approach to auditory interface design, therefore, may require designers to focus more strictly on auditory capabilities. Such interfaces may present the items and objects of the interface in a fast, linear fashion over time rather than attempting to provide auditory versions of the spatial relationships found in visual interfaces.

8.3   Embodied interactions

The experiments described until now assume a passive observer, in the sense that a subject is exposed to a fixed sequence of audiovisual stimuli and is asked to report on the resulting perceptual experience. When a subject is interacting with the stimuli provided, a tight sensorimotor coupling is enabled, which is an important characteristic of embodied perception. According to embodiment theory, a person and the environment form a pair in which the two parts are coupled and determine each other. The term *embodied* highlights two points: first, cognition depends upon the kinds of experiences that are generated from specific sensorimotor capacities. Second, these individual sensorimotor capacities are themselves embedded in a biological, psychological, and cultural context (Dourish 2004).

As described in Chapter 2, the notion of embodied interaction is based on the view that meanings are present in the actions that people engage in while interacting with objects, with other people, and with the environment in general. Embodied interfaces try to exploit the phenomenological attitude of looking at the direct experience and let the meanings and structures emerge as experienced phenomena. Embodiment is not a property of artifacts but rather a property of how actions are performed with or through the artifacts.

The central role of our body in perception, cognition, and interaction has been previously addressed by philosophers (e.g., Merleau-Ponty 1962), psychologists (e.g., Niedenthal et al. 2005), and neuroscientists (e.g., Damasio 2006). A rather recent approach to the understanding of the design process, especially in its early stages, has been to focus on the role of multimodality and the contribution of nonverbal channels as key means of communication, kinesthetic thinking, and more generally, doing design (Tholander et al. 2008). Audiohaptic interactions, described in the following section, also require a continuous action-feedback loop between a person and the environment, an important characteristic of embodied perception. Another approach called embodied sound design, proposes to place the bodily experience (i.e., communication of sonic concepts through vocal and gestural imitations) at the center of the sound creation process (Delle Monache et al. 2018).

The role of the body in HCI has overall recently gained more attention, and interested readers can refer to the book by Höök (2018).

8.4 Audio-haptic interactions

Although the investigation of audio-haptic interactions has not received as much attention as the audiovisual interactions, it is certainly an interesting field of research, especially considering the tight connections existing between the sense of touch and audition. As a matter of fact, both audition and touch are sensitive to the very same kind of physical property – that is, mechanical pressure in the form of oscillations. The tight correlation between the information content (oscillatory patterns) being conveyed in the two senses can potentially support interactions of an integrative nature at a variety of levels along the sensory pathways. Auditory cues are normally elicited when one touches everyday objects, and these sounds often convey useful information regarding the nature of the objects (Ananthapadmanaban and Radhakrishnan 1982; Gaver 1993). The feeling of skin dryness or moistness that arises when we rub our hands against each other is subjectively referred to as the friction forces at the epidermis. Yet it has been demonstrated that acoustic information also participates in this bodily sensation because altering the sound arising from the hand rubbing action changes our sensation of dryness or moistness on the skin. This phenomenon is known as the parchment-skin illusion (Jousmäki and Hari 1998).

The parchment-skin illusion is an example of how interactive auditory feedback can affect subjects' haptic sensation. Specifically, in the experiment demonstrating the rubber-skin illusion, subjects were asked to sit with a microphone close to their hands and then rub their hands against each other. The sound of hands rubbing was captured by a microphone; they were then manipulated in real time and played back through headphones. The sound was modified by attenuating the overall amplitude and by amplifying the high frequencies. Subjects were asked to rate the haptic sensation in their palms as a function of the different auditory cues provided, in a scale ranging from very moist to very dry. Results show that the provided auditory feedback significantly affected the perception of the skin's dryness. This study was extended by Guest et al. (2002) by using a more rigorous psychophysical testing procedure. Results reported a similar increase in smooth-dry scale correlated to changes in auditory feedback but not in the roughness judgments per se. However, both studies provide convincing empirical evidence demonstrating the modulatory effect of auditory cues on people's haptic perception of a variety of different surfaces. A similar experiment was performed combining auditory cues with haptic cues at the tongue. Specifically, subjects were asked to chew on potato chips, and the sound produced was again captured and manipulated in real time. Results show that the perception of potato chips' crispness was affected by the auditory feedback provided (Spence and Zampini 2006). A surprising audio-haptic bodily illusion that demonstrates human observers rapidly update their assumptions about the material qualities of their body is the marble hand illusion (Senna et al. 2014). By repeatedly gently hitting participants' hands while progressively replacing the natural sound of the hammer against the skin with the sound of a hammer hitting a piece of marble, it was possible to induce an illusory misperception of the material properties of the hand. After five minutes, the hand started feeling stiffer, heavier, harder, less sensitive, and unnatural and showed enhanced galvanic skin response to threatening stimuli. This bodily illusion demonstrates that the experience of the material of our body can be quickly updated through multisensory integration. Another interesting example where sounds again affect body perception is shown by Tajadura-Jiménez et al. (2015). Here the illusion is applied to footstep sounds. By digitally varying sounds produced by walking, it is possible to vary one's perception of weight.

Lately, artificial cues are appearing in audio-haptic interfaces, allowing us to carefully control the variations to the provided feedback and the resulting perceived effects on exposed subjects (DiFilippo and Pai 2000; Nordahl et al. 2010; Van den Doel and Pai 1998). Artificial auditory cues have also been used in the context of sensory substitution, for artificial sensibility at the hands using hearing as a replacement for the loss of sensation (Lundborg et al. 1999). In this particular study, microphones placed at the fingertips captured and amplified the friction sound obtained when rubbing hard surfaces.

In the work of Kitagawa et al. (2005), a nice investigation of the interaction between auditory and haptic cues in the near space is presented. The authors show an interesting illusion of how sounds delivered through headphones, presented near to the head, induce a haptic experience. The left ear of a dummy head was stroked with a paintbrush and the sound was recorded. The sound was then presented to the participants who felt a tickling sensation when the sound was presented near to the head but not when it was presented distant from the head. Another kind of dynamic sonic objecthood is obtained through data physicalization, which is the 3D rendering of a data set in the form of a solid physical object. Although there is a long history of physicalization, this area of research has become increasingly interesting through the facilitation of 3D printing technology. Physicalizations allow the user to hold and manipulate a data set in their hands, providing an embodied experience that allows rich naturalistic and intuitive interactions such as multi-finger touch, tapping, pressing, squeezing, scraping, and rotating.

Physical manipulation produces acoustic effects that are influenced by material properties, shape, forces, modes of interaction, and events over time. The idea that sound could be a way to augment data physicalization has been explored through acoustic sonifications in which the 3D-printed data set is superimposed on the form of a sounding object, such as a bell or a singing bowl (Barrass 2016). Since acoustic vibrations are strongly influenced by 3D form, the sound that is produced is influenced by the data set that is used to shape the sounding object. In a similar vein, the design of musical instruments has also inspired the design of new interfaces for human-computer interaction. As stated by Jaron Lanier, musical instruments are the best user interfaces (see Barrass [2016]), and we can learn to design new interfaces by looking at musical instruments. An example is the work of Laput et al. (2015), where structural elements along the speaker-microphone pathway characteristically alter the acoustic output.

In designing multimodal environments, several elements need to be taken into consideration. However, technology has some limitations, especially when the ultimate goal is to simulate systems that react in real time. This issue is nicely addressed by Pai (2005), who describes a trade-off between accuracy and responsiveness, a crucial difference between models for science and models for interaction. Specifically, computations about the physical world are always approximations. In general, it is possible to improve accuracy by constructing more detailed models and performing more precise measurements, but this increased accuracy comes at the cost of latency (i.e., the elapsed time before an answer is obtained). For multisensory models, it is also essential to ensure the synchronization of time between different sensory modalities. Pai (2005) groups all of these temporal considerations, such as latency and synchronization, into a single category called responsiveness. The question then becomes how to balance accuracy and responsiveness. The choice between accuracy and responsiveness depends also on the final goal of the multimodal system design. Often, scientists are generally more concerned with accuracy, so responsiveness is only a soft constraint based on available resources. On the other hand, for interaction designers, responsiveness is an essential parameter that must be satisfied.

8.5 Case study 1: HapticWave

The HapticWave (Tanaka and Parkinson 2016) is an interface that renders sound tangible, developed together with a group of visually impaired musicians and producers to overcome the issue of the strong dominance of visual feedback in music software and interfaces. The HapticWave presents audio for editing in a tactile form by creating a 2D physical plane where sound amplitude is retraced by a motorized slider's vertical movements. By displacing the slider structure left and right, the user is able to scan in time through the sound and feel its amplitude through up and down movements of the slider tip. The HapticWave was developed using participatory techniques as a way of understanding the needs of our users (Tanaka and Parkinson 2016). As musicians, we understood the workplace context under study, but as sighted people, we had no idea what challenges visual impairment posed for our users to be productive in these environments. Meanwhile, we were able to introduce to our users the concepts of cross-modal mapping and multimodal interaction and the innovative technologies of haptic interaction. Through a process of user-centered design, we put in place a series of activities, including interviews, workshops, and brainstorming sessions, to explore and prototype interaction ideas to make audio waveform editing less visually dependent. Surprisingly, the HapticWave received enthusiastic responses from sighted users. This was an unexpected turn, coming from a different type of user than the original user group with whom we had co-designed the device. Sighted musicians expressed an interest in using the device as a way to free themselves from the computer screen while editing or performing music. For example, a DJ saw potential in using the HapticWave to scrub sounds physically instead of using the mouse and computer screen on stage in clubs where stage lights made screens difficult to see. Or without a screen in front of him, he thought he could have a more direct connection with his audience. In this unexpected response, not intended in the original design, the device that had gone through a pragmatic or even conservative design process seemed to unlock and inspire imagination as a romantic interface device.

8.6 Conclusions

This chapter has provided an overview of several experiments whose goals were to achieve a better understanding of how the human auditory system is connected to visual and haptic channels. A better understanding of multimodal perception can have several applications. As an example, systems based on sensory substitution help people lacking a certain sensorial modality to have it replaced by another sensorial modality. Moreover, cross-modal enhancement allows reduced stimuli in one sensorial modality to be augmented by a stronger stimulation in another modality.

Contemporary advances in hardware and software technology allow us to experiment in several ways with technologies for multimodal interaction design, building, for example, haptic illusions with equipment available in a typical hardware store (Hayward 2008) or easily experimenting with sketching and rapid prototyping (Monache et al. 2010; Buxton 2010). These advances in technology create several possibilities for discovering novel cross-modal illusions and interactions between the senses, especially when a collaboration between cognitive psychologists and interaction designers is facilitated. A research challenge is not only to understand how humans process information coming from different senses but also how information in a multimodal system should be distributed to different modalities in order to obtain the best user experience.

As an example, in a multimodal system such as a system for controlling a haptic display, seeing a visual display, and listening to an interactive auditory display, it is important to determine which synchronicities are more important. At one extreme, a completely disjointed distribution of information over several modalities can offer the highest bandwidth, but the user may be confused in connecting the modalities, and one modality might mask another and distract the user by focusing attention on events that might not be important. At the other extreme, a completely redundant distribution of information is known to increase the cognitive load and is not guaranteed to increase user performance. Beyond the research on multimodal stimuli processing, studies are needed on the processing of multimodal stimuli that are connected via interaction. We would expect that the human brain and sensory system have been optimized to cope with a certain mixture of redundant information and that information displays are better the more they follow this natural distribution. Overall, the more we achieve a better understanding of the ways humans interact with the everyday world, the more we can obtain inspiration for the design of effective natural multimodal interfaces.

9 Spatial auditory displays

9.1 Introduction

A unique and powerful dimension inherent in sound is its spatial location. Unlike the visual system, the auditory system does not have a limited field of view. Sounds can be heard and perceived anywhere around a listener. A listener does not have to be facing a sound in order to perceive it. A number of studies have confirmed that auditory signals can direct visual attention to a spatial location (Brock et al. 2002; Spence et al. 2004). A good rule of thumb for knowing when to provide acoustic cues is to recall how we naturally use audition to gain information and explore the environment; that is, the function of the ears is to point to the eyes. Regardless of whether a sound is located in front, behind, above, or below, it can be detected by the listener (Wakefield et al. 2012). When used to process auditory displays, spatial sound can be very effective at enhancing a person's listening experience and conveying additional information to the listener. The auditory system can provide a more coarsely tuned mechanism to direct the attention of our more finely tuned visual analyses, as suggested by the effective linkage between the direction of gaze (eye and head movements) and localization accuracy (Saberi and Perrott 1990; Strybel et al. 1992). This omnidirectional characteristic of acoustic signals will be especially useful in inherently spatial tasks, particularly when visual cues are limited and workload is high – for example, in air traffic control displays for the tower or cockpit (Begault and Wenzel 1992).

In addition to providing location-specific information, when multiple auditory displays are presented concurrently in spatially disparate locations, they can be better segregated into individual streams (Barreto et al. 2007; Marston et al. 2006; Shilling et al. 2000). Without spatial separation, the multiple sound sources will have a greater tendency to fuse together, making them more difficult to understand. The result is the possibility of presenting multiple auditory displays concurrently without sacrificing their intelligibility.

A related concept is augmented audio reality (Cohen et al. 1993), which describes the addition of synthesized, virtual sounds onto real-world audio in an interactive environment. By using virtual content, the human sensory perception of the real world is augmented. Many of these systems are based on mobile

DOI: 10.4324/9781003260202-9

platforms, which allow the user to move around and explore an environment. Often, these systems use spatial auditory displays, in which HRTF-based (see Chapter 2) processing is used and delivered to the listener over headphones. The user is equipped with a system that plays or synthesizes a spatial audio image while simultaneously navigating a real environment, for example, by presenting historic landmark information within a city as a user points a mobile device in the direction of a given landmark.

Recent developments in virtual, augmented, and mixed realities have demonstrated the importance of designing immersive auditory experiences, therefore bringing back to life the field of 3D sound. The goal of spatial sound synthesis is to project audio media into space by manipulating sound sources so that they assume virtual positions, mapping the source channel into 3D space.

Sound is already an important component of virtual and augmented reality (Serafin et al. 2018). Sound in virtual reality (VR) is often experienced through headphones or earplugs, and localization of sound sources in space require accurate recreation of HRTFs.

The history of 3D sound research is long (Davis 2003), and an introduction to the theories related to how humans perceive 3D sound is presented in Chapter 2. However, while in the past 3D sound was merely a niche field of research, important for example in training and simulations, lately it has shown interest and relevance also for the design of interactive experiences in a more broad sense. In this chapter, we focus on spatial sound delivered through headphones and used in virtual and augmented reality installations; however, some concepts can also be translated to spatial sound delivered through a system of loudspeakers. Headphone-based rendering is particularly attractive for mobile virtual and augmented reality applications.

From the technical perspective, one of the still open research questions in 3D sound rendering through headphones is the amount of personalization required. To render spatialized sounds within an interactive experience such as a VR experience, either individualized or generic HRTFs are usually employed. The former require capturing of individual HRTFs and calibration but enable accurate auditory source localization, which may lead to a heightened sense of presence within VR. Personalized HRTFs have been previously measured, starting with the pioneering work of Møller et al. (1995).

However, most research on the perception of personalized HRTFs has been considering static and unimodal conditions. Unimodal comparisons between auditory source localization of virtually rendered sounds using generic versus individualized HRTFs have revealed that the use of generic HRTFs leads to increased confusion over auditory source location (Wenzel et al. 1993). However, it is still not clear whether personalization is necessary for immersive, dynamic multisensory environments. In the previous chapter, we examined several examples of how the different senses affect each others, with a particular focus on audiovisual interaction.

In the work of Berger et al. (2018), it is shown how pairing a visual stimulus with an auditory source in virtual 3D space for a duration as short as

60 seconds is sufficient to induce a measurable improvement in auditory spatial localization in VR. The improvement did not occur when the moving auditory stimulus was not paired with a visual stimulus or when the paired visual stimulus was temporally inconsistent. These results confirm previous research on brain plasticity and adaptation. The development of virtual audio technologies has also led to the recognition of the potential of hearing aids as computational devices to augment listening and sound-based interaction for both hearing-impaired and normally hearing persons (Noceti et al. 2019). For example, microphone arrays arranged on the temples of eyeglasses can be used to increase audio sensitivity in the frontal direction, making human-human or human-machine interaction more effective in noisy environments. Furthermore, audio content can be superimposed over the environmental soundscape through a tiny acoustic prosthesis, opening a wide spectrum of possibilities for sound-mediated interactions, where sound design will become critical for wide acceptance and appreciation.

9.2   Hearables

The concept of hearable, likely introduced by Nick Hunn in 2014, is defined as anything that fits in or on an ear that contains a wireless link, whether that's for audio or remote control of audio augmentation (Plazak and Kersten-Oertel 2018). Hearables represent a wide variety of devices, ranging from wireless audio headphones to smart hearing aids. While hearables are primarily designed for the presentation and recording of audio signals, there are many other possibilities for interaction. Hearables have great potential to blend into our everyday environments by focusing or ignoring information; the fact that hearables are eye-free is, therefore, one of their strongest affordances. Further, hearables are also hands-free, which means that hearables do not impede our ability to visually and tactilely interact with the world. Hearables offer great potential for the future of personal and ubiquitous computing. In particular, ear-mounted wearable devices will play a large role in the evolution of affective computing, especially considering the multitude of biosensors that may be placed on or within the ear.

9.3   Case studies

In the following, we present three different case studies related to the use of immersive binaural audio in interactive applications. The first case study related to people without known disabilities, the second case study to visually impaired people, and the third case study to hearing-impaired people.

9.3.1   *Case study 1: the LISTEN system*

There have been many examples of augmented audio reality (AAR) systems over the past decades. At the Institut de Recherche et Coordination

Acoustique/Musique (IRCAM) in Paris, France, Eckel (2001) developed the LISTEN project for studying audio-augmented environments. Using headphones equipped with a head tracking system, Eckel introduced a platform for navigating through a virtual environment that is superimposed on top of the real environment. Further work on LISTEN resulted in a personalized, augmented environment for a museum guide (Zimmermann and Lorenz 2008), in which virtual soundscapes are presented over headphones. These soundscapes are generated based on the user's position and visit history at the exhibition. Virtual audio tours of cities are becoming rather popular, thanks to the availability of low-cost hardware and software technologies. In such tours, spatially accurate landmarks are represented by 3D auditory displays, providing information about their history, use, and other interesting facts (Bederson 1995; Vazquez-Alvarez et al. 2012).

9.3.2 Case study 2: Soundscape by Microsoft

Soundscape is a project by Microsoft that allows to experience audio played in 3D using a stereo headset. Landmarks around can be heard and therefore enrich the awareness of the surroundings.

By using binaural rendering technologies, users can hear the location of a landmark as coming precisely from the physical location where the landmark is. So for example, if a specific coffee shop is located at 45 degrees from the user, the name of that coffee shop will be told and the location of the sound message will arrive precisely from 45 degrees. Another idea built into Soundscape is the notion of a virtual audio beacon.

For example, if a person is standing on a street corner heading to a restaurant that is one and a half blocks away, Soundscape will play an audio beacon that will sound like it is coming from that restaurant, so no matter which way one is standing or which way one is heading, one can always hear that repetitive clicking sound and know exactly where that restaurant is. It is like seeing with the ears. Soundscape is meant to be used outdoor, and GPS coordinates are used to provide the appropriate sound message. One of the nice aspects of Soundscape is that the beacon sound is in the background, which means that the user can still have a conversation with other people while listening to the instructions. Soundscape enriches the awareness of the surroundings, of what is where in a very natural, easy way. And that really helps to feel more independent and more confident to explore the world beyond what one knows.

9.3.3 Case study 3: SWAN – a system for wearable audio navigation

SWAN (Wilson et al. 2007) is a wearable computer consisting of audio-only output and input via a task-specific handheld interface device. SWAN consists of a small portable computer, an audio processor, audio presentation hardware, input devices, and position- and orientation-tracking technologies. All the components are stored in a shoulder bag,

SWAN aids a user in safe pedestrian navigation and includes the ability for the user to author new data relevant to their needs of wayfinding, obstacle avoidance, and situational awareness support. SWAN addresses the limitations of previous speech-based navigation aids by using nonspeech audio presentation of navigation information whenever possible. SWAN provides an auditory display that enhances the user's ability to keep track of her current location and heading as she moves about, find her way around and through a variety of environments, successfully find and follow a near-optimal and safe walking path to her destination, and be aware of salient features of her environment.

SWAN supports these goals through sophisticated position-tracking technologies, auditory display of navigation routes and environmental features, and implementation of a database of information relevant to the user's navigation needs. SWAN allows users to record their movements or paths through the environment. These paths are used to create a personally relevant set of maps for the user. Additionally, the user can annotate objects found within the environment, including locations, features, and obstacles. To guide the user along a path, SWAN presents a spatialized nonspeech beacon sound that continually indicates the direction the user needs to go (Walker and Lindsay 2003). The beacon's virtual location is updated as the person's location or head orientation changes so as to always be a constant virtual distance away from the user so as to not introduce any volume attenuation. The user simply walks toward the sound, moving from waypoint to waypoint until the destination is reached. When a user approaches a waypoint, the beacon tempo increases until the waypoint is reached, at which point there is a subtle success chime, and the beacon shifts to direct the user toward the next waypoint.

9.3.4   *Case study 4: superhuman hearing*

Hearing-impaired users can also benefit from a properly designed 3D sonic environment. Most research on hearing aids design has been focused on the sense of hearing. However, hearing is a multisensory experience, where cues from other modalities such as vision and proprioception affect what we hear. In the work of Geronazzo et al. (2020), it is described how VR, and more specifically a photorealistic scenario captured using a 360-degree camera, can help design the hearing aids of the future, where users do not just achieve normal hearing but they are also enabled with super-hearing capabilities. Consider, for example, the classic scenario of a cocktail party where it is hard, especially for a hearing-impaired person, to focus on specific conversations.

To achieve the goal, an immersive scenario is created using generalized HRTFs from the SADIE database (Kearney and Doyle 2015). What if one could zoom on a specific speaker? In the work of Geronazzo et al. (2020), it is investigated how different interaction techniques implemented in VR scenarios can be used to empower hearing-impaired users to focus on different people speaking. Such interactions vary from head turning to eye tracking to using a VR controller. Results show that subjects do not really prefer one interaction technique over others, and hearing is a complex multimodal phenomenon. Despite the insights gained from several studies, including the ones presented in this chapter, there remains no inherent, standard, or even clearly best way to use sound to convey the spatial relationships between objects in user interfaces. A major design dilemma, then, involves the extent to which audio interfaces should maintain the conventions of visual interfaces (Mynatt and Edwards 1992), and indeed most attempts at auditory display seek to emulate or translate elements of visual interfaces to the auditory modality. This is very likely a bad design approach. While humans have a higher spatial resolution using vision, they also show a better temporal resolution using audition. These characteristics of the human senses should be adopted when designing auditory interfaces in general, and this is also the case for spatial auditory interfaces: it is very likely that for interfaces with a strong visual component, visuals will be dominant in delivering spatial information, so a highly precise auditory representation of auditory information is likely not needed.

9.4 Conclusions

Research on making HRTFs more readily individualized and more general is ongoing and likely to continue. The development of virtual audio technologies has led to recognition of the potential of hearing aids as computational devices to augment listening and sound-based interaction for both hearing-impaired and normally hearing persons (Noceti et al. 2019). For example, microphone arrays arranged on the temples of eyeglasses can be used to increase audio sensitivity in the frontal direction, making human-human or human-machine interaction more effective in noisy environments. Furthermore, audio content can be superimposed over the environmental soundscape through a tiny acoustic prosthesis, opening a wide spectrum of possibilities for sound-mediated interactions, where sound design will become critical for wide acceptance and appreciation.

10 Synthesis and control of auditory icons

10.1 Generating and controlling sounds

In order to do research in the area of nonspeech audio, one needs to be able to exercise control over a rich and potent sound repertoire. In the past few years, there has been a lot of progress in the development of technologies to support such control. From a practical point of view, the researcher's life is a lot easier than it was when Bly first started her experiments.

In this chapter, we discuss some of the nuts-and-bolts practicalities of working with nonspeech audio. We look at some important hardware and software issues that affect our ability to synthesize and process sounds.

While some of the information in this chapter will date quickly, the underlying issues will remain with us for some time. The objective is to help new researchers get started.

We want to create systems that will impose minimal constraints on possible research. To achieve this, we make a few assumptions:

- Response time: About 5 milliseconds is the upper bound on the response for audio cues.
- Multi-sound/multi-timbre: Not only must we be able to control more than one sound at a time (polyphony), we must have independent timbral control over each (poly-timbre).
- Continuous real-time control: Triggering sound events is not sufficient. We need continuous real-time control over various types of modulation (loudness, pitch, timbre, etc.).
- Processing and synthesis: Signal processing techniques such as filtering and reverberation are important, especially in placing sounds along the foreground/background continuum. The provision of these facilities is as important as sound synthesis.
- Burden on host: Maintaining adequate response time is hard enough without the additional burden of sound. Having the addition of sound degrade the performance of other functions is unacceptable.

Just as visual displays must echo characters as they are typed, so must auditory displays be synchronized with the processes with which they are associated.

DOI: 10.4324/9781003260202-10

But audio interfaces must do more than simply echo an event with a sound. In thinking about response, the continuous shaping of a window in a direct manipulation system is perhaps a better analogy than the echoing of a typed character. In most cases, it is not sufficient simply to trigger a sound at a particular moment. To provide a proper foundation for research, the sound control system must also support the dynamic "shaping" of the sound's attributes. As the visual display of a window stretches when we drag its corner, so must a sound vary continuously as the parameter to which it is associated is manipulated.

We need control over sound, which is rich, immediate, and continuous. However, even with the technology available today, this is not always easy. Much of the difficulty lies within our programming environments, which make it difficult to instrument processes. But even with the appropriate software tools, it can be very difficult to provide the desired control without adversely affecting other aspects of the system's performance.

One way to "save cycles" on the host machine is to delegate the audio processing and synthesis to peripheral hardware. This way, the computational bandwidth demanded from the host is reduced from audio levels down to control levels – a reduction of as much as two orders of magnitude.

While we briefly discuss some aspects of host-generated sounds, our working assumption is that the host is already busy and that most audio work will employ external hardware. We briefly cover "hard" and "soft" synthesis and synthesis versus playback (sampling). We pay particular attention to the control protocol standard in the music business, MIDI, and mention specific products as examples. We also describe another protocol called Open Sound Control (OSC) (Freed 1997), outlining the advantages and disadvantages of MIDI versus OSC.

10.2   Parameterized icons

Auditory icons not only reflect categories of events and objects as visual icons do but are parameterized to reflect their relevant dimensions as well. That is, if a file is large, it sounds large. If it is dragged over a new surface, we hear that new surface. And if an ongoing process starts running more quickly, it sounds quicker.

The possibility of parameterizing icons, whether auditory or visual, has been somehow neglected in interface design. Parameterized icons can serve as more than mere labels for their referents, providing rich sources of information about relevant dimensions, such as size, age, and speed. Parameterization allows single objects or events to be assessed along a number of dimensions. In addition, it creates families of icons that retain perceptual similarity while allowing comparison among members. In general, parameterized icons allow a great deal of information to be conveyed perceptually rather than symbolically.

10.2.1   *Creating parameterized auditory icons*

Unfortunately, it is difficult to parameterize auditory icons because it is difficult to control a virtual source of a sound along relevant dimensions. Standard synthesis techniques have been developed for creating music and thus afford changes in a sound's pitch, loudness, duration, and so forth. But they do not make it easy to change a sound from indicating a large wooden object, for instance, to one specifying a small metal one. It is easy to create a wide variety of beeps and hums using standard synthesis techniques but difficult to create and manipulate sounds along dimensions that specify events in the world.

Because of the limitations of standard synthesis techniques, interfaces using auditory icons have relied on digital sampling in their implementations. Desired sounds are captured by recording them on a computer, shaped by a designer, then played back and manipulated under the control of the interface. This enables the use of much more complex and realistic sounds than can be created by readily available synthesis algorithms. However, there are several drawbacks of sampling that limit its utility as a technique for creating and using auditory icons:

- It is difficult to capture an actual event that sounds like what is desired because sounds are invariably colored by the technologies used to record them.
- Shaping recorded sounds along dimensions relevant to auditory icons is difficult because available software is designed for making music.
- Real-time modification of sounds on playback is even more limited.
- The amount of memory needed for complex auditory interfaces is often prohibitive (on the order of 10 KB per second of sound).

These limitations constrain the possibilities for designing auditory icons and make their creation difficult and time-consuming.

In this chapter, we first describe synthesis algorithms developed as a result of basic research on auditory event perception and present several examples in sufficient detail to allow readers to implement and explore them. These algorithms were developed by one of the authors of this book (Bill Gaver) and allow sounds to be specified in terms of their sources rather than their acoustic attributes. They overcome the limitations of sampling by allowing parametrized auditory icons to be specified along dimensions of virtual source events. We also describe how these algorithms were refined in other research projects.

10.2.2   *Acoustic information for events*

Creating algorithms that allow the synthesis of virtual events implies an understanding of the acoustic information for event attributes – how sounds indicate the material or size of an object, for instance. Event attributes often have very complex effects on sounds, effects that must be described as functions of frequencies and amplitudes over time that specify the partials, or frequency components, that make up a sound. If these functions are understood, source attributes can be specified directly instead of by using separate controls over partial frequencies, amplitudes, and durations. But how can we determine what these functions are?

10.2.3   *Analysis and synthesis of events*

One approach to this problem is suggested by the analysis and synthesis methods (Risset and Wessel 1982) used by computer musicians to capture the relevant properties of traditional instrument sounds (see Figure 10.1). This approach involves recording sounds that vary along dimensions of interest and analyzing their acoustic structure using Fourier analysis or similar techniques. Hypotheses about acoustic information suggested by the analysis can be tested by synthesizing sounds based on simplified versions of the data. For instance, if one supposes that the temporal features of a sound indicate the event that caused it but that its frequency makeup is irrelevant, one might use the amplitude contour from the original sound to modify a noise burst. The hypothesis can then be assessed simply by listening to the result.

In practice, however, it is often difficult to identify the acoustic information for events in the mass of data produced by acoustic analyses. Thus, it is useful to supplement them with analyses of the mechanical physics of the event itself (see Figure 10.2). Studying the physics of sound-producing events is useful both in suggesting perceptible source attributes and in indicating the acoustic information for these attributes. Acoustic analyses help both in checking the

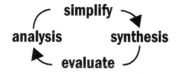

Figure 10.1 Traditional analysis and synthesis.

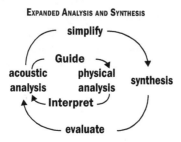

Figure 10.2 Analyzing and synthesizing events requires physical as well as acoustic analyses.

adequacy of physical models and in evaluating particular parameters. Finally, the resulting models can provide the basis for synthesis algorithms that allow sounds to be specified in terms of sources attributes.

In the following sections, we discuss several case studies of events that have been studied in this manner and describe the synthesis algorithms that have resulted. The algorithms have been chosen for their utility in creating auditory icons and are described in order of their complexity. We start with the sounds made by mechanical impacts, which involve a simple interaction of objects. Next, we describe how more complex bouncing, breaking, and spilling sounds can be produced by specifying the temporal patterning of a series of impacts. A third algorithm allows the same virtual object to be hit and then scraped by distinguishing objects from the interactions that cause them to make a sound. Finally, we describe an algorithm for producing machine-like sounds, showing that high-level attributes of complex events may be synthesized directly.

10.2.4   Impact sounds

Many of the sounds we hear in the everyday world involve one solid impacting against another. Tapping on an object, placing it against another, letting it fall – these all involve impact sounds. In the interface, impact sounds are useful in the design of a variety of auditory icons that indicate events such as selecting a file, moving it over another, or attaching one object to another.

Several studies have explored the perceptible attributes of impact events and the acoustic information about them. In this section, we briefly review these studies, then show how the information they provide can be used to create a synthesis algorithm that allows impact sounds to be specified along dimensions of the virtual source.

10.2.4.1   *Mallet hardness, material, and size*

Freed and Martins (Freed 1986) studied people's perception of the hardness of mallets used to strike objects. They recorded the sounds made by hitting cooking pans with mallets of various hardnesses, asked people to judge hardness from the sounds, and used a model of the peripheral auditory system to analyze the acoustic correlates of their judgments. They found that the ratio of high- to low-frequency energy in the sounds and its change over time served as the most powerful predictors of subjects' hardness judgments. To a good approximation, then, mallet hardness is conveyed by the relative presence of high- and low-frequency energy.

We studied the acoustic information available for the length and material of struck wood and metal bars and people's abilities to perceive these attributes (Gaver and Norman 1988). We recorded and analyzed the sounds made by wood and metal bars of several different lengths and developed a model of the physics of impacts that combined analytical solutions to the wave equation for transverse vibrations in a bar (see, for example, Bilbao [2009]) with empirical measurements of damping and resonance amplitudes. This model was used both to aid the interpretation of the acoustic analyses and to synthesize new tokens. The material of the bars had several effects on the sounds they made. Perhaps most importantly, materials have characteristic frequency-dependent damping functions: the sounds made by vibrating wood decay quickly, with low-frequency partials lasting longer than high ones, while the sounds made by vibrating metal decay slowly, with high-frequency partials lasting longer than low ones. In addition, metal sounds have partials with well-defined frequency peaks, while wooden sound partials are smeared over frequency space. These results accord with the physical analyses of Wildes and Richards (1988) of the audible effects of the internal friction characterizing different materials, which show that internal friction determines both the damping and definition of frequency peaks.

Changing the length of a bar, on the other hand, simply changes the frequencies of the sound it produces when struck so that short bars make high-pitched sounds and long bars make low ones. However, the effects of length may interact with the effects of the material. For instance, frequencies change monotonically with length, but the frequency of the partial with the highest amplitude depends on the material and thus may change nonlinearly with length Gaver and Norman (1988). These nonlinearities and the perceptual confusion they cause may be avoided by simplifying the model so that partial amplitudes do not depend on the material.

10.2.4.2 Synthesis algorithm for impact sounds

These results may be captured in a synthesis model that uses frequency and amplitude functions to constrain a formula for describing logarithmically decaying sounds. This formula describes a complex wave created by adding together a number of sine waves with independent initial amplitudes and logarithmic decay rates:

$$G(t) = S_n F_n e^{-dnt} cos(w_n t) \tag{10.1}$$

$G(t)$ is the waveform over time, F_n the initial amplitude, d_n the damping constant, and w_n the frequency of partial n.

This formula has two properties that make it a useful foundation for synthesizing auditory icons. First, its components map well to event attributes. Second, it can be made computationally efficient using trigonometric identities.

10.2.5 Mapping synthesis parameters to source attributes

By constraining the values used in this formula, useful parameters can be defined which correspond well to the attributes of impact sounds discussed previously. The formula involves three basic components: the initial amplitudes of the partials F_n, their damping e^{-dnt}, and their frequencies $cos(w_n t)$. These

Table 10.1 Mapping parameters to events

Term	Effect	Event attribute
F_n	Initial amplitudes	Mallet hardness, force, or proximity
e^{-dnt}	Damping	Material
$\cos(w_n t)$	Partial frequencies	Size, configuration

can be set separately for each partial. However, these three components also correspond to information for mallet hardness and impact force, material, and size and shape, respectively (see Table 10.1). Thus, it is more useful to define patterns of behavior over the partials for each component.

For example, the partial frequencies w_n can be constrained to patterns typical of various object configurations. The sounds made by struck or plucked strings, for example, are quasi-harmonic, so that $w_n = nw_1$. The sounds made by solid plates, in contrast, are inharmonic and can be approximated by random frequency shifts made to a harmonic pattern. The sounds made by solid bars can be approximated by the formula $w_n = (2_n + 1)2/9$. Finally, the sounds made by rectangular resonators are given by the formula $w_n = c/2 \ \overline{(p^2/l^2 + q^2/w^2 + r^2/h^2)}$, where c is the velocity of sound; l, w, and h are the length, width, and height of the box, respectively; and p, q, and r are indexed from 0 (Wildes and Richards 1988). An algorithm based on Formula 1, then, can be constrained so that one of these patterns is used to control the partial frequencies w_n. In addition, w_1 can be specified such that $w_1 \mu$ reflects the size of the object (this affects all the other partial frequencies).

The initial amplitude of the partials, F_n, can be controlled by a single parameter corresponding to mallet hardness. Recalling that Freed and Martin's results (Freed 1986) identified the ratio of high- to low-frequency energy as a predictor of perceived mallet hardness, we might maintain a linear relationship among the partial's initial amplitudes and use the slope from F_1 to control perceived hardness. Thus, $F_n = F_1 + h(w_n - w_1)$, where h is the slope; note that h may be negative so that higher partials have less amplitude than low ones. F_1 (and thus all the amplitudes) may also be changed to indicate impact force or proximity.

Finally, the damping constants for each partial (d_n) can be controlled by a parameter corresponding to the material. A useful heuristic is to set $d_n = w_n d0$ so that high harmonics die out relatively quickly for highly damped materials and last longer for less damped materials (e.g., metal, which has low damping, tends to ring; wood, which is highly damped, tends to thunk). This strategy is suggested both by Wildes and Richards (1988) and Gaver and Norman (1988).

In sum, Formula 1 can be controlled by parameters that make effects corresponding to attributes of impact events. Controlling overall frequency corresponds to the object's size, while the pattern of partial frequencies corresponds to its configuration. The overall initial amplitude corresponds to the force or proximity of the impact, while the pattern of partial amplitudes corresponds to mallet hardness. Finally, the degree of damping corresponds well to the virtual object's material. By controlling these five parameters, then, a wide range of sounds can be created, which vary over several useful dimensions.

10.2.6   *An efficient algorithm for synthesis*

Equation 10.2 is useful in allowing parameters to be defined in terms of source events. It is also attractive because it can be implemented in a computationally efficient way.

An efficient implementation of this formula relies on Euler's relationship

$$e^{iwt} = cos(wt) + isin(wt)$$

to rewrite Equation 10.2 as

$$S_n = Re[(a_n + ib_n)(p + iq)] = Re[(a_n p - b_n q) + i(b_n p + a_n q)] \qquad (10.2)$$

where S_n is the nth sample, a_0 is the initial amplitude, $b_0 = 0$, $i = \sqrt{-1}$, $p = e^{-dt}cos(wt)$, and $q = e^{-dt} t \, sin(\omega t)$.

Samples can thus be generated by calculating p and q, setting a and b to the initial amplitude and 0, and applying Equation 2. The output sample is the real part of the result, and a and b are updated to the real and imaginary parts, respectively (see pseudocode in Table 10.2). Computationally expensive sines and cosines need only be calculated once, and only four multiplications, one addition, and one subtraction are needed for each partial for a given sample. The efficiency of this implementation allows fairly complex impact sounds to be generated in real time on many computers.

Table 10.2 Pseudocode

```
p = cos(freq * 1/samplerate) * power(e, −1 * damping.rate * 1/samplerate);
q = sin(freq * 1/samplerate) * power(e, −1 * damping.rate * 1/samplerate);
a = initial.amplitude;
b = 0;
repeat for duration.in.secs/samplerate: anew = a * p − b * q;
bnew = b * p + a * q; a = anew;
b = bnew; output = anew; end repeat;
```

10.2.7   *Breaking, bouncing, and spilling*

The impact algorithm can serve as a fundamental element in algorithms used to synthesize more complex sounds. For instance, an early example of analysis and synthesis of sound-producing events is a study of breaking and bouncing sounds presented by Warren and Verbrugge (1984). In this study, they used acoustic analyses and a qualitative physical analysis to examine the auditory patterns that characterize these events, and they verified their results by testing subjects on synthetic sounds.

Consider the mechanics of a bottle bouncing on a surface (Figure 10.3 A). Each time the bottle hits the surface, it makes an impact sound that depends on its shape, size, and material (as discussed previously). Energy is dissipated with each bounce so that, in general, the time between bounces and the force of each impact becomes less. Thus, bouncing sounds should be characterized by a repetitive series of impact sounds with decreasing period and amplitude.

When a bottle breaks, on the other hand, it separates into several pieces of various sizes and shapes (Figure 10.3 B). Thus, a breaking sound should be characterized by an initial impact sound followed by several different, overlapping bouncing sounds, each with its own frequency makeup and period.

Acoustic analyses of bouncing and breaking sounds confirm this informal physical analysis. In addition, Warren and Verbrugge (1984) found that people were able to distinguish tokens of bouncing and breaking sounds that were constructed by using these rules to splice tapes of impact sounds together.

BOUNCING AND BREAKING

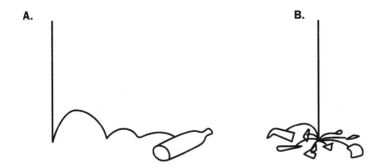

Figure 10.3 Bouncing (A) and breaking (B) sounds are characterized by the temporal patterning of a series of impacts.

Source: After Warren and Verbrugge (1984).

10.2.7.1 Synthesized breaking, bouncing, and spilling

To create bouncing sounds, then, we need simply embed the impact algorithm in another that calls it at logarithmically decaying intervals. To create breaking sounds, the bouncing algorithm is embedded in another algorithm that calls it with parameters specifying sources of different sizes at times corresponding to several logarithmically decaying time series.

Several new event parameters become relevant for these algorithms: the initial height of the virtual object is indicated by the time between the first and second bounce, its elasticity by the percentage difference of delays between bounces, and the severity of breaking by the number of pieces produced. In addition, the asymmetry of the perceived object can be varied by adding randomness to the overall temporal pattern.

It becomes clear upon listening to sounds synthesized using this algorithm that although Warren and Verbrugge (1984) claimed that information for breaking and bouncing depends only on temporal patterning, the perceived event depends on the virtual materials involved as well. For instance, if impacts specifying wooden objects are produced in a temporal pattern typical of breaking, we are liable to hear spilling rather than breaking. Similarly, if each of several virtual objects has different material properties, we again hear several spilling objects rather than breaking.

In sum, the impact algorithm described previously can be used not only to generate the sounds made by mallets of different hardnesses striking virtual objects of a wide variety of shapes, sizes, and materials but can also serve as the basis for more complex bouncing, breaking, and spilling sounds. As such, it serves as a research tool that allows the space of such sounds to be explored. Moreover, it provides an efficient method for generating families of related auditory icons. For instance, parameterized impact, bouncing, breaking, and spilling sounds might be used to differentiate and provide details about the results of actions involving icons, windows, containers, and so forth.

10.2.8 From impacts to scraping

The sounds made by impacts and patterns of impacts are generally useful for creating auditory icons, but it is desirable to have access to sounds made by a wider range of events. In particular, it would be useful to generate the sounds made by the same object being interacted with in different ways. Using such algorithms, auditory interface designers might map a particular file to a particular object and then hit, bounce, or scrape it, depending on the relevant computer interaction.

In order to create such algorithms, it is necessary to separate the specification of a virtual object from that of the interaction that causes it to produce sound. This turns out to be possible because objects tend to vibrate only at certain invariant resonant frequencies. For example, the spectrogram in Figure 10.4 shows the sound made by a piece of glass being hit and then scraped across a rough surface. Note that despite the different temporal patterns of the sounds, the resonant

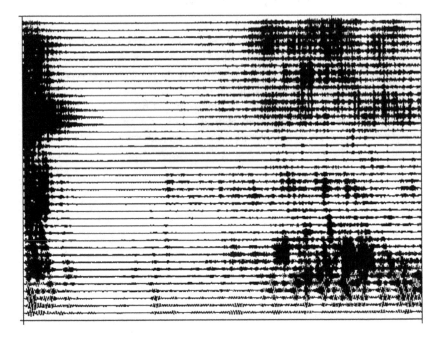

Figure 10.4 Spectrogram of a piece of glass being hit and then scraped: the resonant frequencies remain invariant over different interactions.

modes of each are the same. These modes specify the object, then, while interactions determine the temporal pattern and amount of energy introduced to each.

Because the effects of interactions and objects are distinct, each can be modeled separately. The resonant modes of a virtual object may be modeled as a bank of filters that allow energy to pass at particular frequencies. Interactions, then, can be specified by the pattern of energy passed through the filter bank.

10.2.8.1 *Modeling objects as filter banks*

A simple formula for a bank of one-pole filters is as follows:

$$yn = l_m : F_m(c1_m x_n + c2_m y_{n-1} - c3_m y_{n-2}) \tag{10.3}$$

F_m is an amplitude scalar for partial m, y_n is the nth output, and x_n is the nth input.

$$c1_m = (1 - c3_m)\overline{[(1 - c2m2)/4c3m]}$$
$$c2_m = (4c3_m \cos(2\Pi f_m))/(c3_m + 1)$$
$$c3m = e^{-2\Pi b_m}$$

f_m is the peak frequency, and b_m is the peak bandwidth of partial m.

The parameters used to control the impact algorithm can also be used to control this sort of filter bank. However, manipulating filter bandwidths to control damping actually provides more information for material than do simple manipulations of sine wave damping. Bandwidth *b* is proportional to damping: the narrower the resonance peak of the filter, the longer the resonant response to excitation. This correlation between damping and the smearing of partials in frequency space corresponds well to the characteristics of sounds made by materials such as wood or metal (Gaver and Norman 1988; Wildes and Richards 1988).

10.2.8.2   *Simulating interactions with input waveforms*

A virtual object can be defined by the characteristics of the filter bank described previously. The waveform passes through the filter bank, then models the interaction that causes the object to sound. In this section, we describe two sorts of input waveforms that we have explored. The first models impact forces, the second scraping.

When objects are struck, the input forces are characterized by short impulses such as those shown in Figure 10.5. The energy of such impulses is spread out over many frequencies: the pulse width reflects low-frequency energy, while its angularity reflects high-frequency components. This corresponds to the characterization of mallet hardness by Freed (1986). Hard mallets introduce force suddenly to an object, deforming it quickly, and thus introduce a relatively high proportion of high-frequency energy to the resonant object. Soft mallets, in contrast, deform as they hit the object, introducing energy relatively slowly, and thus, the corresponding impulses are characterized by a high proportion of

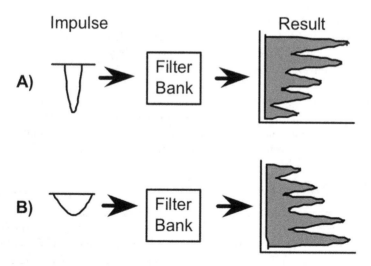

Figure 10.5 Sample impulse waveforms characterizing different impacts (see text).

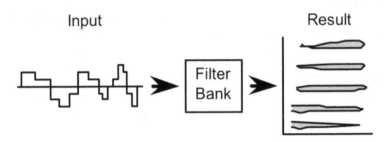

Figure 10.6 A sample force waveform characterizing a scrape with increasing speed.

low-frequency energy. Shaping the impulses used to excite a filter bank, then, is a physically realistic way to control perceived mallet hardness.

When an object is scraped, force is applied more continuously. An informal physical analysis suggests that the pattern of force on an object generated as it is scraped across a surface can be approximated by band-limited noise, where the center frequency of the noise corresponds to dragging speed and the bandwidth to the roughness of the texture (see Figure 10.6). Although these parameters are only approximate, being less well-motivated physically or psychologically than those used to model impacts, experience shows that a wide variety of realistic scraping noises can be produced using these heuristics.

For more refined models of friction and scraping, the reader is referred to Serafin (2004).

In sum, the filter-based algorithm described in this section is based on a physically plausible model of sound-producing events. By separating the parts of the model that specify the object from those specifying the interaction, a wide range of virtual sound-producing events can be simulated. The model can create any of the impact sounds that the algorithm described in the last section can. In addition, it can also be used to create a variety of scraping sounds (and potentially, any other sound involving solid objects).

The ability to generate the sounds of the same object being caused to sound by different interactions offered by this algorithm has great potential for the creation of auditory interfaces. It allows the design of parameterized auditory icons in which the same interface object (e.g., a file) might make sounds indicating a variety of events (e.g., selecting, dragging, opening).

10.2.9 *Machine sounds*

Just as complex interactions such as scraping can be modeled by a few summarizing parameters, so might still more complex events be captured succinctly by high-level descriptions. For instance, another class of sounds useful for auditory icons are those made by small machines. Sampled machine sounds were used effectively in the ARKola simulation (Gaver et al. 1991), indicating ongoing processes that were not visible on the screen. More generally, they might be used to indicate background processes such as printing or compiling in more traditional multiprocessing systems.

A detailed account of the mechanical physics of machinery seems prohibitively difficult. But just as the scraping waveforms described previously model the overall parameters of a complex force rather than each of the contributing details, so an approximate model of machines might capture some of the high-level characteristics of the sounds they produce. In particular, three aspects of machine sounds seem relevant for modeling: First, the overall size of the machine is likely to be reflected in the frequencies of sounds it produces. Second, most machines involve a number of rotating parts that can be expected to produce repetitive contributions to the overall sound. Third, the work done by the machine can be expected to affect the complexity of the sound.

10.2.9.1   FM synthesis of machine sounds

One of the authors has been exploring an efficient algorithm for creating a variety of machine-like sounds that capture these properties. The basic strategy is to synthesize a sound using complex tones that vary in a repetitive way, indicating cyclical motion. The rate at which the virtual machine is working, then, can be indicated by repetition speed, the size of the virtual machine by the base frequency, and the amount of work by the bandwidth of the sounds (see Figure 10.7).

This class of sound may be synthesized efficiently using frequency modulation (FM) synthesis (Chowning 1973). FM synthesis involves modulating the frequency of a carrier wave with the output of a modulating wave. This produces a complex tone with a number of frequency components spaced equally around the carrier wave and separated from one another by the modulating frequency. The number of components (and thus the bandwidth of the sound) depends on the amplitude of the modulating wave (see Figure 10.8). Thus,

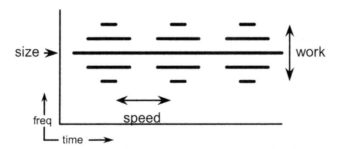

Figure 10.7 Machine sounds can be characterized by a complex wave that varies repetitively over time.

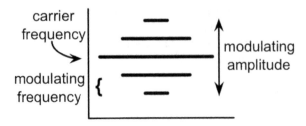

Figure 10.8 FM synthesis, which allows simple control over complex sounds, is well suited for generating machine-like sounds.

machine sounds can be created simply by associating the carrier frequency with the size of the virtual machine, setting the maximum amplitude of the modulator to the amount of work done by the virtual machine, and modulating the amplitude of the modulator according to the speed of the virtual machine.

The resulting sounds are pitched humming noises that pulse at the speed of the virtual machine. When "work" is low, the throbbing is subtle; when it is high, it becomes quite pronounced. Moreover, the quality of the sounds can be varied by changing the ratio of modulating to carrier frequency: when the two are an integral multiple of one another, the resulting sound is harmonic; when they are not, the sound is inharmonic or noisy. Using this algorithm, then, a wide variety of machine-like sounds can be produced for use as indicators of ongoing processes in multiprocessing systems.

10.3   Physics-based simulations

The sound synthesis simulations presented in the previous sections have been widely investigated and also expanded in the computer music community, where simulations of everyday sounds have gone hand in hand with simulations of musical instruments, the latter having seen a wider development.

Sound synthesis by physical models refers to synthesis techniques where the sound is generated by examining the physics of sound production mechanism and is represented using a mathematical equation that is numerically solved. From the first simulations of vibrating strings (Hiller and Ruiz 1971) to the computationally efficient digital waveguides (Smith 1992), several algorithms have been proposed in the last three decades. Here we focus on the algorithms that have been adopted to simulate everyday sounds. The readers interested in learning about physical models to simulate musical instruments are referred to Bilbao (2009) and Smith (2010).

Back in the late '80s, Adrien (1991) proposed modal synthesis as a synthesis technique that considers the modes (the main resonances of any vibrating object). Modal synthesis was adopted by Van Den Doel and colleagues (Van

Den Doel and Pai 2003; Van Den Doel et al. 2001) to simulate the interaction between several everyday objects. In modal synthesis, a vibrating object is modeled by a bank of damped harmonic oscillators that are excited by an external stimulus. The frequencies and dampings of the oscillators are determined by the geometry and material properties (such as elasticity) of the object, and the coupling gains are determined by the location of the force applied to the object. The modal synthesis model is physically well-motivated, as the linear partial differential equation for a vibrating system, with appropriate boundary conditions, has as solutions a superposition of vibration modes.

Perry Cook published an entire book on the topic of sound synthesis with a focus on interactive applications (Cook 2002b). The book is targeted at game developers and HCI researchers who are interested in using efficient physics-based simulations in their implementations. The book adopts several synthesis techniques with a focus on computational efficiency and accessibility to a larger audience. Of particular interest are Cook's physically informed sonic models (Cook 1997). Such models simulate systems where sound is produced by the random collision of many small objects. A good example would be a model of maracas in the world of percussive instruments; however, these models can also be extended to everyday sonic events such as walking on snow or any other activity where several small objects are pseudorandomly interacting together. The idea of linking sound event perception to action has also guided recent designs of technologies for sound and interaction design, focusing on the model of interaction itself rather than sound engines based on conventional sound synthesis techniques. For example, the Sound Design Toolkit (SDT) (Monache et al. 2010) is a software package consisting of a set of physics-based sound synthesis models, especially addressed to sonic interaction design (SID) research and education. SDT is a publicly available software package providing a set of physics-based models for interactive sound synthesis. The palette includes several families of sound models, such as contact phenomena between solids (impact, friction, rolling, crumpling, bouncing, breaking) and liquid-related events and processes (bubbles, dripping, burbling, pouring, splashing). The development of the sound synthesis engines, graphical user interfaces (GUI), and control layers advance together with the realization of interactive workbenches and the evaluation of the system in workshop settings. The authors of the SDT claim that physics-based approach results to be closer to designers' thinking: sounds can be directly described in terms of configurations, geometries, materials and their properties, dynamics of gestures to the point that allows a certain immediate "visualization," and association of the sketched sound with its interactive context, not to mention an intuitive sensory connection with touch. In the SDT, the modal resonator approach is used to simulate the vibrating objects, while more complex simulations of interactions, such as impact and friction (Avanzini and Rocchesso 2001; Serafin 2004), are implemented. The SDT is a modular system that uses physical and modal synthesis to generate sounds based on physical interactions of different bodies and materials. The toolkit is designed as a modular system of patches, with independent modules for objects (such as "metallic ball"), physical properties (such as "weight"), and actions (such as "hitting"). The versatility and modularity of Max/MSP allow quick adaptations to various sensors and systems. Although very versatile and powerful in terms of sound design possibilities, in its current version, the SDT focuses mainly on sound design, and it does not provide a quick and intuitive software package to realize gestural-sound mapping using motion sensors, something that, for example, can be useful in participatory workshops on embodied SID. For producing high-quality sound synthesis, nowadays finite difference schemes (Bilbao 2009; Bilbao et al. 2020) are the most successful techniques. While the effort of deriving physics-based models that are accurate, stable, and efficient is important and laudable, for HCI it is equally important to have simple models that capture the most relevant sonic phenomena in everyday interactions. An alternative approach was offered by Andy Farnell in his book *Designing Sound* (Farnell 2010). *Designing Sound* offers a practical approach to design procedurally based interactive sound effects using the software Pure Data (Puckette et al. 1997). The simulations presented in the book can be considered physically inspired because Farnell provides an intuitive physical explanation of several phenomena, such as bouncing, hitting, and car horns, followed by a possible implementation in Pure Data. The main goal is perceptual fidelity rather than physical fidelity.

10.4   Communicating with sound models

As previously mentioned, another active field of research is the so-called New Interfaces for Musical Expression (NIME), where the inquiries concern how to interact and control sonic material, including also sound models described in the previous sections.

MIDI (Musical Instrument Digital Interface) is a protocol of communication between music devices. MIDI was developed by several commercial synthesizer manufacturers to allow synthesizers to be connected together so that they could share control information, such as the gestures of musicians.

MIDI has many advantages, some being that the file sizes of MIDI data are small, and effects can be applied to individual instruments. However, MIDI also has limited bandwidth and precision.

A popular alternative is Open Sound Control (OSC) (Freed 1997). OSC is an open, efficient, transport-independent, message-based protocol developed for communication among computers, sound synthesizers, and other multimedia devices. OSC is a machine and operating system neutral protocol and readily implementable on constrained, embedded systems. OSC's symbolic names and open-ended hierarchical namespace grew out of frustration with addressing limitations inherent in protocols such as MIDI that rely on short, fixed-length bit fields. One of the nice features of OSC is the ability to define different data types that can be transmitted in a message. Although it is possible to send any data type of any resolution using MIDI system exclusive messages, OSC has provided a standard for software and hardware developers from different vendors. OSC also helps to solve some of the issues outlined by Wessel and Wright (2002), such as latency and the lack of high rate continuous control of traditional interfaces. OSC has, therefore, provided some very useful and powerful features that were not previously available in MIDI, including an intuitive addressing scheme, the ability to schedule future events, and variable data types.

10.5   Evaluation of sound synthesis methods

One of the aims of sound synthesis is to produce realistic and controllable systems for artificially replicating real-world sounds while maintaining a level of parametric control, which is not possible when using sampled sounds. Evaluation of the sound synthesis algorithm is an essential element of the process since it helps to understand both how well the synthesis method performs and how we can improve our system.

Evaluation of a sound synthesis system can take many different forms. Back in 1995, Jaffe presented ten different methods for the evaluation of synthesis techniques (Jaffe 1995). The first four criteria regard the usability of the parameters (e.g., their intuitiveness), if their changes are perceivable, if they are mapped to physical parameters, and if they are well behaved. Other criteria regard the sound produced (e.g., if it maintains its identity during variations), if all classes of sounds can be produced, and if analysis techniques exist for deriving parameters for real-world models. The remaining criteria focus on efficiency and implementation (e.g., how efficient is the technique, if it has an undesirable, unavoidable latency, and how sparse is its parameter control stream). Evaluation of controls and control parameters can be found, for example, in the works of Rocchesso and Fontana (2003), Merer et al. (2013), and Selfridge et al. (2017); human perception of different timbre was investigated by Aramaki et al. (2011), sound identification by Ballas (1993) and McDermott and Simoncelli (2011), and sonic realism by Moffat and Reiss (2018).

One of the most important aspects of evaluating a synthesis method is evaluating the sonic quality of the sound produced. In order to assess sound quality, it is important to perform listening tests with human participants – for example, recording samples and comparing them to the equivalent simulations performed with the synthesis model (Moffat and Reiss 2018; Bech and Zacharov 2006).

Such listening tests have several drawbacks. First of all, the person exposed to the sounds is a mere passive listener. This prevents the model from being used in a real-world context, therefore preventing the experiment from having ecological validity. In addition to this problem, an additional limitation is that the real-time control of the model is missing, so the nuances of how its different parameters vary according to the gestures of the performer are not taken into account. Such listening tests can be compared to the methodologies of the first wave of HCI described at the beginning of this book. Instead, proper evaluations of the sound synthesis tools should move toward second- or even third-wave HCI techniques. Evaluating the control and interaction of a synthesis engine is indeed a vital aspect. There are numerous methods for evaluating these sonic interactions, and in many cases, the control evaluation has to be designed bespoke to the synthesis methods and parametric controls (Heinrichs and McPherson 2014). User listening tests, where participants are able to interact with the synthesis engine through some mapping layer, can be performed to evaluate a series of criteria.

10.6   Conclusions

The algorithms described here allow the synthesis of a variety of everyday sounds specified in terms of attributes and dimensions of the events that cause them. Because they are based on a combination of acoustic and physical analyses and use relatively sophisticated synthesis techniques, they capture a great degree of the richness and complexity of their naturally produced counterparts. Because they are specialized for the classes of events they are to simulate, they are efficient and can generate sounds in real time on many computers. Finally, because they have been designed with potential applications in mind, the events they simulate are useful for auditory icons.

These algorithms vary in their physical accuracy. Some are based on quantitative physical analyses, while others are based on more qualitative, informal descriptions of events. Moreover, even the quantitative analyses are only approximate. For instance, the physics of a struck bar of wood is much more complex than implied by the simple account given here. Insofar as these algorithms are approximate, the sounds they produce will differ from those made by real events.

Nonetheless, these algorithms do produce quite realistic sounds. Listeners comment that they have the impression of hearing an actual event rather than a synthesized sound. Insofar as the sounds do differ from those made by real events, they may be considered "cartoon sounds," sounds that capture the relevant features of their sources just as visual caricatures (or graphical computer icons) capture those of theirs. For the purposes of simulating sound-producing events, then, these algorithms are adequate. For the purpose of creating auditory icons, they show great potential, combining flexibility, intuitive controls, efficiency, and relevance.

We have specified some algorithms here in sufficient detail that readers may implement and explore them in the hope that they will spur further research on parameterized auditory icons or that they can be adapted for interactive, multisensory experiences. Other algorithms have been provided with pointers to articles describing them in detail or to freely available software packages to experiment with. These algorithms certainly open many possibilities for the design of rich auditory interfaces. Impact and scraping sounds can be used to increase the tangibility of graphical objects in direct manipulation interfaces. Bouncing, breaking, and spilling sounds can be used to indicate events in virtual reality systems. Machine sounds might allow us to hear a remote printer as our job reaches the queue, and the characteristics of the sound might tell us how fast the job is printing or how much time it will take. In sum, using these algorithms, we can design interfaces that we can listen to the way we do to the everyday world. As a final note, as mentioned previously, sound synthesis techniques have been merely created to imitate existing musical instruments or everyday sounds. But why just focus only on mere imitation? What about using technologies to extend the sonic possibilities offered by the real world? As Mathews (1963) stated in his seminal paper introducing the first sounds generated by a computer,

> There are no theoretical limitations to the performance of the computer as a source of musical sounds, in contrast to the performance of ordinary instruments. At present, the range of computer music is limited principally by cost and by our knowledge of psychoacoustics. These limits are rapidly receding.

11 Summary and future research

Sounds have been and will continue to be a part of our computing world, just as they are a part of our broader everyday world. From the reassuring click of the keys we hit on keyboards to the steady hum of a healthy processor, sounds provide a multitude of clues about our environment. The topics and work presented here represent a start at designing the use of nonspeech sounds in the computer-human interface. In this way, sounds can play an expanded role in presenting information, and we – designers, developers, and users of interfaces – can take a more active role in accessing and using sounds.

The work presented in this book has shown that sounds already contribute to our ability to gather information about the world around us. Sounds can be used effectively to present information in computing environments and applications. Sounds have the potential to be structured to represent complex information. Sounds, visuals, and touch may also play complementary roles in providing information. Technologies for producing sounds are both capable and available, and much is already known about the nature and perception of sounds. Our challenge is to integrate that knowledge and technology into useable and useful computer-human interfaces.

Consider some areas of current research, such as interactive sonification and sound for multimodal interfaces and augmented, virtual, and mixed realities. Gaver's pioneering work considers how sounds are used in our everyday lives and can be synthesized by computer (Gaver 1989a); since then, much more of this sort of work has appeared in several venues (Van Den Doel et al. 2001; Klatzky et al. 2000; Rocchesso and Fontana 2003; Polotti 2008). Studies of everyday listening provide an understanding of the way in which sounds are currently used and inform decisions about the ways in which sounds might be used. In Chapter 2, we have provided a brief summary of issues in acoustics and psychoacoustics that are likely to be relevant to auditory interfaces. But we also need to explore the perception of higher-level musical structures in order to assess their potential to encode information for users. For instance, Blattner et al. (1989) suggested that variations in motives can be used to signal complex information. What sorts of variation will prove most useful, easiest to relate to the original, and best associated with a particular meaning? Patterson (1982) studied the perceived urgency of sounds, but what about their annoyance?

DOI: 10.4324/9781003260202-11

Understanding how people listen to and react to music seems likely to aid us in designing effective and aesthetic auditory cues. Finally, as prototypes of various applications of sounds appear, we need to observe the resulting work practice and the use of sounds in that practice.

Sounds may complement or work with other interface information; they may replace other interface feedback; they may exist simultaneously but independently of other interface outputs. Bly (1982) and Mezrich et al. (1984) noted that sounds may be particularly well suited to displaying multidimensional data and may make some aspects of data more apparent than graphic displays do. In their pioneering work, Mansur et al. (1985) and Gaver (1986) noted that sounds are useful in that they do not rely on the directed attention of the user; this is, of course, why so many alerts are auditory (Patterson 1982). Gaver further pointed out that sounds are useful for displaying information about changing events and about occluded events or internal mechanisms of objects. Future work will address the question of whether auditory, visual, and tactile components can be designed to create one coherent informational system.

Certainly, auditory interfaces offer potential aid to visually disabled users in gaining access to computers. Morrison and Lunney (in Bly et al. 1985) showed that visually disabled students are able to learn to use auditory representations of infrared spectrograms, and Edwards (1989) created an auditory word processor that visually disabled people could use. This research has been taken further and conveys spatial information using sounds – since then, several auditory interfaces that allow the visually disabled to navigate have been proposed, such as Microsoft Soundscape.

It is interesting that recent artistic practices such as live coding have been making sound creation and manipulation more similar to iterative design processes, with initial sketches being shared and gradually evolving into complex, refined objects. The specialized programming languages and environments for computer music are evolving in the direction of coding as sketching, possibly with direct export of results to larger software frameworks where a variety of sound models can be hosted and made to interact with each other. Machine learning is also revolutionizing the way sound effects are generated, as the example presented by Ghose and Prevost (2020) shows. AutoFoley is a fully automated deep-learning tool that can be used to synthesize a representative audio track for videos. The algorithm is capable of precise recognition of actions as well as inter-frame relations in fast-moving video clips by incorporating an interpolation technique and Temporal Relational Networks (TRN). Several machine learning techniques applied to sound processing, such as the recently introduced differential digital signal processing (DDSP) from Google (Engel et al. 2020), also show promises in how to synthesize sounds for several applications, including auditory interfaces.

As this book shows, the field of auditory interfaces is far from new; however, relatively little work in this domain has yet focused on aspects of inclusion and diversity. The communities focusing on the creation of New Interfaces for Musical Expression (NIME), Digital Musical Instruments (DMIs), and Digital

Audio Effects (DAFX) still consist of a rather homogeneous group of researchers, creators, and practitioners. Some groups are not well represented, and the field is not diverse in the sense that people from various cultural and financial backgrounds, ethnicities, gender identities, and diverse abilities take an active part. Nevertheless, today's increasingly inexpensive tools and systems readily available for the development of interactive interfaces make it an excellent platform for promoting music-making for all. The dissertation of Frid (2019) is a good starting point in this direction.

The increasing awareness of the connections between body gestures, everyday sounds, and human vocalizations is likely to produce new forms of interactions and new tools for designing multisensory objects. In particular, sketching is an expression of biological motion, which can be described by laws that produce visible as well as audible effects (Thoret et al. 2016), with the senses affecting each other for the construction of consistent audiovisual objects. Understanding hand and vocal gestures opens up a truly multisensory domain of sketching.

The sensory convergence of visual and physical metaphors may be key to successful discoveries and to a designerly form of knowledge that can be just as important as scientific understanding (Millet et al. 2013).

As was the case in a survey from two decades ago, examining the audio knowledge of HCI researchers, there is likely still a lack of knowledge in acoustics and music terminology, which prevents the field from growing (see Lumsden and Brewster [2001]).

Given that both musical and everyday sounds are difficult to design, how will new "sound palettes" be created and distributed? The answers to many of these questions will rely on the user model of the sounds, which in turn depends on many of the other research areas suggested here: the kinds of sounds (those that are manipulated and perceived in terms of their acoustic properties or their sources), the applications of sounds, and the relationship between sounds and the other senses.

The creation of auditory displays for the interface is an ongoing challenge. Among the many future challenges for researchers are the design and evaluation of sound for mobile devices and sounds in ecological settings, the use of spatial audio in virtual and augmented realities, and the consideration of increased and widespread usability and personalization of interactions.

Much of the sound produced by today's technology fails to exploit the sophisticated abilities of human hearing. We hope that this book will facilitate this process.

Bibliography

Abe, K, K Ozawa, Y Suzuki, and T Sone. 1999. The influence of verbal information on perception of environmental sounds. *The Journal of the Acoustical Society of Japan* 10: 697–706.

Adams, Mags D, Neil S Bruce, William J Davies, Rebecca Cain, Paul Jennings, Angus Carlyle, Peter Cusack, Ken Hume, C Plack, et al. 2008. *Soundwalking as a methodology for understanding soundscapes.* http://usir.salford.ac.uk/id/eprint/2461/.

Adrien, Jean-Marie. 1991. The missing link: Modal synthesis. In *Representations of musical signals*, 269–298. The MIT Press.

Aesthetic Research Centre of Canada, Barry Truax, and World Soundscape Project. 1978. *The world soundscape project's handbook for acoustic ecology.* ARC Publications: Aesthetic Research Centre: World Soundscape Project.

Aglioti, Salvatore M, and Mariella Pazzaglia. 2010. Representing actions through their sound. *Experimental Brain Research* 206 (2): 141–151.

Alty, James L, and Dimitrios I Rigas. 1998. Communicating graphical information to blind users using music: The role of context. In *Proceedings of the SIGCHI conference on human factors in computing systems*, 574–581. ACM.

American National Standards Institute (1973). *American National Psychoacoustical Terminology.* S3.20. New York: American National Standards Association.

American Institute of Graphic Arts. 1982. *AIGA graphic design USA: The annual of the Aamerican Institute of Graphic Arts*, Vol. 3. Watson-Guptill Publications.

Ananthapadmanaban, T, and V Radhakrishnan. 1982. An investigation of the role of surface irregularities in the noise spectrum of rolling and sliding contacts. *Wear* 83 (2): 399–409.

Aramaki, Mitsuko, and Richard Kronland-Martinet. 2006. Analysis-synthesis of impact sounds by real-time dynamic filtering. *IEEE Transactions on Audio, Speech, and Language Processing* 14 (2): 695–705.

Aramaki, Mitsuko, Richard Kronland-Martinet, and Sølvi Ystad. 2011. Perceptual control of environmental sound synthesis. In *Speech, sound and music processing: Embracing research in India*, 172–186. Springer.

Arons, Barry. 1992. A review of the cocktail party effect. *Journal of the American Voice I/O Society* 12 (7): 35–50.

Attias, Hagai, and Christoph E Schreiner. 1997. Temporal low-order statistics of natural sounds. In *Advances in neural information processing systems 9 (NIPS 1996)*, 27–33. The MIT Press.

Aura, Karine, Guillaume Lemaitre, and Patrick Susini. 2008. Verbal imitations of sound events enable recognition of the imitated sound events. *The Journal of the Acoustical Society of America* 123 (5): 3414–3414.

Avanzini, Federico, Amalia De Götzen, Simone Spagnol, and Antonio Rodá. 2009. Integrating auditory feedback in motor rehabilitation systems. In *Proceedings of international conference on multimodal interfaces for skills transfer (skills09)*, Vol. 232, 53–58. http://www.dei.unipd.it/~avanzini/downloads/paper/avanzini_skills09.pdf.

Avanzini, Federico, and Davide Rocchesso. 2001. Modeling collision sounds: Nonlinear contact force. In *Proceedings of COST-G6 conference digital audio effects (dafx-01)*, 61–66. dafx.de.

Backus, John. 1977. *The acoustical foundations of music*. Norton.

Baldan, Stefano, Stefano Delle Monache, and Davide Rocchesso. 2017. The sound design toolkit. *SoftwareX* 6: 255–260.

Ballas, James A. 1993. Common factors in the identification of an assortment of brief everyday sounds. *Journal of Experimental Psychology: Human Perception and Performance* 19 (2): 250.

Ballas, James A, and James H Howard Jr. 1987. Interpreting the language of environmental sounds. *Environment and Behavior* 19 (1): 91–114.

Ballas, James A, Martin J Sliwinski, and John P Harding III. 1986. Uncertainty and response time in identifying nonspeech sounds. *The Journal of the Acoustical Society of America* 79 (S1): 47–47.

Ballora, Mark, Bruce Pennycook, Plamen C Ivanov, Leon Glass, and Ary L Goldberger. 2004. Heart rate sonification: A new approach to medical diagnosis. *Leonardo* 37 (1): 41–46.

Barrass, Stephen. 1996. Earbenders: Using stories about listening to design auditory interfaces. In *Proceedings of the first Asia-Pacific conference on human-computer interaction APCHI*, Vol. 96. ACM.

Barrass, Stephen. 2013. Zizi: The affectionate couch and the interactive affect design. In *Sonic interaction design*, 235. The MIT Press.

Barrass, Stephen. 2016. Diagnosing blood pressure with acoustic sonification singing bowls. *International Journal of Human-Computer Studies* 85: 68–71.

Barrass, Stephen, and Gregory Kramer. 1999. Using sonification. *Multimedia Systems* 7 (1): 23–31.

Barreto, Armando B, Julie A Jacko, and Peterjohn Hugh. 2007. Impact of spatial auditory feedback on the efficiency of iconic human-computer interfaces under conditions of visual impairment. *Computers in Human Behavior* 23 (3): 1211–1231.

Bech, Søren, and Nick Zacharov. 2006. *Perceptual audio evaluation: Theory, method and application*. Wiley Online Library.

Bederson, Benjamin B. 1995. Audio augmented reality: A prototype automated tour guide. In *Conference companion on human factors in computing systems*, 210–211. ACM.

Begault, Durand R, and Leonard J Trejo. 2000. *3-d sound for virtual reality and multimedia*. NASA Technical Report.

Begault, Durand R, and Elizabeth M Wenzel. 1992. Techniques and applications for binaural sound manipulation. *The International Journal of Aviation Psychology* 2 (1): 1–22.

Benade, Arthur H. 1990. *Fundamentals of musical acoustics*. Courier Corporation.

Berger, Christopher C, Mar Gonzalez-Franco, Ana Tajadura-Jiménez, Dinei Florencio, and Zhengyou Zhang. 2018. Generic HRTFs may be good enough in virtual reality: Improving source localization through cross-modal plasticity. *Frontiers in Neuroscience* 12: 21.

Bernsen, Jens. 1999. *Lyd i design*. Dansk Design Center.

Bilbao, Stefan D. 2009. *Numerical sound synthesis*. Wiley Online Library.

Bilbao, Stefan D, Charlotte Desvages, Michele Ducceschi, Brian Hamilton, Reginald Harrison-Harsley, Alberto Torin, and Craig Webb. 2020. Physical modeling, algorithms, and sound synthesis: The ness project. *Computer Music Journal* 43 (2–3): 15–30.

Biocca, Frank, Jin Kim, and Yung Choi. 2001. Visual touch in virtual environments: An exploratory study of presence, multimodal interfaces, and cross-modal sensory illusions. *Presence: Teleoperators & Virtual Environments* 10 (3): 247–265.

Blattner, Meera M, Robert M Greenberg, and Minao Kamegai. 1992. Listening to the turbulence: An example of scientific audiolization. In *Multimedia interface design*, 87–102. ACM.

Blattner, Meera M, Denise A Sumikawa, and Robert M Greenberg. 1989. Earcons and icons: Their structure and common design principles. *Human-Computer Interaction* 4 (1): 11–44.

Blauert, Jens. 1983. *Spatial hearing: The psychophysics of human sound source localization*. The MIT Press.

Blauert, Jens. 1997. *Spatial hearing: The psychophysics of human sound localization*. The MIT Press.

Bly, Sara A. 1982. Sound and computer information presentation. *Technical report*, Lawrence Livermore National Lab, CA (USA). California University.

Bly, Sara A. 1994. Multivariate data mappings. In *Santa Fe Institute studies in the sciences of complexity-proceedings*, Vol. 18, 405–405. Addison-Wesley Publishing Co.

Bly, Sara A, Steven P Frysinger, David Lunney, Douglass L Mansur, Joseph J Mezrich, and Robert C Morrison. 1985. Communicating with sound (panel session. ACM *SIGCHI Bulletin* 16 (4): 115–119.

Bødker, Susanne. 2006. When second wave HCI meets third wave challenges. In *Proceedings of the 4th nordic conference on human-computer interaction: Changing roles*, 1–8. ACM.

Boff, Kenneth R, and Janet E Lincoln. 1988. User's guide engineering data compendium human perception and performance. *Technical report*, Harry G Armstrong Aerospace Medical Research Lab Wright-Patterson AFB OH.

Bonebright, Terry L, and Michael A Nees. 2007. *Memory for auditory icons and earcons with localization cues*. Georgia Institute of Technology.

Bosi, Marina. 1990. An interactive real-time system for the control of sound localization. *Computer Music Journal* 14 (4): 59–64.

Bowe, Frank. 2000. *Universal design in education: Teaching nontraditional students*. Greenwood Publishing Group.

Boyer, Eric. 2015. *Continuous auditory feedback for sensorimotor learning*. PhD diss, Paris 6.

Brazil, Eoin. 2009. A review of methods and frameworks for sonic interaction design: Exploring existing approaches. In *Auditory display*, 41–67. Springer.

Bregman, Albert S. 1994. *Auditory scene analysis: The perceptual organization of sound*. The MIT Press.

Brewster, Stephen A. 1998. Using nonspeech sounds to provide navigation cues. ACM *Transactions on Computer-Human Interaction (TOCHI)* 5 (3): 224–259.

Brewster, Stephen A, VP Raty, and A Kortekangas. 1996. *Using earcons to provide navigational cues in a complex menu hierarchy Department of Computing Science*. University of Glasgow.

Brewster, Stephen A, Peter C Wright, and Alastair DN Edwards. 1994. A detailed investigation into the effectiveness of earcons. In *Santa Fe Institute studies in the sciences of complexity-proceedings*, Vol. 18, 471–471. Addison-Wesley Publishing Co.

Brewster, Stephen A, Peter C Wright, and Alistair DN Edwards. 1995. Experimentally derived guidelines for the creation of earcons. In *Adjunct proceedings of HCI*, Vol. 95, 155–159. ACM.

Brock, Derek, Janet L Stroup, and James A Ballas. 2002. Effects of 3d auditory display on dual task performance in a simulated multiscreen watchstation environment. In *Proceedings of the human factors and ergonomics society annual meeting*, Vol. 46, 1570–1573. SAGE Publications.

Brown, Megan L, Sandra L Newsome, and Ephraim P Glinert. 1989. An experiment into the use of auditory cues to reduce visual workload. *ACM SIGCHI Bulletin* 20 (SI): 339–346.

Bruce, Vicki, Patrick R Green, and Mark A Georgeson. 2003. *Visual perception: Physiology, psychology, & ecology*. Psychology Press.

Burr, David, Martin S Banks, and Maria Concetta Morrone. 2009. Auditory dominance over vision in the perception of interval duration. *Experimental Brain Research* 198 (1): 49.

Butler, Robert A, and Richard A Humanski. 1992. Localization of sound in the vertical plane with and without high-frequency spectral cues. *Perception & Psychophysics* 51 (2): 182–186.

Buxton, Bill. 2010. *Sketching user experiences: Getting the design right and the right design*. Morgan Kaufmann.

Buxton, William, and Tom Moran. 1990. EuroPARC's integrated interactive intermedia facility (IIIF): Early experiences. *Multi-user interfaces and applications* 11: 34.

Cabe, Patrick A, and John B Pittenger. 2000. Human sensitivity to acoustic information from vessel filling. *Journal of Experimental Psychology: Human Perception and Performance* 26 (1): 313.

Cabot, Richard C, Michael G Mino, Douglas A Dorans, Ira S Tackel, and Henry E Breed. 1976. Detection of phase shifts in harmonically related tones. *Journal of the Audio Engineering Society* 24 (7): 568–571.

Caramiaux, Baptiste, Frédéric Bevilacqua, Tommaso Bianco, Norbert Schnell, Olivier Houix, and Patrick Susini. 2014. The role of sound source perception in gestural sound description. *ACM Transactions on Applied Perception (TAP)* 11 (1): 1–19.

Cardozo, BL, and RAJM Van Lieshout. 1981. Estimates of annoyance of sounds of different character. *Applied Acoustics* 14 (5): 323–329.

Chambers, JM, MV Mathews, and FR Moore. 1974. Auditory data inspection. *Report TM*. SPIE Digital Library.

Chernoff, Herman. 1973. The use of faces to represent points in k-dimensional space graphically. *Journal of the American Statistical Association* 68 (342): 361–368.

Cherry, E Colin. 1953. Some experiments on the recognition of speech, with one and with two ears. *The Journal of the Acoustical Society of America* 25 (5): 975–979.

Chesky, Miriam A Henoch Kris, and M Henoch. 1999. Hearing loss and aging: Implications for the professional musician. *Medical Problems of Performing Artists* 14 (2): 76–79.

Childs, Edward, and Ville Pulkki. 2003. *Using multi-channel spatialization in sonification: A case study with meteorological data*. Georgia Institute of Technology.

Chion, Michel. 1983. *Guide des objets sonores: Pierre Schaffer et la recherche musicale*. Buchet/Chastel.

Chion, Michel. 1985. *Le son au cinéma*, Vol. 5. Cahiers du cinéma.

Chion, Michel. 1994. *Audio-vision: Sound on screen*. Columbia University Press.

Chowning, John M. 1971. The simulation of moving sound sources. *Journal of the Audio Engineering Society* 19 (1): 2–6.

Chowning, John M. 1973. The synthesis of complex audio spectra by means of frequency modulation. *Journal of the Audio Engineering Society* 21 (7): 526–534.

Cohen, Michael. 1993. Throwing, pitching and catching sound: Audio windowing models and modes. *International Journal of Man-Machine Studies* 39 (2): 269–304.

Cohen, Michael, Shigeaki Aoki, and Nobuo Koizumi. 1993. Augmented audio reality: Telepresence/VR hybrid acoustic environments. In *Proceedings of 1993 2nd IEEE international workshop on robot and human communication*, 361–364. IEEE.

Cohen, Michael, and Lester F Ludwig. 1991. Multidimensional audio window management. *International Journal of Man-Machine Studies* 34 (3): 319–336.

Colavita, Francis B. 1974. Human sensory dominance. *Perception & Psychophysics* 16 (2): 409–412.

Coleman, Graeme W, Catriona Macaulay, and Alan F Newell. 2008. Sonic mapping: Towards engaging the user in the design of sound for computerized artifacts. In *Proceedings of the 5th nordic conference on human-computer interaction: Building bridges*, 83–92. ACM.

Connell, Bettye Rose, Mike Jones, Ron Mace, Jim Mueller, Abir Mullick, Elaine Ostroff, Jon Sanford, Ed Steinfeld, Molly Story, and Gregg Vanderheiden. 1997. *The principles of universal design, version 2.0*. NC State University, The Center for Universal Design.

Cook, Perry R. 1997. Physically informed sonic modeling (PHISM): Synthesis of percussive sounds. *Computer Music Journal* 21 (3): 38–49.

Cook, Perry R. 1999. *Music, cognition, and computerized sound: An introduction to psychoacoustics*. The MIT Press.

Cook, Perry R. 2002a. Modeling bill's gait: Analysis and parametric synthesis of walking sounds. In *Audio engineering society conference: 22nd international conference: Virtual, synthetic, and entertainment audio*. Audio Engineering Society.

Cook, Perry R. 2002b. *Real sound synthesis for interactive applications*. CRC Press.

Cox, Trevor J. 2008. Scraping sounds and disgusting noises. *Applied Acoustics* 69 (12): 1195–1204.

Dahlbäck, Nils, Arne Jönsson, and Lars Ahrenberg. 1993. Wizard of Oz studies: Why and how. In *Proceedings of the 1st international conference on intelligent user interfaces*, 193–200. ACM.

Damasio, Antonio R. 2006. *Descartes' error*. Random House.

Davis, Mark F. 2003. History of spatial coding. *Journal of the Audio Engineering Society* 51 (6): 554–569.

Deatherage, Bruce H. 1972. Auditory and other sensory forms of information presentation. In *Human engineering guide to equipment design*. American Institute for Research.

De Campo, Alberto. 2007. *Toward a data sonification design space map*. Georgia Institute of Technology.

Delle Monache, Stefano, Davide Rocchesso, Frédéric Bevilacqua, Guillaume Lemaitre, Stefano Baldan, and Andrea Cera. 2018. Embodied sound design. *International Journal of Human-Computer Studies* 118: 47–59.

Deutsch, Diana. 2013. *Psychology of music*. Elsevier.

DiFilippo, Derek, and Dinesh K Pai. 2000. The AHI: An audio and haptic interface for contact interactions. In *Proceedings of the 13th annual ACM symposium on user interface software and technology*, 149–158. ACM.

Doll, Theodore J, Jeffrey M Gerth, William R Engelman, and Dennis J Folds. 1986. Development of simulated directional audio for cockpit applications. *Technical report*, Georgia Inst of Tech Atlanta Systems Engineering Lab.

Dourish, Paul. 2004. *Where the action is: The foundations of embodied interaction*. The MIT Press.

Duarte, Emanuel Felipe, and M Cećilia C Baranauskas. 2016. Revisiting the three HCI waves: A preliminary discussion on philosophy of science and research paradigms. In *Proceedings of the 15th Brazilian symposium on human factors in computing systems*, 1–4. ACM.

Dubus, Gaël. 2013. *Interactive sonification of motion: Design, implementation and control of expressive auditory feedback with mobile devices*. PhD diss, KTH Royal Institute of Technology.

Dubus, Gaël, and Roberto Bresin. 2013. A systematic review of mapping strategies for the sonification of physical quantities. *PLoS ONE* 8 (12).

Eckel, Gerhard. 2001. Immersive audio-augmented environments: The listen project. In *Proceedings fifth international conference on information visualisation*, 571–573. IEEE.

Ecker, Adam J, and Laurie M Heller. 2005. Auditory? Visual interactions in the perception of a ball's path. *Perception* 34 (1): 59–75.

Edwards, Alistair DN. 1989. Soundtrack: An auditory interface for blind users. *Human-Computer Interaction* 4 (1): 45–66.

Edworthy, Judy, Sarah Loxley, and Ian Dennis. 1991. Improving auditory warning design: Relationship between warning sound parameters and perceived urgency. *Human factors* 33 (2): 205–231.

Ekman, Inger, and Michal Rinott. 2010. Using vocal sketching for designing sonic interactions. In *Proceedings of the 8th ACM conference on designing interactive systems*, 123–131. ACM.

Engel, Jesse, Lamtharn Hantrakul, Chenjie Gu, and Adam Roberts. 2020. DDSP: Differentiable digital signal processing. *arXiv preprint arXiv:2001.04643*.

Eriksson, Martin, and Roberto Bresin. 2010. Improving running mechanics by use of interactive sonification. In *Proceedings of ISon*. interactive-sonification.org.

Ernst, Marc O, and Heinrich H Bülthoff. 2004. Merging the senses into a robust percept. *Trends in Cognitive Sciences* 8 (4): 162–169.

Everitt, Brian S. 1978. *Graphical techniques for multivariate data*. North-Holland.

Farnell, Andy. 2010. *Designing sound*. The MIT Press.

Fernström, M, D Rocchesso, and F Fontana. 2003. Sound objects and human-computer interaction design. In *The sounding object*, ed. by Mondo Estremo. Mondo Estremo.

Fernström, Mikael, F Brazil, and Liam Bannon. 2005. HCI design and interactive sonification for fingers and ears. *IEEE MultiMedia* 12 (2): 36–44.

Flanagan, John C. 1954. The critical incident technique. *Psychological Bulletin* 51 (4): 327.

Fletcher, Harvey, and Wilden A Munson. 1933. Loudness, its definition, measurement and calculation. *Bell System Technical Journal* 12 (4): 377–430.

Flowers, John H, Dion C Buhman, and Kimberly D Turnage. 2005. Data sonification from the desktop: Should sound be part of standard data analysis software? *ACM Transactions on Applied Perception (TAP)* 2 (4): 467–472.

Flowers, John H, Laura E Whitwer, Douglas C Grafel, and Cheryl A Kotan. 2001. *Sonification of daily weather records: Issues of perception, attention and memory in design choices*. Faculty Publications, Department of Psychology.

Foster, Scott H, and Elizabeth M Wenzel. 1992. The convolvotron: Real-time demonstration of reverberant virtual acoustic environments. *The Journal of the Acoustical Society of America* 92 (4): 2376–2376.

Francioni, Joan M, Jay Alan Jackson, and Larry Albright. 1991. The sounds of parallel programs. In *The sixth distributed memory computing conference, 1991. Proceedings,* 570–577. IEEE.

Frauenberger, Christopher, Tony Stockman, and Marie-Luce Bourguet. 2007. A survey on common practice in designing audio in the user interface. In *Proceedings of HCI 2007 the 21st British HCI group annual conference university of Lancaster, UK 21,* 1–9. ACM.

Freed, Adrian. 1997. Open sound control: A new protocol for communicating with sound synthesizers. In *International computer music conference (ICMC).* International Computer Music Association.

Freed, Daniel J. 1986. *Deriving psychophysical relations for timbre.* Michigan Publishing, University of Michigan Library.

Freed, Daniel J. 1990. Auditory correlates of perceived mallet hardness for a set of recorded percussive sound events. *The Journal of the Acoustical Society of America* 87 (1): 311–322.

Frid, Emma. 2019. *Diverse sounds: Enabling inclusive sonic interaction.* PhD diss, KTH Royal Institute of Technology.

Frysinger, SP. 1988. *Pattern recognition in auditory data representation.* Unpublished thesis, Stevens Institute of Technology.

Gardner, William G. 2002. Reverberation algorithms. In *Applications of digital signal processing to audio and acoustics,* 85–131. Springer.

Gardner, William G, and Keith D Martin. 1995. HRTF measurements of a KEMAR. *The Journal of the Acoustical Society of America* 97 (6): 3907–3908.

Gaver, William W. 1986. Auditory icons: Using sound in computer interfaces. *Human-Computer Interaction* 2 (2): 167–177.

Gaver, William W. 1989a. The SonicFinder: An interface that uses auditory icons. *Human-Computer Interaction* 4 (1): 67–94.

Gaver, William W. 1989b. The SonicFinder: An interface that uses auditory icons. In *The use of non-speech audio at the interface* ACM Press, 5.85–5.106. CHI, Austin, TX.

Gaver, William W. 1993. What in the world do we hear?: An ecological approach to auditory event perception. *Ecological Psychology* 5 (1): 1–29.

Gaver, William W, and George Mandler. 1987. Play it again, Sam: On liking music. *Cognition and Emotion* 1 (3): 259–282.

Gaver, William W, and Donald A Norman. 1988. *Everyday listening and auditory icons.* PhD diss, University of California, San Diego, Department of Cognitive Science.

Gaver, William W, Randall B Smith, and Tim O'Shea. 1991. Effective sounds in complex systems: The ARKola simulation. In *Chi,* Vol. 91, 85–90. ACM.

Gaver, William, Thomas Moran, Allan MacLean, Lennart Lövstrand, Paul Dourish, Kathleen Carter, and William Buxton. 1992. Realizing a video environment: EuroPARC's RAVE system. In *Proceedings of the SIGCHI conference on Human factors in computing systems,* June, 27–35. ACM.

Geldard, Frank A, and Carl E Sherrick. 1972. The cutaneous "rabbit": A perceptual illusion. *Science* 178 (4057): 178–179.

Geronazzo, Michele, Luis S Vieira, Niels Christian Nilsson, Jesper Udesen, and Stefania Serafin. 2020. Superhuman hearing-virtual prototyping of artificial hearing: A case study on interactions and acoustic beamforming. In *IEEE transactions on visualization and computer graphics.* IEEE.

Ghose, Sanchita, and John J Prevost. 2020. Autofoley: Artificial synthesis of synchronized sound tracks for silent videos with deep learning. *arXiv preprint arXiv:2002.10981.*

Gibson, James J. 1979. *The ecological approach to visual perception.* Psychology Press.

Gillespie, R Brent, and Sile O'Modhrain. 2011. Embodied cognition as a motivating perspective for haptic interaction design: A position paper. In *2011 IEEE world haptics conference,* 481–486. IEEE.

Giordano, Bruno L, Patrick Susini, and Roberto Bresin. 2013. Perceptual evaluation of sound-producing objects. In *Sonic interaction design.* The MIT Press.

Godøy, Rolf Inge. 2003. Motor-mimetic music cognition. *Leonardo* 36 (4): 317–319.

Godøy, Rolf Inge. 2010. Gestural affordances of musical sound. In *Musical gestures: Sound, movement, and meaning.* Routledge.

Godøy, Rolf Inge, Egil Haga, and Alexander Refsum Jensenius. 2005. Playing "air instruments": Mimicry of sound-producing gestures by novices and experts. In *International gesture workshop,* 256–267. Springer.

Goldstein, Bruce E, and Laura Cacciamani. 2021. *Sensation and perception.* Cengage Learning.

Green, Paul, and Lisa Wei-Haas. 1985. The rapid development of user interfaces: Experience with the Wizard of Oz method. In *Proceedings of the human factors society annual meeting,* Vol. 29, 470–474. SAGE Publications.

Grey, John M. 1977. Multidimensional perceptual scaling of musical timbres. *The Journal of the Acoustical Society of America* 61 (5): 1270–1277.

Grey, John M. 1978. Timbre discrimination in musical patterns. *The Journal of the Acoustical Society of America* 64 (2): 467–472.

Guest, Steve, Caroline Catmur, Donna Lloyd, and Charles Spence. 2002. Audiotactile interactions in roughness perception. *Experimental Brain Research* 146 (2): 161–171.

Haas, Helmut. 1949. *Über den einfluss eines einfachechos auf die hörsamkeit von sprache.* PhD diss, Verlag nicht ermittelbar.

Halpern, D Lynn, Randolph Blake, and James Hillenbrand. 1986. Psychoacoustics of a chilling sound. *Perception & Psychophysics* 39 (2): 77–80.

Haueisen, Jens, and Thomas R Knösche. 2001. Involuntary motor activity in pianists evoked by music perception. *Journal of Cognitive Neuroscience* 13 (6): 786–792.

Hayward, Vincent. 2008. A brief taxonomy of tactile illusions and demonstrations that can be done in a hardware store. *Brain Research Bulletin* 75 (6): 742–752.

Hecht, David, and Miriam Reiner. 2009. Sensory dominance in combinations of audio, visual and haptic stimuli. *Experimental Brain Research* 193 (2): 307–314.

Heinrichs, Christian, and Andrew McPherson. 2014. Mapping and interaction strategies for performing environmental sound. In *2014 IEEE VR workshop: Sonic interaction in virtual environments (SIVE),* 25–30. IEEE.

Hellier, Elizabeth, and Judy Edworthy. 2009. The design and validation of attensons for a high workload environment. In *Human factors in auditory warnings,* 283–304. Routledge.

Hermann, Thomas. 2008. *Taxonomy and definitions for sonification and auditory display.* International Community for Auditory Display.

Hermann, Thomas, and Andy Hunt. 2005. Guest editors' introduction: An introduction to interactive sonification. *IEEE Multimedia* 12 (2): 20–24.

Hermann, Thomas, Peter Meinicke, Holger Bekel, Helge Ritter, Horst M Müller, and Sabine Weiss. 2002. Sonification for EEG data analysis. In *Proceedings of the 2002 international conference on auditory display.* https://pub.uni-bielefeld.de/record/2704060.

Hermann, Thomas, and Helge Ritter. 1999. Listen to your data: Model-based sonification for data analysis. In *Advances in intelligent computing and multimedia systems*. sonification.de.

Hermann, Thomas, and Helge Ritter. 2004. Sound and meaning in auditory data display. *Proceedings of the IEEE* 92 (4): 730–741.

Hermann, Thomas, and Helge Ritter. 2005. Model-based sonification revisited – authors' comments on Hermann and Ritter, ICAD 2002. *ACM Transactions on Applied Perception (TAP)* 2 (4): 559–563.

Hiller, Lejaren, and Pierre Ruiz. 1971. Synthesizing musical sounds by solving the wave equation for vibrating objects: Part 1. *Journal of the Audio Engineering Society* 19 (6): 462–470.

Hong, Dongpyo, Tobias Höllerer, Michael Haller, Haruo Takemura, Adrian David Cheok, Gerard Jounghyun Kim, Mark Billinghurst, Woontack Woo, Eva Hornecker, Robert JK Jacob, et al. 2008. Advances in tangible interaction and ubiquitous virtual reality. *IEEE Pervasive Computing* 7 (2): 90–96.

Höök, Kristina. 2018. *Designing with the body: Somaesthetic interaction design*. The MIT Press.

Hornecker, Eva. 2011. The role of physicality in tangible and embodied interactions. *Interactions* 18 (2): 19–23.

Hug, Daniel. 2009. Investigating narrative and performative sound design strategies for interactive commodities. In *Auditory display*, 12–40. Springer.

Hug, Daniel, Karmen Franinovic, and Yon Visell. 2007. *Sound embodied: Explorations of sonic interaction design for everyday objects in a workshop setting*. Georgia Institute of Technology.

Hutchins, Edwin. 1987. Metaphors for interface design. *Technical report*, California University San Diego La Jolla Inst for Cognitive Science.

Hutchins, EL, JD Hollan, and DA Norman. 1986. Direct manipulation interfaces. In *User centered system design: New perspectives on human-computer interaction*, ed. by Draper Danasw. Lawrence Erlbaum.

Jack, Charles E, and Willard R Thurlow. 1973. Effects of degree of visual association and angle of displacement on the "ventriloquism" effect. *Perceptual and Motor Skills* 37 (3): 967–979.

Jaffe, David A. 1995. Ten criteria for evaluating synthesis techniques. *Computer Music Journal* 19 (1): 76–87.

Jenkins, James J. 1985. Acoustic information for objects, places, and events. In *Persistence and change proceedings of the first international conference on event perception*. Erlbaum.

Jensenius, Alexander Refsum, and Michael J Lyons. 2017. *A NIME reader: Fifteen years of new interfaces for musical expression*, Vol. 3. Springer.

Jensenius, Alexander Refsum, and Marcelo M Wanderley. 2010. Musical gestures: Concepts and methods in research. In *Musical gestures*, 24–47. Routledge.

Jeon, Myounghoon, Bruce N Walker, and Stephen Barrass. 2019. *Introduction to the special issue on sonic information design: Theory, methods, and practice, part 2*. SAGE Publications.

Jousmäki, Veikko, and Riitta Hari. 1998. Parchment-skin illusion: Sound-biased touch. *Current Biology* 8 (6): 190–191.

Kaltenbrunner, Martin, Sergi Jorda, Gunter Geiger, and Marcos Alonso. 2006. The reactable: A collaborative musical instrument. In *15th IEEE international workshops* on enabling technologies: Infrastructure for collaborative enterprises (WETICE '06), 406–411. IEEE.

Kamitani, Yukiyasu, and Shinsuke Shimojo. 2001. Sound-induced visual "rabbit." *Journal of Vision* 1 (3): 478–478.

Kantowitz, Barry H, and Robert D Sorkin. 1983. *Human factors: Understanding people-system relationships.* John Wiley & Sons Inc.

Kearney, Gavin, and Tony Doyle. 2015. An HRTF database for virtual loudspeaker rendering. In *Audio engineering society convention 139.* Audio Engineering Society.

Kelley, John F. 1984. An iterative design methodology for user-friendly natural language office information applications. *ACM Transactions on Information Systems (TOIS)* 2 (1): 26–41.

Kemper, Daniel Hug Moritz, and D Hug. 2014. From foley to function: A pedagogical approach to sound design for novel interactions. *Journal of Sonic Studies* 6 (1): 1–23.

Kersten, Daniel, Pascal Mamassian, and David C Knill. 1997. Moving cast shadows induce apparent motion in depth. *Perception* 26 (2): 171–192.

Kinsler, Lawrence E, Austin R Frey, Alan B Coppens, and James V Sanders. 1999. Fundamentals of acoustics. In *Fundamentals of acoustics,* 4th ed., ed. by Lawrence E Kinsler, Austin R Frey, Alan B Coppens, and James V Sanders, 560. Wiley-VCH. ISBN 0-471-84789-5.

Kitagawa, Norimichi, Massimiliano Zampini, and Charles Spence. 2005. Audiotactile interactions in near and far space. *Experimental Brain Research* 166 (3–4): 528–537.

Klatzky, Roberta L, Dinesh K Pai, and Eric P Krotkov. 2000. Perception of material from contact sounds. *Presence: Teleoperators & Virtual Environments* 9 (4): 399–410.

Kohlrausch, Armin, and Steven van de Par. 1999. Auditory-visual interaction: From fundamental research in cognitive psychology to (possible) applications. In *Human vision and electronic imaging iv,* Vol. 3644, 34–44. International Society for Optics and Photonics.

Kovaric, AF. 1917. New methods for counting the alpha and the beta particles. *Physical Review* 9 (6): 567–568.

Kramer, Gregory, Bruce Walker, Terri Bonebright, Perry Cook, John H Flowers, Nadine Miner, and John Neuhoff. 2010. Sonification report: Status of the field and research agenda. https://digitalcommons.unl.edu/psychfacpub/444/.

Krishnan, Sridhar, Rangaraj M Rangayyan, G Douglas Bell, and Cyril B Frank. 2001. Auditory display of knee-joint vibration signals. *The Journal of the Acoustical Society of America* 110 (6): 3292–3304.

Krumbholz, K, RD Patterson, A Seither-Preisler, C Lammertmann, and B Lütkenhöner. 2003. Neuromagnetic evidence for a pitch processing center in Heschl's gyrus. *Cerebral Cortex* 13 (7): 765–772.

Kubovy, Michael, and David Van Valkenburg. 2001. Auditory and visual objects. *Cognition* 80 (1–2): 97–126.

Kumar, Sukhbinder, Helen M Forster, Peter Bailey, and Timothy D Griffiths. 2008. Mapping unpleasantness of sounds to their auditory representation. *The Journal of the Acoustical Society of America* 124 (6): 3810–3817.

Lamb, Horace. 2004. *The dynamical theory of sound.* Courier Corporation.

Laput, Gierad, Eric Brockmeyer, Scott E Hudson, and Chris Harrison. 2015. Acoustruments: Passive, acoustically-driven, interactive controls for handheld devices. In *Proceedings of the 33rd annual ACM conference on human factors in computing systems,* 2161–2170. ACM.

Laurel, Brenda K. 1986. Interface as mimesis. In *User centered system design*, 67–86. CRC Press.

Lemaitre, Guillaume, Arnaud Dessein, Patrick Susini, and Karine Aura. 2011. Vocal imitations and the identification of sound events. *Ecological Psychology* 23 (4): 267–307.

Lemaitre, Guillaume, Olivier Houix, Yon Visell, Karmen Franinović, Nicolas Misdariis, and Patrick Susini. 2009. Toward the design and evaluation of continuous sound in tangible interfaces: The spinotron. *International Journal of Human-Computer Studies* 67 (11): 976–993.

Leman, Marc. 2016. *The expressive moment: How interaction (with music) shapes human empowerment.* The MIT Press.

Leman, Marc, et al. 2008. *Embodied music cognition and mediation technology.* The MIT Press.

Lesaffre, Micheline, Pieter-Jan Maes, and Marc Leman. 2017. *The Routledge companion to embodied music interaction.* Taylor & Francis.

Li, Teng, Dangxiao Wang, Cong Peng, Chun Yu, and Yuru Zhang. 2018. Speed accuracy tradeoff of fingertip force control with visual/audio/haptic feedback. *International Journal of Human-Computer Studies* 110: 33–44.

Lindsay, Peter H, and Donald A Norman. 1977. *Human information processing: An introduction to psychology.* Academic Press.

Lipscomb, Scott D, and Roger A Kendall. 1994. Perceptual judgement of the relationship between musical and visual components in film. *Psychomusicology: A Journal of Research in Music Cognition* 13 (1–2): 60.

Lövstrand, Lennart. 1991. Being selectively aware with the Khronika system. In *Proceedings of the second European conference on computer-supported cooperative work ECSCW*, 265–277. Springer.

Loy, Gareth. 1985. Musicians make a standard: The midi phenomenon. *Computer Music Journal* 9 (4): 8–26.

Ludwig, Lester F, Natalio Pincever, and Michael Cohen. 1990. Extending the notion of a window system to audio. *Computer* 23 (8): 66–72.

Lumsden, Joanna, and SA Brewster. 2001. *A survey of audio-related knowledge amongst software engineers developing human-computer interfaces.* Glasgow University.

Lundborg, Göran, Birgitta Rosén, and Styrbjörn Lindberg. 1999. Hearing as substitution for sensation: A new principle for artificial sensibility. *The Journal of Hand Surgery* 24 (2): 219–224.

Lunney, David, and Robert C Morrison. 1981. High technology laboratory aids for visually handicapped chemistry students. *Journal of Chemical Education* 58 (3): 228.

Lunney, David, and Robert C Morrison. 1990. Auditory presentation of experimental data. In *Extracting meaning from complex data: Processing, display, interaction*, Vol. 1259, 140–146. International Society for Optics and Photonics.

Mansur, Douglass L, Merra M Blattner, and Kenneth I Joy. 1985. Sound graphs: A numerical data analysis method for the blind. *Journal of Medical Systems* 9 (3): 163–174.

Marston, James R, Jack M Loomis, Roberta L Klatzky, Reginald G Golledge, and Ethan L Smith. 2006. Evaluation of spatial displays for navigation without sight. *ACM Transactions on Applied Perception (TAP)* 3 (2): 110–124.

Mathews, Max V. 1963. The digital computer as a musical instrument. *Science* 142 (3592): 553–557.

May, Keenan R, Brianna J Tomlinson, Xiaomeng Ma, Phillip Roberts, and Bruce N Walker. 2020. Spotlights and soundscapes: On the design of mixed reality auditory environments for persons with visual impairment. *ACM Transactions on Accessible Computing (TACCESS)* 13 (2): 1–47.

McAdams, Stephen, and Albert Bregman. 1979. Hearing musical streams. *Computer Music Journal* 3 (4) (Dec., 1979), pp. 26–43+60 (20 pages).

McDermott, Josh H, Andriana J Lehr, and Andrew J Oxenham. 2010. Individual differences reveal the basis of consonance. *Current Biology* 20 (11): 1035–1041.

McDermott, Josh H, Andrew J Oxenham, and Eero P Simoncelli. 2009. Sound texture synthesis via filter statistics. In *2009 IEEE workshop on applications of signal processing to audio and acoustics*, 297–300. IEEE.

McDermott, Josh H, and Eero P Simoncelli. 2011. Sound texture perception via statistics of the auditory periphery: Evidence from sound synthesis. *Neuron* 71 (5): 926–940.

McGookin, David K, and Stephen A Brewster. 2004. Understanding concurrent earcons: Applying auditory scene analysis principles to concurrent earcon recognition. *ACM Transactions on Applied Perception (TAP)* 1 (2): 130–155.

McGuire, Joan M, Sally S Scott, and Stan F Shaw. 2006. Universal design and its applications in educational environments. *Remedial and Special Education* 3: 166–175.

McGurk, Harry, and John MacDonald. 1976. Hearing lips and seeing voices. *Nature* 264 (5588): 746.

Merer, Adrien, Mitsuko Aramaki, Sølvi Ystad, and Richard Kronland-Martinet. 2013. Perceptual characterization of motion evoked by sounds for synthesis control purposes. *ACM Transactions on Applied Perception (TAP)* 10 (1): 1–24.

Merleau-Ponty, M. 1962. *Phenomenology of perception Routledge*. UK [France, 1945].

Mezrich, Joseph J, S Frysinger, and R Slivjanovski. 1984. Dynamic representation of multivariate time series data. *Journal of the American Statistical Association* 79 (385): 34–40.

Millet, Guillaume, Anatole Lécuyer, Jean-Marie Burkhardt, Sinan Haliyo, and Stéphane Regnier. 2013. Haptics and graphic analogies for the understanding of atomic force microscopy. *International Journal of Human-computer Studies* 71 (5): 608–626.

Moffat, David, and Joshua D Reiss. 2018. Perceptual evaluation of synthesized sound effects. *ACM Transactions on Applied Perception (TAP)* 15 (2): 1–19.

Møller, Henrik, Michael Friis Sørensen, Dorte Hammershøi, and Clemen Boje Jensen. 1995. Head-related transfer functions of human subjects. *Journal of the Audio Engineering Society* 43 (5): 300–321.

Monache, Stefano Delle, Pietro Polotti, and Davide Rocchesso. 2010. A toolkit for explorations in sonic interaction design. In *Proceedings of the 5th audio mostly conference: A conference on interaction with sound*, 1–7. ACM.

Monk, Andrew. 1986. Mode errors: A user-centred analysis and some preventative measures using keying-contingent sound. *International Journal of Man-machine Studies* 24 (4): 313–327.

Muller, Michael J, and Sarah Kuhn. 1993. Participatory design. *Communications of the ACM* 36 (6): 24–28.

Murphy, Emma, Ravi Kuber, Philip Strain, Graham McAllister, and Wai Yu. 2007. *Developing sounds for a multimodal interface: Conveying spatial information to visually impaired web users*. Georgia Institute of Technology.

Mynatt, Elizabeth D. 1994. Designing with auditory icons: How well do we identify auditory cues? In *Conference companion on human factors in computing systems*, 269–270. ACM.

Mynatt, Elizabeth D, and W Keith Edwards. 1992. Mapping GUIs to auditory interfaces. In *Proceedings of the 5th annual ACM symposium on user interface software and technology*, 61–70. ACM.

Nees, Michael A, and Bruce N Walker. 2007. *Listener, task, and auditory graph: Toward a conceptual model of auditory graph comprehension*. Georgia Institute of Technology.

Neuhoff, John G, Joseph Wayand, and Gregory Kramer. 2002. Pitch and loudness interact in auditory displays: Can the data get lost in the map? *Journal of Experimental Psychology: Applied* 8 (1): 17.

Niedenthal, Paula M, Lawrence W Barsalou, Piotr Winkielman, Silvia Krauth-Gruber, and François Ric. 2005. Embodiment in attitudes, social perception, and emotion. *Personality and Social Psychology Review* 9 (3): 184–211.

Noceti, Nicoletta, Luca Giuliani, Joan Sosa-Garciá, Luca Brayda, Andrea Trucco, and Francesca Odone. 2019. Designing audio-visual tools to support multisensory disabilities. In *Multimodal behavior analysis in the wild*, 79–102. Elsevier.

Nordahl, Rolf, Amir Berrezag, Smilen Dimitrov, Luca Turchet, Vincent Hayward, and Stefania Serafin. 2010. Preliminary experiment combining virtual reality haptic shoes and audio synthesis. In *International conference on human haptic sensing and touch enabled computer applications*, 123–129. Springer.

Nymoen, Kristian, Rolf Inge Godøy, Alexander Refsum Jensenius, and Jim Torresen. 2013. Analyzing correspondence between sound objects and body motion. *ACM Transactions on Applied Perception (TAP)* 10 (2): 1–22.

Ortega, Laura, Emmanuel Guzman-Martinez, Marcia Grabowecky, and Satoru Suzuki. 2009. Auditory dominance in time perception. *Journal of Vision* 9 (8): 1086–1086.

Otto, Norman C, Richard Simpson, and Jason Wiederhold. 1999. *Electric vehicle sound quality, Technical report*. SAE Technical Paper.

Pai, Dinesh K. 2005. Multisensory interaction: Real and virtual. In *Robotics research: The eleventh international symposium*, 489–498. Springer.

Patterson, Roy D. 1982. *Guidelines for auditory warning systems on civil aircraft*. Civil Aviation Authority.

Patterson, Roy D. 1989. Guidelines for the design of auditory warning sounds. *Proceedings of the Institute of Acoustics* 11 (5): 17–25.

Patterson, Roy D. 1990. Auditory warning sounds in the work environment. *Philosophical Transactions of the Royal Society of London. B, Biological Sciences* 327 (1241): 485–492.

Pauletto, Sandra. 2014. Film and theatre-based approaches for sonic interaction design. *Digital Creativity* 25 (1): 15–26.

Pauletto, Sandra, Daniel Hug, Stephen Barras, and Mary Luckhurst. 2009. Integrating theatrical strategies into sonic interaction design. In *4th conference on interaction with sound: Audio mostly 2009; Glasgow; United Kingdom; 2 September 2009 through 3 September 2009*, 77–82. ACM.

Pierce, John Robinson. 1992. *The science of musical sound*, Vol. 174. WH Freeman.

Plazak, Joseph, and Marta Kersten-Oertel. 2018. A survey on the affordances of "hearables." *Inventions* 3 (3): 48.

Plenge, Georg. 1974. On the differences between localization and lateralization. *The Journal of the Acoustical Society of America* 56 (3): 944–951.

Polotti, Pietro. 2008. *Sound to sense, sense to sound: A state of the art in sound and music computing.* Logos Verlag Berlin GmbH.

Posner, Michael I, Mary J Nissen, and Raymond M Klein. 1976. Visual dominance: An information-processing account of its origins and significance. *Psychological Review* 83 (2): 157.

Puckette, Miller S, et al. 1997. Pure data. In *ICMC.* International Computer Music Association.

Rath, Matthias, and Davide Rocchesso. 2005. Continuous sonic feedback from a rolling ball. *IEEE MultiMedia* 12 (2): 60–69.

Rayleigh, Lord. 1907. XII. On our perception of sound direction. *The London, Edinburgh, and Dublin Philosophical Magazine and Journal of Science* 13 (74): 214–232.

Recarte, Miguel A, and Luis M Nunes. 2003. Mental workload while driving: Effects on visual search, discrimination, and decision making. *Journal of Experimental Psychology: Applied* 9 (2): 119.

Repp, Bruno H, and Amandine Penel. 2002. Auditory dominance in temporal processing: New evidence from synchronization with simultaneous visual and auditory sequences. *Journal of Experimental Psychology: Human Perception and Performance* 28 (5): 1085.

Risset, Jean-Claude. 1969. Pitch control and pitch paradoxes demonstrated with computer-synthesized sounds. *The Journal of the Acoustical Society of America* 46 (1A): 88–88.

Risset, Jean-Claude. 1986. Pitch and rhythm paradoxes: Comments on "auditory paradox based on fractal waveform" [j. acoust. soc. am. 7 9, 186–189 (1986)]. *The Journal of the Acoustical Society of America* 80 (3): 961–962.

Risset, Jean-Claude, and David L Wessel. 1982. Exploration of timbre by analysis and synthesis. *The Psychology of Music* 2: 151.

Robart, Ryan L, and Lawrence D Rosenblum. 2009. Are hybrid cars too quiet? *The Journal of the Acoustical Society of America* 125 (4): 2744–2744.

Rocchesso, Davide. 2011. *Explorations in sonic interaction design.* Logos Berlin.

Rocchesso, Davide, and Federico Fontana. 2003. *The sounding object.* Mondo Estremo.

Rocchesso, Davide, Stefano Delle Monache, and Stephen Barrass. 2019. Interaction by ear. *International Journal of Human-Computer Studies* 131: 152–159.

Rocchesso, Davide, Pietro Polotti, and Stefano Delle Monache. 2009. Designing continuous sonic interaction. *International Journal of Design* 3 (3).

Roe, Cynthia J, William H Muto, and Tyler Blake. 1984. Feedback and key discrimination on membrane keypads. In *Proceedings of the human factors society annual meeting,* Vol. 28, 277–281. SAGE Publications.

Roederer, Juan G. 2012. *Introduction to the physics and psychophysics of music.* Springer.

Rossing, Thomas D. 2007. *Springer handbook of acoustics.* Springer.

Rossing, Thomas D, and NH Fletcher. 1991. *The physics of musical instruments.* Springer.

Saberi, Kourosh, and David R Perrott. 1990. Minimum audible movement angles as a function of sound source trajectory. *The Journal of the Acoustical Society of America* 88 (6): 2639–2644.

Sanders, Mark S, and Ernest James McCormick. 1987. *Human Factors in engineering and design,* 7. McGraw-Hill Education 7: 155.

Sanders, Mark S, and Ernest James McCormick. 1998. Human factors in engineering and design. *Industrial Robot: An International Journal.*

Scaletti, Carla, and Alan B Craig. 1991. Using sound to extract meaning from complex data. In *Extracting meaning from complex data: Processing, display, interaction ii,* Vol. 1459, 207–219. International Society for Optics and Photonics.

Schafer, R Murray. 1993. *The soundscape: Our sonic environment and the tuning of the world*. Simon and Schuster.

Schaffert, Nina, Klaus Mattes, and Alfred O Effenberg. 2010. Listen to the boat motion: Acoustic information for elite rowers. In *Human interaction with auditory displays – proceedings of the interactive sonification workshop*, 31–38. https://interactive-sonification.org.

Scharf, Bertram, and S Buus. 1986. Strategy and optimization in human information processing. In *Handbook of perception and human performance*, ed. by Audition IK Boff, L. Kaufman, and J. Thomas, Vol. I. John Wiley & Sons.

Scharf, Bertram, and Adrianus JM Houtsma. 1986. Loudness, pitch, localization, aural distortion, pathology. In *Handbook of perception and human performance, vol. 1: Sensory processes and perception*, ed. by Kenneth R. Boff, Lloyd Kaufman, and James P. Thomas, Wiley-Interscience.

Schleicher, Dennis, Peter Jones, and Oksana Kachur. 2010. Bodystorming as embodied designing. *Interactions* 17 (6): 47–51.

Schmid, Carmen, Christian Büchel, and Michael Rose. 2011. The neural basis of visual dominance in the context of audio-visual object processing. *NeuroImage* 55 (1): 304–311.

Schutz, Michael, and Scott Lipscomb. 2007. Hearing gestures, seeing music: Vision influences perceived tone duration. *Perception* 36 (6): 888–897.

Sekuler, Allison B, and Robert Sekuler. 1999. Collisions between moving visual targets: What controls alternative ways of seeing an ambiguous display? *Perception* 28 (4): 415–432.

Sekuler, Robert. 1997. Sound alters visual motion perception. *Nature* 385 (6614): 308.

Selfridge, Rod, David Moffat, Joshua D Reiss. 2017. Real-time physical model for synthesis of sword swing sounds. In *Proceedings of SMC conference*. Sound and Music Computing.

Sengers, Phoebe, and Bill Gaver. 2006. Staying open to interpretation: Engaging multiple meanings in design and evaluation. In *Proceedings of the 6th conference on designing interactive systems*, 99–108. ACM.

Senna, Irene, Angelo Maravita, Nadia Bolognini, and Cesare V Parise. 2014. The marble-hand illusion. *PLoS ONE* 9 (3).

Serafin, Stefania. 2004. *The sound of friction: Real time models, playability and musical applications*. PhD diss, Department of Music, Stanford University.

Serafin, Stefania, Michele Geronazzo, Cumhur Erkut, Niels C Nilsson, and Rolf Nordahl. 2018. Sonic interactions in virtual reality: State of the art, current challenges, and future directions. *IEEE Computer Graphics and Applications* 38 (2): 31–43.

Serra, Xavier, Marc Leman, and Gerhard Widmer. 2007. *A roadmap for sound and music computing*. The S2S2 Consortium.

Shams, Ladan, Yukiyasu Kamitani, and Shinsuke Shimojo. 2000. Illusions: What you see is what you hear. *Nature* 408 (6814): 788.

Shams, Ladan, Yukiyasu Kamitani, and Shinsuke Shimojo. 2002. Visual illusion induced by sound. *Cognitive Brain Research* 14 (1): 147–152.

Shaw, Edgar AG. 1974. Transformation of sound pressure level from the free field to the eardrum in the horizontal plane. *The Journal of the Acoustical Society of America* 56 (6): 1848–1861.

Shepard, Roger N. 1964. Circularity in judgments of relative pitch. *The Journal of the Acoustical Society of America* 36 (12): 2346–2353.

Shilling, Russell D, Tomasz Letowski, and Russell Storms. 2000. *Spatial auditory displays for use within attack rotary wing aircraft*. Georgia Institute of Technology.

Singh, Nandini C, and Frédéric E Theunissen. 2003. Modulation spectra of natural sounds and ethological theories of auditory processing. *The Journal of the Acoustical Society of America* 114 (6): 3394–3411.

Slawson, A Wayne. 1968. Vowel quality and musical timbre as functions of spectrum envelope and fundamental frequency. *The Journal of the Acoustical Society of America* 43 (1): 87–101.

Smith, Julius Orion. 1992. Physical modeling using digital waveguides. *Computer Music Journal* 16 (4): 74–91.

Smith, Julius Orion III. 2000. Personal communications.

Smith, Julius Orion. 2010. *Physical audio signal processing: For virtual musical instruments and audio effects*. W3K Publishing.

Smith, Stuart Orion, R Daniel Bergeron, and Georges G Grinstein. 1990. Stereophonic and surface sound generation for exploratory data analysis. In *Proceedings of the SIG-CHI conference on human factors in computing systems*, 125–132. ACM.

Sonnenwald, Diane H, B Gopinath, Gary O Haberman, William M Keese, and John S Myers. 1990. Infosound: An audio aid to program comprehension. In *Twenty-third annual Hawaii international conference on system sciences*, Vol. 2, 541–546. IEEE.

Speeth, Sheridan Dauster. 1961. Seismometer sounds. *The Journal of the Acoustical Society of America* 33 (7): 909–916.

Spence, Charles, and Jon Driver. 1997. Audiovisual links in exogenous covert spatial orienting. *Perception & Psychophysics* 59 (1): 1–22.

Spence, Charles, John McDonald, and Jon Driver. 2004. Exogenous spatial cuing studies of human crossmodal attention and multisensory integration. In *Crossmodal space and crossmodal attention*, 277320. Oxford University Press.

Spence, Charles, and Massimiliano Zampini. 2006. Auditory contributions to multisensory product perception. *Acta Acustica United with Acustica* 92 (6): 1009–1025.

Stanton, Neville A, and Judy Edworthy. 2019. Auditory warnings and displays: An overview. In *Human factors in auditory warnings*, 3–30. Routledge.

Stevens, Robert D, Alistair DN Edwards, and Philip A Harling. 1997. Access to mathematics for visually disabled students through multimodal interaction. *Human-Computer Interaction* 12 (1–2): 47–92.

Storms, Russell L, and Michael J Zyda. 2000. Interactions in perceived quality of auditory-visual displays. *Presence: Teleoperators & Virtual Environments* 9 (6): 557–580.

Strybel, Thomas Z, Carol L Manllgas, and David R Perrott. 1992. Minimum audible movement angle as a function of the azimuth and elevation of the source. *Human Factors* 34 (3): 267–275.

Susini, Patrick, Nicolas Misdariis, Guillaume Lemaitre, and Olivier Houix. 2012. Naturalness influences the perceived usability and pleasantness of an interface's sonic feedback. *Journal on Multimodal User Interfaces* 5 (3–4): 175–186.

Tajadura-Jiménez, Ana, Maria Basia, Ophelia Deroy, Merle Fairhurst, Nicolai Marquardt, and Nadia Bianchi-Berthouze. 2015. As light as your footsteps: Altering walking sounds to change perceived body weight, emotional state and gait. In *Proceedings of the 33rd annual ACM conference on human factors in computing systems*, 2943–2952. ACM.

Tanaka, Atau, Olivier Bau, and Wendy Mackay. 2013. 11 the a20: Interactive instrument techniques for sonic design exploration. *Sonic Interaction Design*. The MIT Press.

Tanaka, Atau, and Adam Parkinson. 2016. Haptic wave: A cross-modal interface for visually impaired audio producers. In *Proceedings of the 2016 CHI conference on human factors in computing systems*, 2150–2161. ACM.

Terhardt, Ernst. 1974. Pitch, consonance, and harmony. *The Journal of the Acoustical Society of America* 55 (5): 1061–1069.

Terhardt, Ernst. 1978. Psychoacoustic evaluation of musical sounds. *Perception & Psychophysics* 23 (6): 483–492.

Terhardt, Ernst, and G Stoll. 1981. Skalierung des wohlklangs (der sensorischen konsonanz) von 17 umweltschallen und untersuchung der beteiligten hörparameter. *Acta Acustica United with Acustica* 48 (4): 247–253.

Thieberger, Ed M, and Charles Dodge. 1995. An interview with Charles Dodge. *Computer Music Journal* 19 (1): 11–24.

Tholander, Jakob, Klas Karlgren, Robert Ramberg, and Per Sökjer. 2008. Where all the interaction is: Sketching in interaction design as an embodied practice. In *Proceedings of the 7th ACM conference on designing interactive systems*, 445–454. ACM.

Thomas, James Philip, and Maggie Shiffrar. 2010. I can see you better if I can hear you coming: Action-consistent sounds facilitate the visual detection of human gait. *Journal of Vision* 10 (12): 14–14.

Thoret, Etienne, Mitsuko Aramaki, Lionel Bringoux, Sølvi Ystad, and Richard Kronland-Martinet. 2016. Seeing circles and drawing ellipses: When sound biases reproduction of visual motion. *PLoS ONE* 11 (4).

Tractinsky, Noam, Adi S Katz, and Dror Ikar. 2000. What is beautiful is usable. *Interacting with Computers* 13 (2): 127–145.

Truax, Barry. 2001. *Acoustic communication*. Greenwood Publishing Group.

Tukey, John Wilder. 1970. *Exploratory data analysis: Limited preliminary*. Addison-Wesley Publishing Company.

Väljamäe, Anastasiia, Tony Steffert, Simon Holland, Xavier Marimon, Rafael Benitez, Sebastian Mealla, Aluizio Oliveira, and Sergio Jorda'. 2013. A review of real-time EEG sonification research. International Conference of Auditory Display.

Van den Doel, Kees, Paul G Kry, and Dinesh K Pai. 2001. Foleyautomatic: Physically based sound effects for interactive simulation and animation. In *Proceedings of the 28th annual conference on computer graphics and interactive techniques*, 537–544. ACM.

Van den Doel, Kees, and Dinesh K Pai. 1998. The sounds of physical shapes. *Presence* 7 (4): 382–395.

Van den Doel, Kees, and Dinesh K Pai. 2003. Modal synthesis for vibrating objects. In *Audio Anectodes*. AK Peter.

Van der Burg, Erik, Christian NL Olivers, Adelbert W Bronkhorst, and Jan Theeuwes. 2008. Pip and pop: Nonspatial auditory signals improve spatial visual search. *Journal of Experimental Psychology: Human Perception and Performance* 34 (5): 1053.

Vanderveer, Nancy J. 1980. *Ecological acoustics: Human perception of environmental sounds*. Cornell University.

Vassilakis, Pantelis N. 2005. Auditory roughness as a means of musical expression. *Selected Reports in Ethnomusicology* 12 (119–144): 122.

Vazquez-Alvarez, Yolanda, Ian Oakley, and Stephen A Brewster. 2012. Auditory display design for exploration in mobile audio-augmented reality. *Personal and Ubiquitous Computing* 16 (8): 987–999.

Vi, Chi Thanh, Damien Ablart, Elia Gatti, Carlos Velasco, and Marianna Obrist. 2017. Not just seeing, but also feeling art: Mid-air haptic experiences integrated in a multisensory art exhibition. *International Journal of Human-Computer Studies* 108: 1–14.

Vogt, Katharina. 2010. *Sonification of simulations in computational physics*. PhD diss, University of Gratz.

Von Békésy, Georg, and Ernest Glen Wever. 1960. *Experiments in hearing*, Vol. 8. McGraw-Hill.

Von Helmholtz, Hermann. 1912. *On the sensations of tone as a physiological basis for the theory of music*. Longmans, Green.

Vos, Joos, and Rudolf Rasch. 1981. The perceptual onset of musical tones. *Perception & Psychophysics* 29 (4): 323–335.

Voss, Richard F, and John Clarke. 1975. "1/f noise" in music and speech. *Nature* 258 (5533): 317–318.

Wakefield, Gregory H, Agnieszka Roginska, and Thomas Santoro. 2012. Auditory detection of infrapitch signals for several spatial configurations of pink noise maskers. In *41st international congress and exposition on noise control engineering 2012, internoise 2012*, 4446–4456. https://nyuscholars.nyu.edu/en/publications/auditory-detection-of-infrapitch-signals-for-several-spatial-conf.

Walker, Bruce N, and DM Lane. 1994. *Auditory display: Sonification, audification, and auditory interfaces*. Westview Press.

Walker, Bruce N, and Jeff Lindsay. 2003. *Effect of beacon sounds on navigation performance in a virtual reality environment*. Georgia Institute of Technology.

Walker, Bruce N, Amanda Nance, and Jeffrey Lindsay. 2006. *Spearcons: Speech-based earcons improve navigation performance in auditory menus*. Georgia Institute of Technology.

Wallach, Hans. 1940. The role of head movements and vestibular and visual cues in sound localization. *Journal of Experimental Psychology* 27 (4): 339.

Warren, William H, and Robert R Verbrugge. 1984. Auditory perception of breaking and bouncing events: A case study in ecological acoustics. *Journal of Experimental Psychology: Human Perception and Performance* 10 (5): 704.

Welch, Robert B, and David H Warren. 1980. Immediate perceptual response to intersensory discrepancy. *Psychological Bulletin* 88 (3): 638.

Wenzel, Elizabeth M, Marianne Arruda, Doris J Kistler, and Frederic L Wightman. 1993. Localization using nonindividualized head-related transfer functions. *The Journal of the Acoustical Society of America* 94 (1): 111–123.

Wenzel, Elizabeth M, FL Wightman, and SH Foster. 1988. A virtual acoustic display for conveying three-dimensional information. In *Proceedings of the human factors society 32nd annual meeting, Anaheim*. ACM.

Wessel, David L. 1979. Timbre space as a musical control structure. *Computer Music Journal* 3 (2) (Jun., 1979), pp. 45–52 (8 pages).

Wessel, David L, and Matthew Wright. 2002. Problems and prospects for intimate musical control of computers. *Computer Music Journal* 26 (3): 11–22.

Westerkamp, Hildegard. 1974. Soundwalking. *Sound Heritage* 3 (4): 18–27.

Wildes, Richard P, and Whitman A Richards. 1988. Recovering material properties from sound. In *Natural computation*. The MIT Press.

Williamson, John, Roderick Murray-Smith, and Stephen Hughes. 2007. Shoogle: Excitatory multimodal interaction on mobile devices. In *Proceedings of the SIGCHI conference on human factors in computing systems*, 121–124. ACM.

Wilson, Jeff, Bruce N Walker, Jeffrey Lindsay, Craig Cambias, and Frank Dellaert. 2007. Swan: System for wearable audio navigation. In *2007 11th IEEE international symposium on wearable computers*, 91–98. IEEE.

Yeung, Edward S. 1980. Pattern recognition by audio representation of multivariate analytical data. *Analytical Chemistry* 52 (7): 1120–1123.

Zatorre, Robert J, Joyce L Chen, and Virginia B Penhune. 2007. When the brain plays music: Auditory – motor interactions in music perception and production. *Nature Reviews Neuroscience* 8 (7): 547–558.

Zimmermann, Andreas, and Andreas Lorenz. 2008. Listen: A user-adaptive audioaugmented museum guide. *User Modeling and User-Adapted Interaction* 18 (5): 389–416.

Zölzer, Udo. 2011. *Dafx: Digital audio effects*. John Wiley & Sons.

Zwicker, Earl, and Ernst Terhardt. 1980. Analytical expressions for critical-band rate and critical bandwidth as a function of frequency. *The Journal of the Acoustical Society of America* 68 (5): 1523–1525.

Zwicker, Eberhard, and Hugo Fastl. 2013. *Psychoacoustics: Facts and models*, Vol. 22. Springer.

Index

Note: Page numbers in *italics* indicate a figure and page numbers in **bold** indicate a table on the corresponding page.

CPSIA information can be obtained
at www.ICGtesting.com
Printed in the USA
LVHW050845180623
749271LV00039B/351